Burt Bacharach & Hal David

What The World Needs Now

By Robin Platts

All rights reserved under article two of the Berne Copyright Convention (1971).
No part of this book may be reproduced or transmitted in any form or by any means,
electronic or mechanical, including photocopying, recording, or by any information storage
and retrieval system without permission in writing from the publisher.
We acknowledge the financial support of the Government of Canada through
the Book Publishing Industry Development Program for our publishing activities.
Published by Collector's Guide Publishing Inc.
Box 62034, Burlington, Ontario, Canada, L7R 4K2
Printed and bound in Canada
Burt Bacharach & Hal David – What The World Needs Now
by Robin Platts

Copyright © 2003 C.G. Publishing / Robin Platts ISBN 1-896522-77-7

Burt Bacharach & Hal David

What The World Needs Now

By Robin Platts

Table Of Contents

Introduction	5
Chapter 1: Big Bert And Little Bert	7
Chapter 2: My Heart Is An Open Book	13
Chapter 3: Show And Tell	16
Chapter 4: Dionne	22
Chapter 5: Hitmakers!	27
Chapter 6: Love, Sweet Love	36
Chapter 7: What's It All About?	40
Chapter 8: Let The Music Play	45
Chapter 9: The Look Of Love	51
Chapter 10: Promises, Promises	61
Chapter 11: Nothing's Worrying Me	69
Chapter 12: Close To You	75
Chapter 13: Long Ago Tomorrow	80
Chapter 14: Lost Investments	83
Chapter 15: Knowing When To Leave	87
Chapter 16: I Took My Strength From You	91
Chapter 17: It Was Almost Like A Song	94
Chapter 18: The Best That You Can Do	96
Chapter 19: What the World Needs Now	101
Chapter 20: Something Even Non-believers Can Believe In	109
The Songs	110
Discography	153

Acknowledgements

Special thanks to all those who agreed to be interviewed for this book: Burt Bacharach, Hal David, Rose Marie Jun, Gene Pitney, Phil Ramone, Ray Stevens, B.J. Thomas, Steve Tyrell and Dionne Warwick.

I'd also like to thank everyone else who offered their assistance: Davide Bonori, Henry Carr, John Koenig, Sue Maine, Claudia Marx, Nancy Munoz, Mark Miester (whose excellent Bacharach Web site can be found at www.bacharachonline.com), and Rob Pingel, Vee Platts, and Karen Sherry. And a very big thank you to Georgina Saksa at Casa David.

Dedicated to Mary Standell, who encouraged my interest in Bacharach and David songs, little realizing it would become an obsession.

Introduction

They were the last of their kind.

By the 1960s the American popular song was rapidly falling into the hands of a new breed, the singer-songwriter. And yet the songwriting team of Burt Bacharach and Hal David flourished in that decade, continuing and developing a tradition that stretched back decades before them. They were the latest in a lineage that included the Gershwins, Irving Berlin, Rodgers and Hart and Cole Porter, but they peaked in the era of the Beatles, Bob Dylan and the Rolling Stones. In an era of youthful voices expressing the perspective of a new generation, Bacharach and David stormed the charts with sophisticated, adult songs. But they bridged the generation gap, too, their work sounding equally at home when delivered by old school crooners like Frank Sinatra or young upstarts like Arthur Lee and Love. Other songwriting teams came after Bacharach and David, but none achieved the fame that they did, and no one after them produced such an amazing body of work: *What The World Needs Now Is Love, Raindrops Keep Fallin' On My Head, I Say A Little Prayer, The Look Of Love, Walk On By* and *Alfie* are just a few of the classic songs Bacharach and David wrote together.

Bacharach and David's songs have a distinctive sound and appeal, but there is no formula. One number is mature and sophisticated, the next simple and sincere, while the next might be all of the above and more. Both Bacharach (music) and David (lyrics) made full use of their palettes, exploring a dynamic range of words and sounds, textures and rhythms. Their selection of vocalists was as varied as the musical settings with which they were backed: a touch of harpsichord between the verses, marimba, flugelhorn, and maybe a cheesy organ to emphasize certain phrases. The lyrics were clever and witty, but never without honesty and heartfelt sincerity. Burt and Hal were consummate professionals, yet everything they wrote seemed to come straight from the heart, and their professionalism served only to convey those feelings more effectively.

And yet those simple emotions were conveyed in music and lyrics that were very artfully constructed – songs that were actually much more complex than they sounded. Bacharach and David made it sound easy, but it wasn't. They took the American songwriting tradition to an exciting new place, with groundbreaking words, rhythms and melodies.

This book is not a biography of Burt Bacharach and Hal David. It is the story of their music, the collaboration – the story of the songs and how and why they were written. The second half of the book is a reference guide, with details about every song they wrote together and a discography of some of the innumerable recordings of their work. My words cannot capture the magic of these songs so I suggest that, before continuing, you slap an LP by Burt Bacharach or Dionne Warwick on the turntable, or put a CD in the player. Then read on and, to borrow a line from Hal David, let the music play…

BURT BACHARACH AND HAL DAVID

Chapter 1: Big Bert And Little Bert

Kansas City, Missouri, May 1928.

Bert Bacharach was hard at work, drawing up a list of names for the baby girl his wife Irma was expecting. When the baby arrived, on the twelfth, his efforts proved to have been in vain. It was a boy.

"In a moment of fatherly pride," Bert recalled many years later in the SATURDAY EVENING POST, "I decided the Bacharach family was ready for a Big Bert and a Little Bert."

But the senior Bacharach reflected on his own youth and decided it was unfair to inflict his own given name on his newborn son. Bertram, he decided, "might be considered a nice name in classy circles, but it was comparable to Algernon, Percy or Reginald in Atlantic City, where I went to grammar school."

So Little Bert became Little Burt.

When Burt was eight, his father (who had previously worked for a department store) became a newspaper columnist. His column was a huge success, syndicated for 19 years by King Features. He became well known for his writings on men's fashion and wrote two books, BERT BACHARACH'S BOOK FOR MEN and RIGHT DRESS, in the 1950s.

When Burt was two, the Bacharach family relocated to Kew Gardens, Queens, New York. After that, they moved to Forest Hills, Long Island, where mother Irma suggested that little Burt, now eight, take piano lessons.

"Burt threw himself into his instruction and absorbed absolutely everything offered to him," his father recalled, although Burt's musical future was far from apparent at the age of eight. At that stage, Burt's piano teacher regarded him as a good student, but not brilliant.

BURT BACHARACH AND FATHER BERT POSE FOR A JIM BEAM AD

Burt Bacharach & Hal David

"What a drag for a kid," Burt recalled in a mid-'60s NEWSWEEK profile. "Practicing the piano. But what else did I have to do?" Like most other boys his age, Burt was crazy about sports and girls but, he lamented, "I was too short for either."

Hoping that music would improve his social standing, the young Bacharach immersed himself in it, spending hours in front of the radio listening to symphonies. He wasn't immediately drawn to classical music. In the long Sunday car rides back to New York after visiting relatives Philadelphia, Irma would tune in the New York Philharmonic, but Burt wasn't impressed. He found most of the Philharmonic's repertoire – heavy on the Beethoven and Strauss – too serious and sad, even depressing.

Before too long, Burt "heard some music that cut through the drudgery: Debussy, Ravel's 'Daphnis et Chloe: Suite No. 2.' That was an opening for me. I had a similar experience when I heard what the bebop generation in jazz was doing: Dizzy Gillespie and Thelonius Monk and Charlie Parker. They were just in another world, musically – a very fresh world. So that was kind of exciting. It caught my interest."

By the time he was 13, Burt's parents sensed where his future lay, and sat him down for a family conference. "His mother and I told him we thought he had a good future in music," recalled his father in the SATURDAY EVENING POST. "But that only he could determine what he wanted to do." Burt told his folks he was sticking with music, although he was later to claim he had said it just to please his mother.

Before that, Burt had imagined he might end up in the men's clothing business. "That's where my dad had affiliations," he told the CBS SUNDAY MORNING show. "I thought it was the easiest, most accessible job that my dad might introduce me (to)."

Burt attended Forest Hills High School, studying music after school with Boleslav Marinu. Before long, he was playing piano in a band, performing at dances and at the local community center. Those performances helped Burt meet girls and generally improve his social standing. Finally, he felt like he belonged.

Until his mid-teens, Burt's burgeoning passion for music still co-existed with his dream of being a football player. The final piece of the puzzle fell into place in the early '40s, when a 15- or 16-year-old Burt sneaked into New York's Spotlight Club to catch a set by Dizzy Gillespie. Bacharach had never heard Gillespie before that night and the performance was a revelation. From that moment on, Bacharach knew that his future was music – not to please his parents, not to improve his social standing, but because the muse had grabbed him and wouldn't let go.

After high school, Bacharach decided to study music at college, but found that it was difficult to gain entrance to the top American music colleges. Having heard great things about the Music Conservatory at McGill University in Montreal, he decided to head up to Canada to pursue his studies.

Wowing the Dean with a Debussy piece on the piano, Burt secured the one available place in the program. Halfway through the young musician's performance, the Dean stopped him, saying, "We must have that lad." Burt was accepted and studied at McGill for the next three years.

As impressed as the Dean was with his playing, Bacharach didn't exactly have his pick of higher learning institutions. McGill "was one of the few schools that I could get into at that time," he says. "My high school grades were that bad. So (McGill) was not my first choice. I would rather have gone to Oberlin or Eastman, but I wasn't accepted."

Bacharach's studies at McGill didn't provide him with much musical inspiration. "I don't remember developing," he says, "kind of just marching through the three years that I was there."

Although he had not yet started composing, Bacharach was already a skilled pianist. During his first year at McGill, Bacharach won top honours in the Canadian Scholastic Piano Competition, in which he competed against thousands of budding pianists.

"I didn't study composition (at McGill)," Bacharach points out. "I studied piano. It was not a great music school at the time. I know it's evolved into a much better music school now than when I was there."

Bacharach may not have grown much through his courses at McGill, but he did find some inspiration in Montreal's thriving jazz scene.

"I did hear some good music," he says. "I used to hang out at (jazz clubs) Rockhead's Paradise and Café St-Michel. So that had some influence on me – hearing Oscar Peterson, hearing the Maynard Ferguson Big Band. There was some good musicianship going on there."

"Being in Montreal was very different from being in the States," Bacharach says. "It felt a little more European."

While at McGill, Bacharach wrote his first song, *The Night Plane To Heaven*. Burt wrote the song with "a man that I roomed with, a young man named Don Smith. It was probably not such a memorable song. I can't remember any more than that."

The Night Plane To Heaven was published, but went nowhere. Although his studies may still have been "a bore," Bacharach stuck it out, realizing the importance of formal musical training. He has always been a firm believer in the importance of being able to read and write music. In his own case, his formal grasp of music has given him the ability to get his musical ideas down on paper no matter where he is, without the aid of a piano or a tape recorder.

In fact, Burt found that writing away from the piano caused him to develop more interesting melodies and beats.

"When you're sitting at the piano, you tend to go to what's familiar and you can get trapped by pretty chords," he explained in an interview with MOJO. "And you go by the step, by the beat. If you get away from the piano and hear the melodic contour as well as the harmonisation in your head, you're hearing a long vertical line. I like to take a long look at the song."

In the summer, between semesters at McGill, Bacharach hooked up with a small jazz combo back in Forest Hills. With them, he got his first professional engagement, playing the summer season at a hotel in the Catskills. The engagement ended rather abruptly when the hotel burned down.

Bacharach left McGill after three years but, in 1972, the university gave the composer an Honorary Degree in Music.

Bacharach went on to study composition with Henry Cowell, at the Music Academy of the West, and with Darius Milhaud at the Mannes School of Music. Milhaud was an important influence on Bacharach's work. He taught the young composer not to be afraid of being melodic, telling him, "Don't ever be worried about something that people can remember, whistle or sing." Bacharach never forgot those words.

In 1950, Burt was drafted into the U.S. army for his two years of compulsory service. He wasn't much of a soldier, but his military stint did lead to new musical opportunities.

The other young soldiers nicknamed Burt "the maestro." He was often seen conducting an imaginary orchestra in the barracks and, when in a new town, sought out the local concert hall while the other soldiers headed for the bars. Bacharach was eventually recruited to tour army bases and army hospitals across the U.S., doing a program he called "Bach To Bacharach."

Burt's army stint took him to post-war Germany. In Garmisch, near Munich, the young GI supervised the entertainment at Casa Carioca, a nightclub in the U.S. army's recreation center. The elaborate club had its own ice rink, underneath the movable dance floor, and a convertible roof that slid open to reveal the sky.

Somewhere not far from Garmisch was a village called Bacharach. The village was more than just a namesake to Burt – it was where his grandparents had lived years earlier, before coming to America.

In Garmisch, Burt met a singing soldier named Vito Farnola, who performed under the stage name Vic Damone. After Burt's army stint ended in 1952, Bacharach and Damone toured America extensively, with Burt acting as Vic's conductor/arranger.

After that, Bacharach worked with the Ames Brothers, Polly Bergen and Imogene Coca. He even toured North Africa as a half-time act for the Harlem Globetrotters. He also worked with singer Paula Stewart, who became his wife in 1953. (They divorced in '58.)

Hearing the mediocre material being pitched to these acts by song pluggers,

BURT BACHARACH

Bacharach decided to try his hand at songwriting, figuring he could do at least as well as the stuff these other songwriters were turning out. To that end, he returned home to New York and rented a small office in the Brill Building, the hub of the *Tin Pan Alley* songwriting industry.

Located at 1619 Broadway, the Brill Building was the natural place for a budding songsmith to set up shop. Tough economic times during the Depression had forced the building's owners to rent space to music publishers. Initially, three publishers inhabited the Brill Building — Southern Music, Mills Music and Famous Music. Before long, other companies, such as Fred Fisher Music and Irving Caesar Music, moved in.

By the mid-'50s, the Brill Building was a thriving song factory, with eager writers hustling on each floor to get their works published. If they struck out on one floor, they'd hop in the elevator and try their luck on the next, and so on. There were arrangers who would knock off an arrangement for 10 dollars and there were demo studios where writers to put their ten-dollar arrangements on tape. On every floor of the building, musicians, record companies, managers and recording artists jostled for a shot at the charts.

The Brill Building was at its height during the late '50s and early '60s, as various songwriting teams fashioned the songs that ruled the era's charts: Gerry Goffin and Carole King (whose hits included *Up On The Roof*, *One Fine Day* and *Will You Love Me Tomorrow*), Barry Mann and Cynthia Weil (*You've Lost That Lovin' Feeling*, *We Gotta Get Out Of This Place*, *I Just Can't Help Believing*), Jerry Leiber and Mike Stoller (*Hound Dog*, *On Broadway*, *Love Potion No. 9*), Jeff Barry and Ellie Greenwich (*River Deep, Mountain High*, *I Can Hear Music*, *Be My Baby*) and Doc Pomus and Mort Shuman (*Save The Last Dance For me*, *Sweets For My Sweet*, *This Magic Moment*). And, by 1957, Burt Bacharach and Hal David.

Bacharach and David arrived at the Brill Building during an era of transition. Rock and roll was changing the music industry in many ways, and songwriters and publishers were hit hard. After rock and roll and its offshoots took hold, songs and their publication as sheet music became much less important than they had been previously, the emphasis now being placed on recordings, on particular versions of songs.

Burt Bacharach & Hal David

When Bacharach first set up his office at the Brill, he was happy just to get a song published. Already displaying the work ethic that would push him to the top of the charts in the '60s, Burt's goal was to turn out four songs a day.

During his 10 months in the rented office, Bacharach was met with plenty of rejection. To pay the bills, he did weekend gigs as an accompanist/conductor, working with Joel Grey, Georgia Gibbs and Steve Lawrence. Weekdays, Bacharach toiled away in his little office, learning the craft of songwriting, but produced no hits. His first recorded song was *Keep Me In Mind*, co-written by Jack Wolf and recorded by Patti Page in 1954. It didn't chart.

In 1955 and 1956 Bacharach continued to write with Wolf, their other collaborations including *How About* and *It's Great To Be Young*. Burt also wrote with Wilson Stone (their *Desperate Hours* was cut by the legendary crooner Mel Torme), Edward Heyman (*Beauty Isn't Everything* and *Whispering Campaign*) and Sammy Gallup (*My Dreamboat Is Drifting* and *Uninvited Dream*).

Although Bacharach's early efforts were not as ambitious as his '60s work, he was already pushing the boundaries of pop songwriting. But, in those early days, his more adventurous work met with resistance from powerful record company A&R men.

"They'll never be able to dance to it," the A&R men would complain. If he would just change a certain idiosyncratic three-bar phrase to a more conventional four bars, they told him, his song would get recorded. And Burt, eager for a hit but happy just to get a song *recorded*, listened. Changes were made and the young composer's ideas were compromised.

"I listened (to the A&R men) and ruined some good songs," he told NEWSWEEK years later. "What I've found is that if it's a good tune people will find a way to dance to it."

If Bacharach's early compositions sound less inventive than his later efforts, some of the blame has to go to record company interference. Also, the talented composer needed a lyricist whose flair for words could match his way with a melody. In 1956, he found just the man for the job.

Chapter 2: My Heart Is An Open Book

By the summer of 1956, Burt Bacharach was still in the Brill Building, but was now working for Famous Music. Eddie Wolpin, the general manager of Famous, suggested he try pairing up with a lyricist named Hal David, who had already written a number of hits.

David was seven years older than Bacharach, born in Brooklyn in May 1921. Hal's first musical experience was taking violin lessons as a child.

"I wrote for my own amusement when I was a kid," he recalls. "All through school. I had a little band in Brooklyn."

During the summers of his high school years, Hal's band played Saturday night shows in "boarding-room type Borscht-circuit hotels."

As Hal grew older, it became clear that he had a way with words. He wrote parody songs for the Saturday night shows he played with his band and, in writing these, he felt more strongly about the lyrics than he did about the music.

Hal's lyrical inclinations grew, fostered by the supportive environment in which he and his two brothers were raised. Many years later, in an interview for the SONGWRITERS SHOWCASE radio show, Hal fondly recalled his old school, Thomas Jefferson High.

"It was a great school. They encouraged those of us who had some interest in the arts and writing and painting..." The three David sons "all got involved in the arts, while my mother and father were cutting corned beef and pastrami (in their deli). How it happened, I don't know..."

Hal's older brother Mack was already having success as a songwriter (Mack wrote music as well as lyrics), and Hal was eager to follow in his footsteps, at least a far as lyrics were concerned.

Mack David's songwriting successes included *I Don't Care If The Sun Don't Shine*, *Candy*, *Cherry Pink and Apple Blossom White*, *It Must Be Him*, and the songs for Walt Disney's CINDERELLA.

Although Hal wanted to become a lyric writer, Mack did not encourage him. The older brother felt the life of a lyricist was too difficult and that Hal should get a job in advertising or write for a newspaper. Hal took Mack's advice and aimed for a newspaper career. After high school, he enrolled in the New York University School of Journalism, but his studies were soon interrupted by the Second World War.

"When I was drafted into the army, I was sent overseas – after a month of basic training in Los Angeles," Hal recalls. "And the day we got over to Hawaii, there was a longshoremen's strike. The head of the union at the time was a man named Harry

Bridges. He was a communist, and he called a strike during the middle of World War Two. So we had to unload our own ships. It was backbreaking work."

After a day of hard labour, a sign caught David's eye: 'U.S. Army show – Auditions at the U.S.O. Building in Honolulu.'

The next day, David headed over to the U.S.O. Building to audition for the Central Pacific Entertainment Section (CPES). The CPES – whose members also included comedian Carl Reiner and actor Werner Klemperer (best remembered as "Colonel Klink" on *Hogan's Heroes*) – served under Major Maurice Evans. In civilian life, Evans was a successful actor, known at that time for his Shakespearian roles, but subsequently best known as Dr. Zaius, the simian villain in the late '60s film classic PLANET OF THE APES.

"They were looking for singers, dancers, writers, what have you," David recalls. "And there was a line coming out of the U.S.O. Building of soldiers seeking to get into an army show. When it was my turn to audition, they asked me what I did. And I said, 'Well, I'm a writer. I write songs, I write sketches, I write this, I write that.' I had written for the NEW YORK POST. So that intrigued Maurice Evans. And he said, 'We'll get you in on a 30 day detached service and see how it works out.'

"The next day they had a truck to take me down to the CPES, which was at the University of Hawaii in Oahu, just outside of Honolulu," David continues. "There I went to Evans' office and he took me into the auditorium that was our theatre, Farrington Hall. And there was George Schaffer, the young fellow who was directing. George asked me to do some writing. They were all happy with my stuff. And I stayed there for close to three years."

David's army stint convinced him that songwriting, not journalism, was where his future lay.

"I loved the writing of songs," he says, "and that's what I decided to do. They were wonderful shows. It was a wonderful experience for me and for all of us."

Under Evans' direction, the unit put on various productions to which Hal contributed joke sketches and song lyrics. Teaming up with composer Roger Adams, he began writing songs to entertain the troops.

In 1943, on the basis of the songs he wrote for the CPES, David became a member of the American Society of Composers, Authors and Publishers (ASCAP). After the war, David continued to write, at first with Roger Adams.

"Roger came from a theatrical family," David says. "He knew a lot of people, and I knew some people through my brother. We started making the rounds. We didn't do so well with the publishers, but we started writing special material for nightclub performers. And that's how I made a living, writing special material – basically comedic material – trying to break through. And, being around, I met some composers in the pop field. And I started writing with them as well as Roger, and I began to get published."

Inevitably, David soon found himself at the Brill Building.

"The Brill Building became my hangout," he recalls. "There was a restaurant (in the building), the Turf, where the writers would gather at lunchtime, where I would go and have lunch. I'd meet a lot of the other writers – when I could afford to eat at the Turf. Or else I'd be eating at a hog dog stand or something!"

HAL DAVID

At first, Hal listened to the advice of music publishers, who suggested that he write songs that aped "last week's hit." He did so, with little success, and then decided that, if he was going to fail anyway, he may as well do so on his own terms. He began writing lyrics that were much more personal. So began the approach that characterized his subsequent body of work: the events of the songs are imagined, but the feelings expressed in the words come from his own experience.

From his earliest days as a lyricist, David has strived to write about people and feelings, rather than ideas and things. Many of his best lyrics (including *A House Is Not A Home* and *What The World Needs Now Is Love*) have stressed the importance of love over material things.

In 1945, Hal penned lyrics for a number of songs, including *If It's For Me, I'm Not Home* (with Leonard Whitecup) and *You Could Sell Me The Brooklyn Bridge* (with Roc Hillman). He also wrote some numbers with his brother Mack during this period, including *The Lady With The Light In The Harbour* and *The Sands Of San Jose* – the latter showing that Hal was already exploring the lyrical possibilities of the California town's name two decades before he and Burt Bacharach wrote *Do You Know The Way To San Jose?*

In the late '40s, David worked with a number of different collaborators, but wrote regularly with two in particular. With Don Rodney, he wrote *Funny Little Money Man, I'd Rather Be Wrong Than Be Sorry, Peek-a-boo, Strummin' On The Old Banjo, Get Me One Of Those* and numerous others. Hal also wrote extensively with Arthur Altman, penning *Me And Your Cigarette, Blue For A Boy, Pink For A Girl, The Wall Between Us, True Love* and many others.

David had little success until 1947, when one of his songs caught the ear of bandleader Sammy Kaye. Two years later, Hal had his first hit with Kaye's recording of *The Four Winds And The Seven Seas*, co-written with Don Rodney. Five different artists charted with *The Four Winds And The Seven Seas* in 1949: Sammy Kaye, Mel Torme, Vic Damone, Herb Jeffries and Guy Lombardo all scored hits with the song, the most successful being that by Kaye, which reached No. 3.

Another brush with the charts came in 1950, when Frank Sinatra cut *American Beauty Rose*, penned by David, Arthur Altman and Red Evans. *American Beauty Rose* was recorded by Sinatra in 1951 and charted at No. 26. Another version, by Eddy Howard, reached No. 21.

From 1951 to 1958, David wrote mainly with Leon Carr (*For the Life Of Me, Let's Have A Meeting Of The Lips, Take The Note The Bluebird Wrote*, and the hit *Bell Bottom Blues*) and Lee Pockriss (*You Won't Have To Cry Over Me, I Could Be A Mountain* and the hit *My Heart Is An Open Book*).

By the mid-'50s, Hal was writing lyrics at one of the Brill Building's bigger publishing companies, Famous Music. It was there that he met Burt Bacharach in 1956. Eddie Wolpin suggested that Burt and Hal try writing together and, after a year or so, the charts beckoned.

Chapter 3: Show And Tell

"We used to meet every day at Famous Music," says Hal David, recalling the early days of his partnership with Burt Bacharach. "I'd come in with some titles and some ideas for songs, lines. Burt would come in with opening strains of phrases or what might be part of a chorus section. It was like 'Show And Tell': I'd show him what I had thought of and he'd show me what he had thought of. And whatever seemed to spark the other would be the start of whatever song we started to write that day. I'd write four lines or six lines of a lyric and he'd have a melody and, very often, we'd sit in the room and write the song together – sort of pound it out. I'd be writing lyrics and he'd be writing music and, all of a sudden, we'd have the structure of a song, which we'd keep working on. We didn't write songs so quickly that they were done overnight or that day. I'd take home his melody and he'd take home my lyrics and so, very often, we'd be working on three different songs at one time."

The setting was by no means glamorous, but certainly typically of the Brill Building era: a cramped room, a window that didn't open and a well-worn upright piano. The smoke from David's cigarettes would fill the office as the pair worked away, breaking mid-day to send out for liverwurst sandwiches from a nearby deli.

Among Burt and Hal's earliest efforts together were *Peggy's In The Pantry* (recorded ... Cherry Parsons), *The Morning Mail* (recorded by the Gallahads), *Tell The Truth And The Devil, Your Lips Are Warmer* and *Warm And Tender*. Their song *I Cry More*, sung ... Dale, showed up in the film DON'T KNOCK THE ROCK.

Bacharach and David's efforts during 1957 included *I Could Kick Myself, The Last Time I Saw My Heart, The Night That Heaven Fell* (recorded by Tony Bennett), *Saturday Night in Tia Juana'* and *Third from the Left*. They also collaborated with Paul Hampton on *Paradise Island*.

MARTY ROBBINS – STORY OF MY LIFE LP

The duo's first success came in 1957, when Marty Robbins recorded *The Story Of My Life* for Columbia Records. Driven by a whimsical whistling hook, the Mitch Miller-produced single peaked at No. 15, and reached the top spot on the country chart. Although *The Story Of My Life* turned out to be a country record, that wasn't Bacharach and David's original intention.

"I thought I was writing a pop song," Hal said years later in an interview with BILLBOARD, "and I found out it was a country song."

In Britain, *The Story Of My Life* was a No. 1 hit for Michael Holliday in 1958 and two other versions, by Alma Cogan and Dave King, also charted there. *The Story Of My Life* was swiftly followed into the charts by another Bacharach/David collaboration, Perry Como's *Magic Moments*, a No. 27 hit.

Bacharach and David didn't have a set formula for writing together. Sometimes the words came first, sometimes the music, and sometimes words and music grew at the same time, each feeding off and building upon the other. In the case of *Magic Moments*, the Bacharach melody came first and David, using a method that was a staple of his lyric-writing career, listened to the tune until it spoke to him. His lyric for *Magic Moments* grew out of what the melody said to him and such was his enthusiasm that he even wrote lyrics for a section that Bacharach had intended to be instrumental. Bacharach warmed to the idea and what was intended as an instrumental became the verse of the song.

Although pleasant and eminently humble, Burt and Hal's first two hits gave little indication of what was to come.

"Our first two big songs... didn't exactly break new ground," Hal observed many years later in a LOS ANGELES TIMES interview.

After that initial double-shot, things died down a little, but Burt and Hal continued to write together.

Burt Bacharach & Hal David

MARLENE DIETRICH – MORE OF THE BEST CD

Despite those early songwriting successes, Burt remained active as an arranger/conductor. In 1958, Marlene Dietrich hired him as her musical director.

"I was on my way to California to try to learn something about film scoring and maybe get a chance to score a movie," Bacharach told US magazine. "And I got a call from Peter Matz, a friend who conducted for both Dietrich and Noel Coward. Matz was in a bind and asked whether I would consider, like, working with her. I said, shoot, yes, that would be great! I went to see her the next day at the Beverly Hills Hotel in one of the villas. She was intimidating, you know, just this legend."

"It's quite a job," Bacharach told BILLBOARD in 1960, "but Marlene thinks I'm the only one who can handle her music. It's a lot of fun to work with Marlene. She really is a friend."

With Dietrich, Bacharach began performing his signature "magic act" – standing up at the piano, playing with his left hand and conducting with his right. However, in his early shows with Dietrich, Burt was invisible for most of the performance.

"They used to put a scrim in front of me," he told the New York Times years later. "Not that she was trying to hide me, but they used the scrim for lighting effects. Then, for the last three numbers, they'd open the scrim and – lo and behold! – there'd be a Jewish piano player."

Although he was touring extensively with Dietrich, Bacharach's work as a composer began to take up an increasing amount of his time. Luckily for Burt, Dietrich "didn't want to work that hard, so I had chunks of time on my hands for writing songs." Burt toured regularly with Dietrich until 1962 and made periodic appearances with her after that.

"My respect and my love for the musician Burt Bacharach is matched by my love and my respect for the man," Dietrich said in the liner notes for Burt's first LP. "No matter how many curtains open and close between me and the audience—his approval is what I am seeking. What happiness to sing to his melodies and orchestrations which carry me like a magic carpet to the theatres of the world."

Dietrich was certain that her musical director would one day be as famous as she was. She once called Frank Sinatra to tell him that he should record Bacharach and David's early number *Warm And Tender*.

"She probably believed in me more as a writer at the time than I believed in myself," Bacharach said in an interview for the TV show BIOGRAPHY.

Bacharach also worked as nightclub piano man during this period. In 1958, he did a stint playing regular gigs at the Bayview on Fire Island. These evenings, in the 11 p.m. to 2 a.m. slot, Bacharach played some of his own work but favoured old standbys.

"He knows the showtunes and the standards," said VARIETY in a review of one of Burt's Bayview gigs, "and the Islanders who (huddle) around the piano or hug the tables seldom ask for more. The keyboarding, like the room, is unpretentious and informal."

Despite all his other obligations, Bacharach still found time to write with Hal David. From 1958 to 1961, Bacharach/David collaborations included the Jane Morgan single *With Open Arms* (which reached No. 39), the Four Coins' *Wendy Wendy* (a No. 72 hit), Connie Stevens' *And This Is Mine* and a couple of Drifters B-sides.

Despite their initial success together, both Bacharach and David continued to work with other writers. Bacharach wrote with Bob Hilliard (the Drifters' *Please Stay* and *Mexican Divorce*) and co-wrote the Shirelles' hit *Baby, It's You* with Hal's brother, Mack. Burt and Mack also penned the theme to a cheesy horror flick called THE BLOB in 1958, the eponymous theme becoming a hit for the Five Blobs, a studio group fronted by Bernie Nee.

During this period, Hal David saw his lyrics reach the charts via *Johnny Get Angry* by Joannie Sommers, *Sea Of Heartbreak* by Don Gibson, *The Charanga* by Merv Griffin, *Outside My Window* by the Fleetwoods and Sarah Vaughan's million-selling *Broken-Hearted Melody*. Hal also wrote a number of songs with Sherman Edwards, including *I'm Liking This*, *Kissin' On The Red Light* and the Patti Page hit *You'll Answer To Me*.

"It seemed everyone was bouncing around," Bacharach recalled in Joe Smith's OFF THE RECORD: AN ORAL HISTORY OF POPULAR MUSIC. "It was almost incestuous. I'd write with Hal David three times a week, and then I'd switch off and write with Bob Hilliard in the morning, and then in the afternoon Bob would write with the same composer Hal had just finished with."

Between 1958 and 1962, much of Burt's time was spent touring with Dietrich, but he still devoted time to songwriting, and sought to improve his skills. He even sought advice from another songwriting team, Leiber and Stoller, about writing songs and making records with a more contemporary feel.

"We didn't teach him how to write music, hardly," said Mike Stoller in an interview with the British Film Institute, "but he was very curious about the effects and rhythms we used, and the instruments we used. He adopted those in his recordings."

Indeed, Bacharach's music evolved significantly during this period - from the lightweight sing-along style of *Magic Moments* and *The Story Of My Life* to the sophisticated, contemporary rhythm and blues sound of his early '60s work with Dionne Warwick and Lou Johnson. His love of jazz and classical music also came to bear as his style developed.

Bacharach worked on a number of Drifters sessions with Leiber and Stoller during 1961, as an arranger and a writer. The group recorded two songs he co-wrote with Bob Hilliard, *Please Stay* and *Mexican Divorce*.

As more and more Bacharach and David numbers appeared in the BILLBOARD singles chart, the songwriting-partner swapping came to an end. But although Burt and Hal began to write together more or less exclusively, they had yet to find a voice that suited all their material, so they continued to pitch their songs to a variety of different artists. In 1961, Chuck Jackson's recording of *I Wake Up Crying* made No. 59 in the pop charts. The following year, Tommy Hunt peaked at No. 119 with the first recording of *I Just Don't Know What To Do With Myself*, while Babs Tino went two positions higher with *Forgive Me (For Giving You Such A Bad Time)*.

In 1962, Burt and Hal began a fruitful collaboration with Gene Pitney, best known at that time for his 1961 hit *A Town Without Pity*.

"When I first started recording, Bacharach and David were just another two writers coming around when I had a session," recalls Pitney, "trying to get a song in. But I could tell right away that they were different from the majority of writers. They had that something about them."

Listening to Bacharach perform the duo's numbers at the piano in an office at the Brill Building, Pitney was impressed not only by the songs, but by the composer's vocal delivery.

"Most times Burt would play the song on piano and let me have a run at it," he says. "He sings his own songs so great that you can never do it as well. I don't mean technically, just that he puts so much of Burt into the music that you can't get him out, even when you are singing the song! His nuances and subtle shading on his melodies is very difficult to copy. I had to try to make the songs my own and not try to emulate Burt."

By this point, Bacharach and David were doing most of their sessions at a New York studio called Bell Sound.

"I can always see Burt conducting the orchestras in Bell Sound," recalls Pitney. "His command was electrifying. The musicians had so much respect that they would be absolutely quiet and do his every bidding. The guitarists would bring in several guitars to see which one fit the particular song and again do whatever they could for Burt."

"Any Bacharach session was a great one," says Pitney. "The air was always crackling with emotion and creativity. I find it hard to work the way most songs are recorded today, without any orchestra in the studio, and all tracks having been done beforehand. To watch the masters at work while I was singing the vocals was a complete rush that prompted that extra 10 per cent out of my performance. To see the string section bowing and Gary Chester wailing away on the drums, and Bucky Pizzerelli playing those great licks on guitar. It doesn't get any better than that!"

In May of 1962, Pitney reached No. 4 with (*The Man Who Shot*) *Liberty Valance*, the first of his four Bacharach/David-authored singles. Although it got plenty of radio play, the song was not featured in the John Wayne film of the same title.

The studio, Paramount Pictures, was keen to feature the "(The Man Who Shot) Liberty Valance)" in the film, but the director, John Ford, refused. It wasn't so much that he didn't like the song, but simply didn't want any song in his picture.

"A bit of trivia that I learned about five years ago is that the music that did end up in *Liberty Valance* was the old score from a Henry Fonda film called *Young Mister Lincoln*," says Pitney. "The only connection I could find was that they were both directed by John Ford."

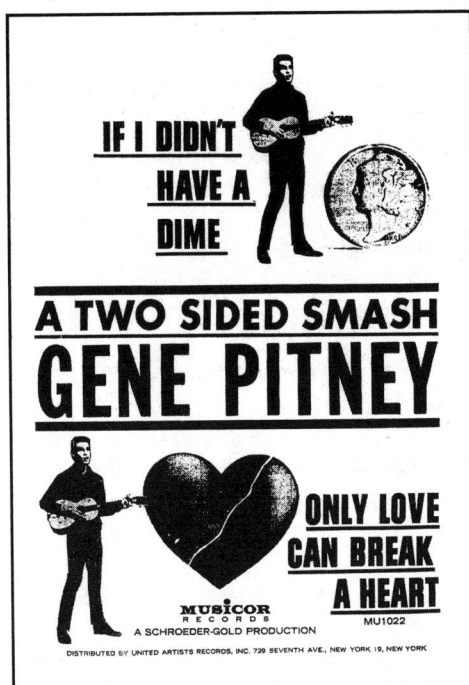

AN AD FOR GENE PITNEY'S *ONLY LOVE CAN BREAK A HEART* SINGLE

Pitney subsequently charted with three other Bacharach/David numbers — *Only Love Can Break A Heart* (which reached No. 2), *True Love Never Runs Smooth* (No. 21) and *24 Hours From Tulsa* (No. 17). He also recorded *Donna Means Heartbreak*, a song Hal wrote with Paul Hampton.

24 Hours From Tulsa features one of Hal David's more memorable lyrics from this period.

"I wrote that to a melody that Burt wrote and that's what the melody said to me," David recalls. "Music speaks to a lyric writer, or at least it should speak to a lyric writer. And that's what the music said to me. And why it did, I don't know. I don't think I had ever been to Tulsa. I've always kind of liked what I call 'narrative songs' — story songs. And when I hear music, very often I hear a story. The fact that it was Tulsa, as opposed to Dallas, is not terribly meaningful, but the sound of 'Tulsa' rang in my ear."

Although *Liberty Valance* was a hit for Pitney, his subsequent Bacharach and David-penned film theme, *The Fool Killer*, flopped. Aside from being less overtly commercial than his other Bacharach-David records, it was hindered by the fact that it wasn't included in the movie of the same name.

"I'm not sure what happened with *'Fool Killer'*, says Pitney, "but my gut feeling is that the publisher Aaron Schroeder was playing a bit of a game with the film studio and Bacharach and David. Aaron was the best at getting songs out there and fought hard for his songs and sometimes he did what he had to do and burned one party or the other."

Several other Bacharach and David songs were reportedly intended for Pitney, but didn't happen.

"I'm not sure if I ever turned down a Bacharach and David song," says Pitney. "I know Burt played me *Trains And Boats And Planes* one day after he finished it and I told him that it wasn't very good. Yikes. Where was my head that day!!"

What The World Needs Now Is Love was also reportedly written with Pitney in mind.

"I didn't know about *What The World Needs Now*," Pitney says. "Probably a publishing problem again. Schroeder tried to get the publishing on any song I recorded and Bacharach and David were shrewd enough to know they should keep it if they could. You can lose some great songs that way."

"I think our relationship ended when Burt and Hal started using Dionne (Warwick) for the majority of their songs," says Pitney. "I am sure this was publishing coming to the fore again. I couldn't be the vehicle for their songs if they were to keep the publishing so I was taken out of the Bacharach and David picture."

Chapter 4: Dionne

In 1962, six years after they started writing together, Bacharach and David found the perfect voice for their songs. The catalyst for their success was a college student from New Jersey.

Marie Dionne Warrick was born on December 12, 1940, in Newark, New Jersey. That she became a singer was no great surprise. Gospel music was a big part of her family's life, and her aunts and uncles had a highly regarded vocal group, the Drinkard Singers.

As a child, Dionne had a keen interest in music, learning to play the piano and showing great promise as a singer. At 14, she and sister Delia formed their own vocal group, the Gospelaires. The group won an amateur contest at the Apollo Theater and soon found work singing background on recording sessions.

In 1959, Dionne won a scholarship to study music at Hartt College in West Hartford, Connecticut. ("You've practically got to be a music major to sing Bacharach music," she told NEWSWEEK in 1970.) By 1962, her time was divided between her music major at Hartt and session work.

By 1961, the Gospelaires were in demand for recording sessions, their voices gracing sides by Bobby Darin, the Shirelles and Chuck Jackson.

Burt Bacharach first encountered Dionne when the Gospelaires sang backup on a Drifters session in 1961. The song was one Burt had written with Bob Hilliard, *Mexican Divorce*, and the 21-year-old Dionne, with her hair in pigtails and wearing jeans and dirty white sneakers, caught the composer's ear.

"We had been doing a lot of background work with different producers," says Warwick. "Burt approached me and asked if I'd do some demonstration records of songs he was going to write with a new songwriting partner, whose name happened to be Hal David."

"The group was dynamite," said Burt. "But there was something about the way (Dionne) carried herself that made me want to hear her sing by herself. After I did, she started to do all our demos."

"She was a background singer on a lot of the recording dates," recalls Hal David. "And she came to Burt, wanting to do some demo records for him. He invited her up to Famous Music and she sang for both of us. We both were very impressed and we went in and did a couple of demo songs with her. The first one was *It's Love That Really Counts* and then we did *Make It Easy On Yourself*."

The demo of *It's Love That Really Counts* was impressive enough to get Dionne signed to Florence Greenberg's Scepter Records label.

Greenberg had entered the music business in the late '50s. At that time, she was a housewife in her 30s, with no previous experience in the music business. But she knew what she liked, and her instincts eventually paid off. Greenberg formed a label called Tiara, on which she put out the debut single by a girl group called the Shirelles. After the group's debut single enjoyed some success, Decca Records offered Greenberg $4000 for the label and the Shirelles' contract. She took the offer, using the $4000 to start another label, Scepter, in 1959. Decca soon lost interest in the Shirelles and sold them back to Greenberg, whose faith in the group was rewarded in 1960 by a No. 1 single, Goffin and King's *Will You Love Me Tomorrow*.

Scepter soon established itself as one of America's most important R&B labels. By the mid-'60s, the R&B sound was increasingly being accepted by pop fans.

"The country and the music business have finally come to recognize R&B music for what it really is," noted Scepter vice-president Marvin Schlacter in an interview with

AN EARLY SCEPTER RECORDS WARWICK AD

MAKE WAY FOR DIONNE WARWICK LP

BILLBOARD, "and have come to accept it as a tremendous influence on today's pop music."

"Florence was quite a gal," says Steve Tyrell, a Texan who started at Scepter in 1964 as a staff producer. "She had some very intuitive creative instincts, but I don't know where they came from, and I don't think she did either! But she definitely had 'em. She's the one that signed Dionne Warwick, she's the one that gave Burt and Hal the deal to produce."

When Burt and Hal played Greenberg the demo of *It's Love That Really Counts*, meaning to pitch the song, the label boss was more impressed by the singer. Greenberg signed Warwick almost immediately, and also gave Bacharach and David a production deal.

"They took the (demo of) *It's Love That Really Counts* to Scepter," says Warwick, "and Florence Greenberg didn't care for the song but she wanted the voice. I was in school at the time, so that was the last thing on my mind. And, as long as it didn't interfere with my education – my mom would never have stood for it – we finally got to the point where we started to record."

"Florence said, 'I'll sign her and let you guys write and produce for her,'" says Tyrell. For the first time, Burt and Hal would have complete control over how the songs were recorded. This was especially important to Burt, who had been frustrated about the way his music was changed to suit the tastes of record labels and producers.

Bacharach may have initially seen music as a way to improve his social status in school but, by the late '50s, music was his passion. When he conducted, the music seemed to consume him. His compositions were of huge importance to him and he became very protective of them.

"He'd hear the whole record in his head when he was writing a song," says Tyrell. From that point on, what Burt and Hal heard in their heads would be, more or less, what was released.

"We had total creative freedom," Bacharach recalled in the liner notes for the Dionne Warwick CD FROM THE VAULTS, "and after Hal and I wrote a song, the only person we had to run it by was Dionne."

"Before we started to record Dionne," says David, "we went through, for the most part, Famous Music, and they pitched the songs. In those days, very often you'd go and play things live (with Burt singing at the piano) for Mitch Miller or whomever you were playing things for and then, if they liked the song, you'd go and make a demo. Sometimes you'd do a demo (first), if you were sending something out to California or somewhere else. If it was in New York, it would be (played) live."

A VEE JAY RECORDS AD

Eddie Wolpin took Dionne's demo of *Make It Easy On Yourself* to Vee-Jay Records. The label placed the song with Jerry Butler, who recorded it and had a No. 20 hit. The record was a breakthrough for Bacharach, since it was one of the first times he had been actively involved in a record's production.

Not everyone was enthusiastic about the record: Dionne had assumed that the song would be her debut single, and was not pleased to hear that Burt and Hal had given it to Butler.

"Dionne was much perturbed," Hal remembers, "because she thought that was her song."

"When I finally decided, 'Okay, I'll record,' one of the songs that I wanted was *Make It Easy On Yourself*," Dionne says. "And that's when they informed me that song had already been given to Jerry Butler. And one thing led to another, and my final words were basically, 'Don't make me over, don't even try.' And out of that, Hal David wrote a song called *Don't Make Me Over*."

Bacharach and David did their first session with Warwick on August 18, 1962, at Bell Sound in midtown Manhattan. Most of New York's key studios were located in the area, many within easy walking distance of the Brill Building. Bacharach and David's early sessions were done in Bell Sound's Studio A, with Eddie Smith engineering. On that first session with Dionne, Burt and Hal produced three tracks: *I Smiled Yesterday*, *Unlucky* and *Don't Make Me Over* – the latter written by Bacharach and David in response to the misunderstanding over *Make It Easy On Yourself*.

Having had a great deal of studio experience with the Gospelaires, the transition to being a recording artist in her own right was an easy one for Warwick.

"Being a session singer, I was quite accustomed to the studio," she says, "the only difference being that I was in the lead vocal booth, while everybody else was in the other booth."

Scepter released *Don't Make Me Over* at the end of 1962. A spelling error on the record label meant that Dionne Warrick was billed as "Dionne Warwick." As the record raced up the charts, there was no time to correct the spelling and from that moment on, the singer was known as Dionne Warwick. By January 1963, the first release by the newly rechristened Ms. Warwick had climbed to its peak chart position of No. 21.

Don't Make Me Over was just the beginning of a stunning run of singles for the Bacharach-David-Warwick team. The partnership would yield no less than 36 hits over the next 10 years, in addition to many more classic album tracks and B-sides. With Dionne, Burt and Hal perfected the style that made them famous. As Burt himself liked to put it, these records were "three-and-a-half minute movies," with different levels of musical intensity and lyrics that told a story.

During this period, Warwick continued to sing on Bacharach and David's demos. A few of these recordings even showed up on her records: Dionne's demo version of *It's Love That Really Counts* turned up on her first LP, PRESENTING DIONNE WARWICK, as did *Make It Easy On Yourself*. Florence Greenberg gave the demo of *It's Love That Really Counts* to the Shirelles, who released it as a B-side, charting at No. 102.

Dionne continued to do back-up work after signing to Scepter. She added her voice to Timi Yuro's recording of *The Love Of A Boy*, which peaked at No. 44 at the end of 1962. The song was familiar to Warwick, since she sang the demo version, which eventually showed up on the flip of her *Anyone Who Had A Heart* 45.

During her years at Scepter, Dionne worked with other producers as well as Bacharach and David. Her singles and many of her album tracks were done with Burt and Hal, but her early albums also featured recordings produced by Scepter's main producer Luther Dixon and Florence Greenberg's son Stan.

Chapter 5: Hitmakers!

With Dionne Warwick as the perfect voice for their songs and a burgeoning sideline in movie themes, Bacharach and David hit their stride in the early '60s. However, Warwick's next two singles, *This Empty Place* and *Make The Music Play*, did not match the success of *Don't Make Me Over* – peaking at No. 84 and No. 81, respectively – and Bacharach and David continued to pen hit songs for other artists. Their other successes of 1963 included Bobby Vinton's Blue On Blue (a No. 3 hit in June), Bobby Vee's *Anonymous Phone Call* (No. 110 in January) and the Gene Pitney singles *True Love Never Runs Smooth* and *Twenty Four Hours From Tulsa*.

Another Bacharach and David classic, Jack Jones' *Wives And Lovers*, was unleashed in late 1963. The track clicked with record buyers and peaked at No. 14 in the charts. Like *(The Man Who Shot) Liberty Valance*, *Wives And Lovers* is often assumed to be the theme song from the movie of the same name. In fact, says Hal David, this is not quite true.

"WIVES AND LOVERS was the title of a film," he explains. "We were asked to write what would be called an 'exploitation song.' It wasn't going in the film, but it was meant to come out and, every time it got played, the name of the film would be performed. It was a song to promote the film, but it was never in the film. It was never meant to be in the film. Exploitation songs were very common in those days."

"I never thought for a moment that *Wives And Lovers* had a ghost of a chance of being a hit," says David. "It just seemed too hip and sophisticated for its time."

Wives And Lovers proved that, in pushing the boundaries in terms of rhythms and arrangements, Burt and Hal could be even more successful than when they listened to the suggestions of the A&R men.

"Very often our most uncommercial songs become the biggest hits in the country," Hal pointed out in a 1964 BILLBOARD interview. "*Wives And Lovers* is an example. It was an assignment from Paramount Pictures. As we saw it, the only honest approach was to do it off-beat musically. So we wrote it as a jazz waltz."

Initially, Jones's label Kapp Records saw the track as *too* off-beat, and promoted the other side of the single. But Kapp's West Coast promotion man Gil Frazen was convinced that *Wives And Lovers* was the hit side and pushed the song until he was proven correct.

Although Dionne Warwick was quickly becoming Burt and Hal's vocalist of choice, she did not initially get first refusal of all their material. In the 1963-64 period, singer Lou Johnson first recorded some of their best new songs. Johnson had recently signed to Big Top Records, and the label's publishing company Hill & Range (located, naturally, in the Brill Building) had hooked him up with Bacharach and David. Although he didn't have much chart success with Bacharach and David material, Johnson was the first to record *Reach Out For Me* and *Message To Martha* (AKA *Message To Michael*) – both of which later provided hits for Warwick.

LOU JOHNSON'S *REACH OUT FOR ME* SINGLE

Towards the end of 1963, Bacharach and David charted with Lou Johnson's recording of *Reach Out For Me*, which made it No. 74. Johnson is one of the unsung heroes of the Bacharach and David story. The songwriters had high hopes for Johnson, but his versions didn't really catch on, and it was left to others to score with the songs Johnson recorded first. Nonetheless, Johnson's versions are regarded as essential by Bacharach/David purists and he was, in those early days, their male equivalent to Dionne Warwick.

As the quality of their collaborations improved and the hits became more frequent, Burt and Hal reached a point where they no longer worked with other writers. Recalls David, "I don't think we ever said to each other, 'Hey, let's write together exclusively', we just started to."

Meanwhile, in early 1963, Bacharach began a side career as a recording artist. He had previously released a one-off single entitled *The Searching Wind* in 1958, and put out a single entitled *Move It On The Backbeat* – credited to Burt and the Back Beats – at the beginning of '63. Neither disc had charted and Burt's own recording career didn't begin in earnest until he signed to Kapp Records in the summer of 1963.

Bacharach's first Kapp release was the single *Saturday Sunshine*, a pleasant track that sneaked into the Billboard Top 100, peaking at No. 93 in July.

Over the years, some of Bacharach and David's biggest hit records have been re-recordings of songs that were not successful when they were first released or which first appeared only as B-sides or album cuts. A perfect case-in-point is *(They Long To Be) Close To You*: the song made its first appearance in late 1963, on the flip side of *Blue Guitar*, a No. 42 hit by actor Richard Chamberlain, the star of TV's *Dr. Kildare*. The song would be re-recorded a number of times, but the best-known version would not appear until 1970, when the Carpenters took it to No. 1. Dionne sang on the demo of *Close to You*, as she did with many early Bacharach/David numbers, and her demo was issued on the B-side of a single.

At the end of 1963, Warwick met up with Burt and Hal at Burt's apartment, to rehearse songs for an upcoming session. The songwriting duo played her a short new segment that they were working on. Dionne loved it immediately and jokingly demanded, "What are you waiting for? Finish it off!"

To her surprise and delight, Bacharach and David did just that. By the next morning, they had a newly completed song, *Anyone Who Had A Heart*.

The song became part of the next Bacharach/David/Warwick studio session. Usually, the studio and musicians for these sessions were booked in three-hour blocks, with the aim of getting three or four songs recorded. Some artists finished in less than three hours, still having to pay the musicians their three-hour minimum fee. This never happened when Bacharach and David were in the studio. With Burt and Hal trying to capture the best possible take of each song, their sessions frequently went into overtime, sometimes to the tune of thousands of dollars in musician's fees.

The *Anyone Who Had A Heart* session was running behind schedule, and it became clear that there would only be time to complete two tracks. The two options for recording after *Anyone Who Had A Heart* were a promising song called *In The Land Of Make Believe* or another new number, *Walk On By*. Burt, Hal and Dionne wisely opted for the latter and unknowingly made two big hits in one session. When the session was done, the challenge was deciding which track to put out first – both *Walk On By* and *Anyone Who Had A Heart* were much too good to be used as a B-side.

"We had done 'Walk On By' and 'Anyone Who Had A Heart' at the same recording session," says Hal David. "And we couldn't make up our minds which record to go with first. And we went back and forth and back and forth and finally elected to come out with 'Anyone Who Had A Heart'. And so 'Walk On By' was always meant to be the next one."

Although *In the Land Of Make Believe* pales next to *Walk On By* and *Anyone Who Had A Heart*, it did catch the attention of one important listener. In a 1993 MELODY MAKER profile, Steely Dan's Donald Fagen chose the track as a piece of music that had significantly influenced him.

"This is a straight ahead pop song in intent, but Burt Bacharach is brilliant," said Fagen. "He was Marlene Dietrich's musical director for a while, and he utilized a lot of French classical music for her stuff. Poulenc and Debussy were his models and, when applied to soul and gospel, it had this very ethereal effect, especially with Dionne Warwick's voice. I love this combination of classicism and soul. Walter Becker and I were both huge fans of Burt Bacharach records and they were definitely an influence."

The *Walk On By / Anyone Who Had A Heart* session was proof that, in the few years since *The Story Of My Life* and *Magic Moments*, Bacharach and David had evolved into a truly brilliant songwriting team. Their run of chart success had given them the clout to produce their own sessions and be more adventurous, but the catalyst was Dionne Warwick. Her voice could seemingly navigate any melody or lyric that they could write. With that voice at their disposal, it seemed that nothing was impossible.

"The more she could do musically, the more chances we could take," Bacharach told the LOS ANGELES TIMES. "And she did it almost effortlessly. The range didn't matter; the difficulty didn't matter. I don't think there was another singer who could have listened, taken direction and then delivered the way Dionne did."

Although Bacharach's melodies are notoriously challenging for most vocalists, for Warwick they were a piece of cake.

"They weren't difficult to me at all," says Warwick. "And I think that had a lot to do with the fact that they were written for me. I just kind of understood what Burt was doing musically. And how can you not understand lyrically with Hal David's writing?"

Warwick relished the challenge of recording Bacharach's tricky melodies.

"Because of my background in music and being able to read, I loved recording his stuff," she says, "based on the fact that it was like taking an exam every time I went to the studio. It was almost, 'Okay, let's see if you can do this one.' But I didn't find anything complicated about what he was writing. I know a lot of people who have subsequently tried to record some of these things have even approached me and said, 'You know, you've got to be a little bit sick – nobody can sing this stuff but you!'"

In January of 1964, the stunning *Anyone Who Had A Heart* became Dionne's first Top 10 hit, reaching No. 8. Across the Atlantic, the song fared even better, though not via Warwick's version. While the songs of Bacharach and David have always been hugely popular in Britain, the recordings that hit the U.K. charts were sometimes different versions, often by British artists. Such was the case with *Anyone Who Had A Heart*: in Britain, the big hit was Cilla Black's recording, which reached No. 1 in February '64. During the same month, Dionne Warwick's recording of the song reached No. 42 in Britain, while Mary May's version reached No. 49.

Warwick was peeved about Black's version, feeling it was little more than a carbon copy of her record.

"It was exactly like mine," she says of Black's recording. "You know, if I had coughed or sneezed, that's what she would've done."

Warwick had even greater chart success with her next 45, reaching No. 6 with one of Bacharach and David's most enduring compositions, *Walk On By*. Scepter had reportedly intended *Walk On By* to be the B-side of Warwick's new 45, with the gorgeous *Any Old Time Of The Day* earmarked as the hit side. But the influential New York D.J. Murray the K flipped the record and another Bacharach/David B-side was transformed into a hit.

Warwick usually got first refusal of Burt and Hal's songs – at least on "songs that we thought were right for her," Burt says. "With songs like *Blue On Blue* or *The Man Who Shot Liberty Valance* – kind of white-bread songs – we wouldn't do that. But a lot of songs were written directly for how Dionne would be, for her voice."

Bacharach told the LOS ANGELES TIMES that many of his and Hal's songs "were written with the concept that they were suitable for only one artist, made with (that artist) in mind. You hear Dionne singing in your head, and that's how you do the song. But (the covers) show the songs can be done another way."

The number of Bacharach and David songs that didn't suit Dionne's voice was decreasing rapidly as the songwriting team developed an instinctive relationship with the singer.

"Dionne was such a spokesperson for their songs," says Phil Ramone, who engineered many of the classic Bacharach/David/Warwick dates, "in the way that she delivered the songs. I recorded with Burt and Hal in London. I recorded the Dusty Springfield session for *The Look Of Love* and a couple of other songs that they'd done away from Dionne. And you could clearly feel that Dionne felt, 'Oh my God, every time we do a song, I want it first.' And, after PROMISES, PROMISES, I guess they made her a promise about that."

Dionne's voice was a perfect fit, able to negotiate Bacharach's often-tricky melodies, while conveying the emotion of David's lyrics.

"She always interprets my lyrics in a way that sounds as though she had written them herself," said Hal.

"There's so much simple truth in his lyrics that it's almost like singing gospel," Dionne wrote in her foreword to Hal's book WHAT THE WORLD NEEDS NOW AND OTHER LOVE LYRICS. "You can hear that gospel sound in my voice no matter which of his songs I'm singing."

"We were writing songs that had a rhythm and blues background," says David. "Which was something which was very comfortable and natural for us. And it was right up Dionne's alley. We were writing like that before we met Dionne. And as that became more successful, we kept writing like that. But we were very eclectic and varied in our work. Fortunately she was so good, she could do it all."

Bacharach was generally pretty strict with his singers in the studio, insisting that they sing his melodies exactly as he wanted. Warwick soon became an exception and the composer allowed her to have room for her own interpretation.

"I used to make suggestions to her," Bacharach said in the mid-'60s. "No more. I know what she does will be a jewel."

More often than not, Bacharach and David's non-Warwick songs were movie themes. "In addition to writing for and recording Dionne," says Hal, "we were doing things like writing for Paramount, songs like *Wives And Lovers*, *The Man Who Shot Liberty Valance*." With a few exceptions – such as *What The World Needs Now Is Love*, *This Guy's In Love With You* and *One Less Bell To Answer* – just about every non-Warwick Bacharach and David hit from the mid-'60s to the early '70s was written for a specific movie assignment.

On Bacharach and David's movie assignments, the film studios had input in selecting the vocalists "to a limited extent," Hal explains. "*The Man Who Shot Liberty Valance* was a song that they were having lots of trouble getting a record on. And Burt and I went and played it for Aaron Schroeder who loved it. Then we played it for Gene Pitney. We got that record ourselves. And *Wives And Lovers* – we played it for Jack Jones and he recorded it. Very often we were able to go and get the record ourselves, but sometimes the film company did."

By 1964, buoyed by their success with Warwick, Bacharach and David could afford to take their time perfecting their songs and their records. It wasn't just talent that made their songs so great, but also determination and hard work.

"Before we even think of recording," Hal told BILLBOARD, "we completely finish and polish the strongest song we feel we can write at that time... It often takes from two to three months to produce a single record. This includes the inception of a song, through thorough rehearsing, careful planning of the arrangement and careful planning of the choral background. The work is intensive in preparation down to the recording mixing and mastering."

Warwick says she would rehearse with Bacharach and David "when I was available, because I was also on the road. I'd go over to Burt's apartment or to Famous Music, usually the day before (the session). Sometimes it was a couple of days before and we'd have the background group in too. But it didn't really take that much time."

Although Bacharach and David spent a great deal of time perfecting their songs before rehearsing them with Warwick, they were open to making the occasional change.

"Sometimes we would come up with something in the background that would cause a reaction to either change a melody and/or a time signature or something of that nature," says Warwick. "But, by and large, whatever they wrote was what they wrote and that's what we sang."

Even after they finished recording and mixing a track, Burt and Hal still oversaw the final transition to vinyl.

"Unfortunately there has to be a gradual diminishing of sound quality," Burt told BILLBOARD in 1964, "from the original tape sound of the (recording) 'date' – down to a monaural mix, then the 'final catastrophe' when it goes into and out of a pressing plant." To minimize the "final catastrophe," Bacharach and David actually went so far as to select which plants their records were pressed at on a case-by-case basis.

"We find that there is a difference in various songs and 'dates' we do," said Burt, "(depending on) whether a compression or injection pressing method was used. Thus we always get pressings from at least two plants on every 'date' and we choose the record closest to the original tape sound. Not many songwriters and producers go out inspecting pressing plants."

Bacharach said that he and David typically heard each song hundreds of times before the record was pressed: roughly 450 times in writing and rehearsing with the artist, followed by another 80 times through for Burt as he worked on the arrangement at home.

"We then do maybe 24 takes in the studio," Bacharach said. "We listen to the playbacks, remix and listen to the acetates. After 1000 listenings we must force ourselves to listen to the record as if we had just thought of it and were hearing it in completed form for close to the very first time. Believe me, this is the hardest thing of all."

Bacharach said that his greatest moment of excitement came not in hearing the finished pressing, but in hearing the song come to life in the studio. David, on the other hand, was more thrilled by hearing a new record on the radio.

"When I hear the record for the first time on the radio," he told BILLBOARD, "and I hear it coming out the way we conceived it, I then get closest to my original excitement that I felt when we first wrote the song."

Unlike Bacharach, David preferred the writing process to the recording process. Hal said that working in the studio "has never been as satisfying as writing a song... Perhaps because record styles are very changeable." Hal felt that, unlike records themselves, great songs were perennial.

Before Bacharach and David proved themselves as hitmakers, the journey from the excitement of a newly written song to a finished record was often fraught with compromise. Bacharach has often recalled that, in the early years of his collaboration with Hal David, they would agree to musical compromises in order to conform to a record label's notion of what was 'commercial'. A&R men questioned the commercial viability of his innovative (in pop music terms) time signatures. Although he made concessions in the early years, Bacharach felt the record companies were wrong to underestimate record buyers' ability to assimilate unusual rhythms.

"People buying my records don't know what 7/8 time is," he told BILLBOARD in an early '70s interview, "they're accepting a total sound."

In spite of the fact that Bacharach's music was challenging and complex, it always seemed perfectly natural to David.

"I never, from the very beginning, found Burt's music to be difficult," he told the LOS ANGELES TIMES. "I never heard the songs in three, or four, or seven or eight. They just seemed exactly the way they were supposed to be, even with all the three-bar phrases and unusual rhythms." Hal didn't realize that they were "breaking rules" until he started to notice studio musicians struggling over the unorthodox changes.

In the summer of 1964, Dusty Springfield hit No. 6 with *Wishin' And Hopin*, a song previously released by Dionne Warwick as the B-side of *This Empty Place*. Burt had apparently suggested that Dusty cover the song – one of many Bacharach/David B-sides that were revived as hits.

Burt Bacharach & Hal David

Springfield recorded the song as an album track, but New York disk jockey Jack Lacey was so taken with *Wishin' And Hopin* that he played it every day. The response to the airplay on the album convinced Springfield's label to pull the track as a single, and *Wishin' And Hopin* shot up the singles charts.

The latter months of 1964 saw Dionne Warwick chart with two more of Burt and Hal's tunes, *You'll Never Get To Heaven (If You Break My Heart)* and *Reach Out For Me*, which reached No. 34 and No. 20, respectively.

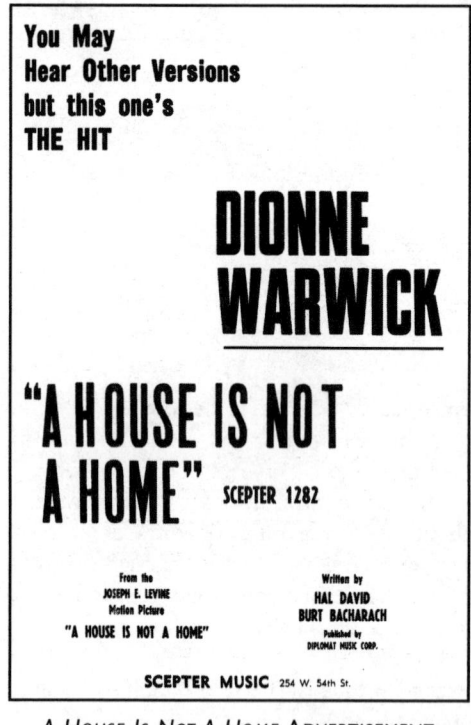

A HOUSE IS NOT A HOME ADVERTISEMENT

Burt and Hal's next movie assignment was the theme song for a Shelley Winters film called A HOUSE IS NOT A HOME. The movie has since been forgotten, but the Bacharach/David theme song has become a standard. Brooke Benton recorded the first version, taking it to No. 75 in August 1964. Warwick's version - the flipside of *Reach Out For Me* — was slightly more successful, peaking at No. 71.

In Britain, Dusty Springfield scored a hit with the Bacharach/David classic *I Just Don't Know What To Do With Myself*, while Bobby Goldsboro scored a domestic hit (No. 74) with the pleasant-but-not-classic *Me Japanese Boy I Love You*. Although he is not credited as such, Burt reportedly produced the latter track. *Me Japanese Boy* had a revival in the 1990s, when it was recorded by Japan's Pizzicato Five.

In September, Lou Johnson charted with the first recording of the perennial *(There's) Always Something There To Remind Me*. Although not a big hit, Johnson's version made it to No. 49, two positions higher than the Sandie Shaw rendition, which was released three months later. (In Britain, Shaw's version was a No. 1 hit.)

Late 1964 also saw the first appearance of another Bacharach/David standard – one that has been recorded under three different titles. The first single release, by Lou Johnson, was entitled *Kentucky Bluebird* (peak chart position: No. 104), while Jerry Butler's version (also released in '64) was called *Message To Martha*.

Other notable Bacharach/David releases in 1964 included Paul Anka's *From Rocking*

VIDEO RELEASE OF SEND ME NO FLOWERS

Horse To Rocking Chair and Doris Day's *Send Me No Flowers*. The latter track was the theme for the Rock Hudson/Doris Day comedy of the same name, but the film features a different recording than the single – not uncommon in the '60s when movie songs were often re-recorded for record release. Though it's an appealing song – featured prominently in the movie – *Send Me No Flowers* only climbed to No. 135 in the BILLBOARD singles chart.

The American charts of 1964 were dominated by British acts, in the wake of the Beatles and the "British Invasion." Although American artists suddenly found it tougher to crack the charts, Bacharach and David's success kept growing. The British invasion didn't seem to adversely affect them. In fact, a number of English acts of the time recorded their songs. The previous year, the Beatles had cut *Baby It's You* for their first album and seemed to have some admiration for Bacharach and David's work.

"His songs are a lot more musical than the stuff we write," said Paul McCartney of Bacharach, "and a lot more technical. None of us can read or write music."

In March 1965, Bacharach released another 45, *Don't Go Breaking My Heart*, on the Kapp label. As with many of Burt's own recordings, the vocals on his *Don't Go Breaking My Heart*" were performed by a session vocalist. While the A-side was one of Bacharach's best solo recordings, it did not chart, but the flip – *Trains And Boats And Planes* – reached No. 4 in the U.K. Both sides of the single turned up on Bacharach's first LP, HIT MAKER!, which, like subsequent efforts, mixed instrumental and vocal renditions of Bacharach/David material. The debut album featured guest vocals by Tony Middleton and Joel Grey. The album spawned several subsequent variations/reissues, one of the most common being BURT BACHARACH PLAYS HIS HITS. The most familiar design features a swingin' '60s girl on the front and it was this cover that Mike Myers displayed prominently in his hit movie AUSTIN POWERS.

The HIT MAKER! album was recorded in London, and one of the players was a young session guitarist named Jimmy Page. Although Page achieved fame with the very un-

Bacharach-like Yardbirds and Led Zeppelin, Page was impressed with Burt's professionalism and the respect the musicians had for him. Future Zeppelin bassist John Paul Jones added some low end to some of Bacharach's recordings during this period.

The HIT MAKER! LP didn't do much business in the United States, but was a Top 10 hit in Britain. The British had always had an affinity for Bacharach and David's songs. Their first two hits together, *The Story Of My Life* and *Magic Moments*, had charted higher in Britain than in America, each reaching the top of the singles charts. Since then, Bacharach and David's songs had been mainstays of the British pop charts. Bacharach became a star in Europe even before he did in the States. Pundits raved about the "Bacharach Sound," and the composer spent a great deal of time in Europe in the mid-'60s.

In 1965, Scepter released the fourth Dionne Warwick album, THE SENSITIVE SOUND OF DIONNE WARWICK. Although Bacharach-David-Warwick sessions were done almost exclusively in New York, there were exceptions. THE SENSITIVE SOUND OF DIONNE WARWICK LP was recorded at Pye Records' studios in London.

"I was on tour, and Burt was in London, so it was very timely," Dionne recalled in the liner notes for her LOVE SONGS CD. "We did the session at the studios of Pye Records, which was the British licensee for Scepter. Of course, Burt and I were not quite accustomed to stopping in the middle of a song while the entire orchestra put down its batons… and went for a [typically British] tea break!"

Chapter 6: Love, Sweet Love

The stereotype of the "professional songwriter" suggests a hack, churning out by-the-numbers songs just to get a hit. This was never the case with Bacharach and David Both Burt and Hal put their heart and soul into their songwriting and their focus was on writing good songs rather than writing hits. Although they were professional songwriters, their songs were just as sincere, heartfelt and honest, as any Bob Dylan or Beatles songs.

"I think what you write is what you are," Burt explained in an interview with SELECT magazine. "Look at Hal David, you could say, `Oh man, he looks like a regular guy. He could be a dentist.' Then he'll unleash these extraordinary lyrics. It's not peoples' eccentricities or how they dress; there's a deeper core that comes through their craft." Sammy Cahn famously observed that Bacharach was the only professional songwriter who *didn't* look like a dentist.

"He's a terribly nice guy," Burt said of Hal in a NEWSWEEK interview. "When he writes 'What the world needs now is love, sweet love,' he believes it."

"Hal David is a man who feels things deeply," said Dionne Warwick. "He has a lot to say to a lot of people and he says it in his lyrics."

"Hal is so very important in that twosome," says Gene Pitney. "I don't know of anyone else, except maybe Bernie Taupin, who can paint a picture so unique and, a lot of the time, do it with very simple words. *Only Love Can Break A Heart* and *24 Hours From Tulsa* show this very well. Go to the other extreme and who could write *What's New Pussycat* and make it come out like it did?"

"He's kind and gentle," said Bacharach of David, "which is important when you have to stay in a room with him all day."

"We have always had a happy collaboration," said Hal in 1968. "We respect each other's talent and make accommodations to suit each other. When either of us finds himself unenthused about (the other's ideas), we express our feelings in the gentlest terms."

If a lyric or a musical idea didn't appeal to both composer and lyricist, they would usually drop it and move on. In certain cases, though, a rejected idea would stay in the mind of its creator. In those cases, the idea was often revived and used.

"At those times," said Hal, "we defer to the judgement of the believer. Some of our best songs have been written because one of us believed in something so strongly that the other went along."

Bacharach and David's next big hit was a good example of this. *What The World Needs Now is Love* was several years in the making — initially abandoned, but revived because of Hal's belief in it. Hal had come up with the idea for the lyric in 1963, but he didn't finish it until two years later.

One day in 1963, Hal was in his car, driving into New York City, when two lines suddenly came into his mind: "What the world needs now is love, sweet love/No, not just for some, but for everyone..."

After coming up with the first part of the lyric, Hal was stuck. "I kept thinking of lines like 'Lord we don't need planes that fly higher or faster...', and they all seemed wrong," he wrote in 1968. "But the idea stayed with me. In 1965, the next line came to him — "Lord, we don't need another mountain." The rest of the lyrics came easily, as did the music Burt supplied for the much-delayed words.

Bacharach and David reportedly offered the song to Gene Pitney first but it didn't happen, so they offered it to Dionne. Warwick was not taken with the song and passed on it. However, she points out, the song in its original form sounded very different from the version that became a hit.

"I think it was written for a Gene Pitney session," says Warwick. "But it never got on the session. And it sounded like a Gene Pitney song – you know, a cowboy song. Nothing like the final edition."

Bacharach also doubted the tune's potential and it was left to Hal David to suggest reviving it for a Jackie DeShannon session almost a year later. At that point, DeShannon's biggest claim to fame was that she had cut the original version of the Jack Nitzche/Sonny Bono composition *Needles And Pins* – a No. 84 hit in 1963.

A JACKIE DESHANNON 45

"There wasn't great enthusiasm for (*What The World Needs Now*)," recalls Hal. "I had great enthusiasm for it. We were asked by Liberty Records to record Jackie, who is a great singer and a good songwriter, too. We were in an office in the RKO building and we played a number of songs to Jackie. I suggested to Burt that we play *What The World Needs Now Is Love* to her. And we did and Jackie said, 'That's the one I want to do.' Jackie was the catalyst – she was really excited about doing that song."

"It was an old song that Hal had to encourage Burt to play for me," DeShannon told GOLDMINE. "When it first came out, radio stations would say it's a waltz, you can't dance to it."

"My records with them were very heartfelt and soulful," DeShannon continued. "It was a natural combination. The records with them were cut live – no overdubs, no punch-ins. *What The World Needs Now* was done in the second take."

DeShannon's enthusiasm helped transform *What The World Needs Now*, and the result was a Top 10 hit. DeShannon followed it with another Bacharach/David-composed side, *A Lifetime Of Loneliness*, which reached No. 66. DeShannon was very enthusiastic about *A Lifetime Of Loneliness*, calling it "one of the greatest records I've ever done."

In May, *Trains And Boats And Planes* made another appearance in the British charts, this time as a No. 12 hit for Billy J. Kramer and the Dakotas, a Liverpool group managed by Beatles manager Brian Epstein. Kramer's version reached No. 47 in the U.S.

That summer, another movie soundtrack assignment resulted in one of Burt and Hal's most enduring compositions. A truly memorable song – delivered in the singer's inimitably gutsy style – *What's New Pussycat?* took Welsh newcomer Tom Jones to No. 3 in the singles chart. (Jones had previously cut Bacharach and David's *To Wait For Love*, as the B-side of his first hit *It's Not Unusual*.)

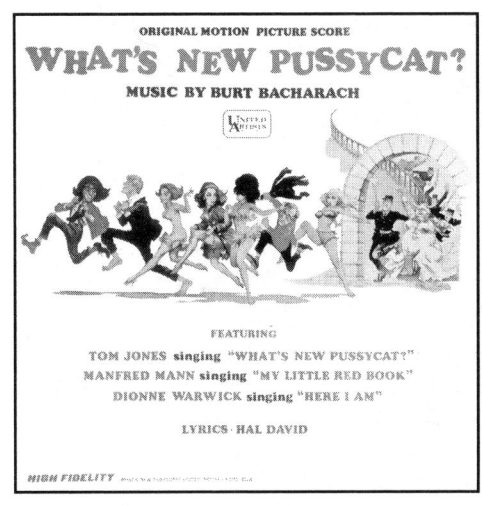

WHAT'S NEW PUSSYCAT? LP

As was usually the case with their movie assignments, the title was the starting point for the song. Hal recalls that the title came from Woody Allen, who scripted WHAT'S NEW PUSSYCAT?, but it's been said that Allen borrowed the phrase from Warren Beatty.

Bacharach and David were in London for a Dionne Warwick engagement when they ran into the film's producer Charlie Feldman. Feldman had already assigned the score and songs for PUSSYCAT to someone else, but was apparently unhappy with the results. At the suggestion of his girlfriend, a big Bacharach and David fan, Feldman asked Burt and Hal to take over.

After mulling over the title, Bacharach composed the first part of the melody – "What's new pussycat, whoa whoa whoa...' – and sang it for David over the phone. Hal set to work on the rest of the words and finished the song with Bacharach in a London hotel suite on Easter Sunday morning.

As well as the title song and a Bacharach score, WHAT'S NEW PUSSYCAT? featured two other Bacharach/David compositions, the lovely *Here I Am* (performed by Dionne Warwick) and the driving *My Little Red Book* (performed by Manfred Mann). The latter tune got a radical makeover from L.A. upstarts Arthur Lee and Love a year later, a rendition that reportedly did not meet with Bacharach and David's approval, but fared better on the charts than the Manfred Mann version, reaching No. 52. Lee stripped the slightly awkward rhythm and chord sequence down and really made the song work, turning it into a garage rock standard.

"That was an odd [composition], really, atypical of what I wrote," Bacharach told the LOS ANGELES TIMES many years later. "Then Arthur Lee came along and cut his version and had a hit. I've just had to get used to people making radical changes on my songs, stand back and objectively look at it and see if I liked what they'd done."

Like Manfred Mann's *My Little Red Book* (which stalled at No. 124) and Tom Jones' title song, Dionne Warwick's contribution to WHAT'S NEW PUSSYCAT? was released as a single, in the summer of '65. *Here I Am* initially peaked at No. 65, but climbed to No. 45 in February 1966. The single is noteworthy for its B-side, another recording of *(They Long to Be) Close to You*. Dionne's next single, *Looking With My Eyes*, only reached No. 64, but she was back in the Top 40 in January 1966 with *Are You There (With Another Girl)*. *Make It Easy On Yourself* returned to the charts at the end of 1965, this time performed by the British duo the Walker Brothers, who took the song to No. 16.

Warwick's *Here I Am* also appeared as the title track of her next LP. The HERE I AM album was evidence of the evolution of the Bacharach/David/Warwick partnership. The trio was moving away from the R&B style of their early sides and moving into music that was often even more complex and challenging.

Chapter 7: What's It All About?

By the mid-'60s, Burt Bacharach was a star. He seemed to epitomize the hip lifestyle, so much so that Mike Myers recruited him in the '90s to bring a touch of Swinging '60s authenticity to his hit movie AUSTIN POWERS.

In 1965, Bacharach married Angie Dickinson, a glamorous actress and honorary member of the Rat Pack. The couple bought a house in Beverly Hills, and spent most of their time there for the next decade.

Hal David remained in Long Island. Although the Bacharach-David songwriting partnership continued, the working set-up changed. In the late '60s and early '70s, Bacharach and David would work together for three to four months out of each year, splitting that time between their respective hometowns. During writing periods, Hal would spend a month in California, and then Burt would spend a month in New York, with a further month of work completed via long distance phone calls. When it was time to bring the latest batch of songs to life in the studio, Burt would jet back to New York for the recording sessions.

"I moved to California when I married Angie," Bacharach recalls. "Hal would come out and we'd do some writing out there. And I had an apartment in New York – we could write there. A lot of the work we did, we'd initiate in the work spot – in the office – and at the end of the day we'd break. And Hal would continue working at home, as I would. We both worked very well independently of each other. We'd both want to get away from each other – from the collaboration – because you don't feel as much pressure. You're at home, you go to the piano, go eat dinner, come back, work a little bit. Find a solution and call each other on the phone, sing it for Hal. I did that with *A House Is Not A Home*."

"He moved out to L.A., but he kept his apartment in New York for many years after that," says David. "I stayed in New York. And we worked out a schedule where when I came out to L.A., I checked into the Beverly Wilshire Hotel. We tended to work for about a week to 10 days in New York – he would fly in – then take about a week to 10 days off. And then I'd fly out to California and we'd work about a week to 10 days there. It was back and forth and back and forth. That situation went on for a long, long time."

"The system works well," said Bacharach of the bi-coastal collaboration. "The separation keeps our outlooks fresh... If we spent more time with each other socially, we'd have less to bounce off each other."

"We were working a lot," Hal points out. "We were recording Dionne, so we always needed a lot of songs. For the most part, we recorded Dionne in New York. In fact, most of our records were done in New York. Phil Ramone was our recording engineer, and we recorded for the most part at A&R Studios."

Bacharach was a natural in concert and on television. Handsome and well-dressed, he quickly became a sex symbol. In a NEW YORK TIMES profile, writer Albert Goldman described his "handsome, purely American face, an image blown back from the Kennedy years, with those sun crinkles in the eyes, that trace of silver in the thick, choppy hair..."

Burt's flamboyant (but heartfelt) performance style added another dimension to his celebrity. NEWSWEEK described his "calisthenically emotional style of conducting that involves doing simultaneous knee bends at the pianos, swivelling to fire musical directions at the different sections of the band, using his hands like Karate choppers, generating an excitement among the musicians and – especially when he sang a little – among the audience."

"I'm not trying to prove anything as a conductor," he told the magazine in 1970. "Or as a pianist. Technically, I'm probably rotten at both. But it's heartfelt, it's honest. It's my music. I'm free and I don't care what I look like."

What made Bacharach so compelling to watch was the way he seemed to get lost in his music. His performance style wasn't put on; he was simply pouring his heart and soul into it.

Bacharach seemed to be glamorous almost in spite of himself. When in California, he liked to compose in his bathing suit on his terrace, away from the piano. But the reasons for this very California approach were practical: Burt simply felt that writing at the piano interfered with his melodies. His formal musical training meant that he didn't need to compose at an instrument. When a winning melody came into his head, he could simply write down the musical notation on paper. In his method of writing, as in the songs themselves, Bacharach simply did what felt right to him.

"I'm not trying to break rules," the composer told NEWSWEEK. "Just writing what's satisfying to me."

In April 1966, Dionne Warwick reached No. 8 with *Message To Michael*, her own version of the song that had previously been recorded as *Kentucky Bluebird* and *Message To Martha*.

Significantly, *Message To Michael* was one of the few Warwick singles not produced by Bacharach and David. Apparently, Hal and Burt were strongly opposed to changing the lyrics to a female perspective, feeling that 'Martha' was the only name that would work. The French singer Sacha Distel had recorded a version but had decided to scrap it. Dionne, who was a huge star in France, laid her own vocal over Distel's backing track. The result was another classic Bacharach/David/Warwick record, the first made without Burt and Hal's direct involvement.

"Hal kept saying, 'It's not a girl's song, it's a boy's song'," says Warwick. "As it turns out, I was in Paris, at the Olympia Theatre, performing with Sacha Distel. And Florence Greenberg happened to also be there. She was thinking of signing him to the label, and *Message To Martha* was one of the songs that he was going to record. And I went in and basically did a demo of the lyrics (over Distel's finished track), so that he could get the English enunciation, and changed the name from 'Martha' to 'Michael' to suit me."

"Dionne's vocal was so brilliant that it was obvious we had subconsciously written the song for her even while we thought we were writing for a man," Hal said later. "I don't mind being wrong if, in the final analysis, everything turns out right."

The decision to release Dionne's *Message To Michael* as a single was largely due to the efforts of Steve Tyrell. By 1966, Tyrell was working promotion and A&R for Scepter Records.

MESSAGE TO MICHAEL 45

"I was the one that was in touch with the radio," says Tyrell. "I heard Dionne's version of *Message To Michael*, and I begged them to release that. I remember getting in an elevator with Burt and Hal and following them down into Times Square, begging them to let me put that song out. The next day they called Florence and said, 'Look, Steve is so into this tune – tell him he can put it on the B-side, but he shouldn't promote it.'"

Tyrell didn't exactly obey the last instruction.

"When that song came out," he recalls, "I got right on a plane, I flew to New Orleans, and I went to WTIX. Buzz Bennett was the guy's name – he was a big radio guy. And I said, 'Hey, man, I got something for you right here,' and I played it for him. And he walked right into the control room and put it on the radio. Because it opened, 'Fly away to New Orleans...' And in one week it was a smash. I don't even remember what the side was that Burt had wanted to put out!"

Burt and Hal's initial reluctance about the record was partially due to the fact that they did not produce Dionne's recording of *Message To Michael*.

"Because Burt wasn't there, and he's such a perfectionist, it probably wasn't as good as it could have been if Burt had been there," says Tyrell. "So that's why he didn't like it – he probably heard flaws in it. But I was only hearing Dionne and the song, and I heard no flaws in it. I heard it being just a smash. I refused to let them not put that record out."

In May 1966, Jackie DeShannon released her third Bacharach and David-penned single, *Come And Get Me*. The track was on par with *What The World Needs Now* and *A Lifetime Of Loneliness*, but fared poorly on the charts, peaking at No. 83 – despite BILLBOARD'S prediction that the "rockin' lyric ballad from the pen of Burt Bacharach and Hal David and an exciting performance by Miss DeShannon will put her back on top of the charts." DeShannon released one more Bacharach/David single after that, *Windows And Doors*. An excellent, slightly folky number, it failed to crack the top 100 – "bubbling under" at No. 108 – and was the last record DeShannon made with Bacharach and David.

PROMISE HER ANYTHING VIDEO

The first half of 1966 saw the release of three Bacharach/David movie theme songs: the first two were Trini Lopez's *Made In Paris* and Tom Jones' *Promise Her Anything* – the former written for a continental Ann-Margret/Louis Jordan romp, the latter the theme to an Arthur Hiller-directed comedy starring Warren Beatty as a struggling soft-porn film director.

Made In Paris and *Promise Her Anything* were only minor hits (No. 113 and No. 74, respectively), but were brilliant, dynamic records. Both discs – unusually for Bacharach and David records – were driven by electric guitar riffs. Those two tracks were perhaps the closest Burt and Hal got to rock and roll, although many cover versions have since proven that much of their catalogue can be made to rock.

Bacharach and David's third movie theme of 1966 was by no means rock and roll, but a ballad that became one of the duo's best-known compositions and one of their personal favourites.

Ironically, the song *Alfie* – considered by many to be Bacharach and David's finest collaboration – almost didn't happen. When Ed Wolpin asked the duo to pen the theme song for Paramount, they were initially uninterested.

Burt Bacharach & Hal David

"Writing a song about a girl with a beautiful name can be exciting," wrote Hal in his book WHAT THE WORLD NEEDS NOW. "A song about a man called 'Alfie' did not seem too exciting at the time."

David felt that the title *Alfie* suggested "a music hall comedy song - maybe for Gracie Fields. And I said, 'I don't think we can do it.' They said, 'Give it a try.' And we tried for a bit and came back and said, 'It's not for us.'"

Paramount persisted and Hal, having read the script, gave the lyrics one more try. This time, he found a way to make it work, and delivered one of his deepest, most thoughtful lyrics. Burt set the words to music and another classic was born. Hal didn't even see the film before writing the song; he first viewed it when it played at a local movie house in Long Island.

ALFIE was based on the stage play of the same name, by Bill Naughton. Terence Stamp had starred in the stage version, but the film cast Michael Caine as the womanizing lead, a sometime-chauffeur whose interest in women was very one-dimensional. Alfie doesn't spend much time pondering the meaning of life, but at the end of the film he briefly wonders, "What's it all about?" This line gave Hal the starting point for his lyrics.

Alfie became one of Bacharach and David's most-covered songs. From the movie soundtrack itself came the first version of *Alfie*, performed by Cher, which peaked at No. 32 in August 1966. Across the Atlantic, Cilla Black fared even better with the song, her version (conducted by Bacharach) reaching No. 9 in Britain. Early '67 would see the release of versions by Dionne Warwick (a No. 18 hit), Dee Dee Warwick and Bacharach himself (his debut single on A&M Records).

The reasons for the multiple *Alfies* squaring off in the charts were down to complex dealings between movie companies and record labels. Burt and Hal assumed that Dionne would perform *Alfie*, but the British film company insisted on Cilla Black, who was a bigger star in Britain at that time.

"Because (the film) was subsidized by British money, they wanted a British artist to record it," says Warwick.

Back in the States, the movie's American distributor United Artists wanted the theme done by an artist on one of their record labels, and selected Cher, then half of the duo Sonny & Cher and an Imperial Records artist.

To add to all this confusion, while the British prints of the film featured Cilla's version, and the American ones featured Cher, some prints of the movie did not feature the song at all, substituting a jazz theme by Sonny Rollins.

Despite the movie companies' insistence on Cher and Cilla Black, Burt and Hal knew who their best interpreter was. They cut a version with Dionne Warwick, and her version became the biggest hit (in America at least) and probably the best-remembered version.

However, since Warwick's *Alfie* came after a number of other versions, Scepter didn't initially see it as a chart contender.

"We recorded (Dionne's version of) *Alfie* and *Trains And Boats And Planes* on the same session," says Steve Tyrell. "*Alfie* was put on the B-side of *Trains And Boats And Planes*. We didn't think it was a hit."

"We decided to put out *Trains And Boats And Planes*," Tyrell recalls. "And someone said, what should we put on the back? And someone said, put *Alfie* on there. So we put out *Trains*, and it was a huge hit. And then Dionne got chosen to sing *Alfie* on the Academy Awards. And as soon as she did it, she got a huge ovation. And the next week, we got radio stations to turn it over, and it became one of their all-time classic songs."

Bacharach had initially rejected the idea of Dionne recording *Trains And Boats And Planes*, feeling that the song was "too country" for Warwick. Burt and Hal had reportedly considered the song as a vehicle for Gene Pitney, but problems with the singer's management put an end to the Bacharach-David-Pitney collaboration.

Chapter 8: Let The Music Play

The session for Dionne Warwick's *Alfie* was one of the first dates Bacharach and David did with engineer Phil Ramone at A&R Studios.

Warwick's early sessions with Bacharach and David had been done at Bell Sound Studios, conveniently located near the Scepter Records offices in Manhattan. On one occasion, when Bell Sound was fully booked, Burt and Hal decided to try out A&R, an independent facility located at 112 West 48th Street.

A&R had been founded in 1961, by Ramone and musician Jack Arnold, the initials of their surnames providing the studio with its name. Arnold had departed in the early '60s, but Ramone remained, working as the studio's engineer. As well as being a fine engineer, Ramone was determined to keep up with the latest recording technology. When A&R first opened, it had a three-track tape machine – the standard at the time – but before too long Ramone upgraded, and A&R became the first independent studio to house a four-track machine.

Another perk of working at A&R was its location, directly above Jim & Andy's lounge, a popular hangout for session musicians. There was even a phone link between the bar and the studio, so that producers could rope in players at a moment's notice.

"They had made some big records at Bell Sound," says Ramone. "And it was booked or something, so they came over to A&R and tried me. My reputation as an engineer was starting to get some good marks. I had been working with Leiber and Stoller, Jeff

Barry and Ellie Greenwich. I'd had a couple of years under my belt, to get me to a place where people actually knew who I was. There was an instant feeling between Burt and Hal and myself. Plus Dionne – we got a great sound on her."

"And after that, when Bell sound was busy again, they came back," says Ramone. "They were loyal to the guy they worked with at Bell."

Nevertheless, Ramone's engineering skills and studio facilities were soon enough to convince Burt and Hal to make A&R their studio of choice. They continued to work at A&R up to and including their last sessions with Warwick in the early '70s.

Despite the presence of multitrack recording equipment, Bacharach and David sessions were usually done live, with no overdubs.

"In those days, everything was live," recalls Ramone. "We only had one room at the time for a big orchestra. So the isolation between the orchestra and the vocals was rather critical, but we had a good booth. The group was in one booth, Dionne was in the other. Burt worked at the piano, looking in at the control room. I had him set up so that he could look in to me, you know, for anything he wanted from me. And the mix had to be really nice in the room. I would come out and talk to them about things I needed. And we moved rapidly because in those days people tried to do four songs in three hours."

The musicians, producers and singer would all arrive at the studio at roughly the same time, ready to record.

"There was very little rehearsing (in the studio)," Warwick recalls. "The engineer would get a sound and then we'd record. Everything was live."

"I certainly miss it an awful lot," says Warwick of the live recording approach of the era.

Although they had become producers out of self-defence, Bacharach and David had become a very skilled production team, their two different styles complementing each other and ensuring that the final recording was faithful to their intent as songwriters.

"Burt was in control of the music, really," says Steve Tyrell. "And he knew exactly what he wanted to happen. If he got confused or something, he would go into the bathroom - and act like he was taking a bathroom break – and he'd go in there and try and get his brain together, to try to figure out what was going on that wasn't right."

"He was a consummate maestro," says Tyrell. "He knew what was happening. But it's one thing to know what's happening, and another to get the performances out of people. Because those records were recorded live, all at one time – with Dionne singing, the strings playing, the horns playing, the rhythm section, and the background vocals. Everybody was in there, and Burt was standing in the middle. And sometimes there'd be a key lick in the song. And he'd be conducting, and there'd be two keyboards – Paul Griffin used to play the main piano part and Burt would go and double the main licks on piano himself, while the song was being recorded."

Typically, Hal David's role in the studio was subtler than that of Bacharach, but his contribution should not be underestimated.

"Burt was the musician and the arranger – in addition to being a marvellous composer, he's a very good arranger," says David. "So I think that, when it came to things musical, I would defer to him more often than not. But in terms of basic feelings about the production, my feelings would get expressed and, very often, would be the direction we'd go."

"Hal was always next to me," says Ramone. "And he voiced his feelings and opinions about how the lines were being read or other things. He's a quiet man, so when he speaks, everybody stops to hear what he has to say. He was always very subdued and said what he felt was right. He dealt with the song from a larger picture – he didn't usually stop and say, you know, 'The guitar part could've been hotter.' He'd say things like that, but he was more about the intent of the song; he looked out for their musical interests from that point of view."

"Hal was very much involved in the overview of what was happening," recalls Tyrell. "Burt was in the studio with the musicians, conducting, and coming into the control room for playbacks. And Hal was sitting right next to Phil Ramone, listening to the entire feel of the record – were the words really coming through, was the tempo right. He was listening from a different perspective. He wrote the words, and he was interested in whether the content of the song was coming across, whether it was coming across emotionally. Hal knew what the song was supposed to be saying. And it made for a really good team."

Ramone quickly became an important part of the team.

"Phil was Burt's sonic and musical collaborator," says Tyrell. "Phil was a violin player, he had great ears. Burt trusted Phil to get the stuff down on tape, sounding right. And he was a very big part of the team. Phil was classically trained and he could hear harmonics and he could hear pitch really well, and intonation. When you're in the studio with a whole bunch of musicians, and you're trying to record four songs in three hours, there's a lot of stuff going on."

When the team started out, they would try to do four songs per session – standard practice in those days. Before long, they reduced this number to three.

"They finally decided to only do three songs per session," recalls Ramone, "which was breaking the mould again. Because people didn't spend a ton of money making an album. You came in prepared. They had obviously rehearsed with Dionne away from the studio. Nobody did what we did later on in life, which was take your time, get what it is you needed and if you got one song per three hours, it'd be a miracle."

As Bacharach and David became more and more successful, "the sessions became like events," recalls Tyrell. "(Disc jockey and self-styled Fifth Beatle) Murray the K was always there. Burt's father and mother were always there. And Cissy Houston was always singing, and John Houston her husband and probably a very young Whitney would come to the sessions all the time. Cissy would bring the whole family. It was a family affair."

"I'd have to make my little speech," recalls Ramone. "I'd say to them, 'I'm thrilled that you're all here. Cheer us on, but I really need for you guys not to talk while we're trying to work.' Sometimes the noise in the control room was louder than in the studio."

Some family members showed their support in non-verbal ways. During the *Alfie* session, Ramone's mother had knitted a scarf for Bacharach. The track turned out to be a big hit and, after that, the presence of Mrs. Ramone and her knitting needles in the back of the control room was seen as a lucky charm.

In addition to the assorted family members, Florence Greenberg was a frequent visitor to the A&R control room, checking in on her hitmaking team.

In the mid-'60s, A&R moved into a new, larger space on Seventh Avenue, in the former location of one of Columbia Records' studios.

"We had lots more room," says Ramone. "And Burt experimented once in a while with a bigger orchestra. Burt preferred a smaller string section, almost like an ensemble sound, with a solo flugelhorn or an oboe, things like that. He never overbuilt the orchestra. And he built such power into it, that when the brass came in or things like that happened, it was so emotional in the room."

Bacharach himself didn't always play on the sessions, but when he did, something magical happened.

"As I got to know him better, I kept begging him never to leave the piano," recalls Ramone. "He'd say, 'Oh, I don't keep time that well...' When he'd stay in the control room for a while, I'd say to him, 'I think we're safe here, but I think you need to go out there.' He inspires musicians, totally."

From 1964 to '68, Bacharach/David/Warwick sessions were done on four-track tape machines.

"By '68, everybody was eight-track," says Phil Ramone. "But people didn't think in those terms. They thought of the mono mix as being the most important, and the fact that I had rigged the studio so we could do stereo and mono at the same time and they would not have different qualities. A lot of producers did not want to go back and remix for stereo. I mixed it that way, in case something ever changed in the business. Well, it changed. And we revisited these tracks, and because I could make

BURT BACHARACH & HAL DAVID

them sound exactly the same even with two speakers versus one, I think they understood that they were in a far better territory. The mixing and the style of their mixes, as they made them, were very sensitive to the way they heard the song."

"I think I learned incredible patience," Ramone says of his years in the studio with Burt and Hal, "and respect for the artists and musicians."

The respect was mutual.

"The players played for those guys," says Ramone. "They loved to play on those dates. They loved Dionne. Nobody had any temperament; it was always about how good we could make something, or how much better. I think that's a pivotal point for people like me, when I started to move into production. I knew as an engineer you needed a lot of psychology to be able to talk to a musician who might be rough at the edges about what you asked him to do – if you asked him to play a little quieter in one spot, or asked for a nice crescendo, when they're looking up at you going, 'What do you know about those words?'"

"Many times, when Burt was playing and (the session musicians) were playing," says Ramone, "I would walk out and either talk to him or Gary the drummer and say, 'You know, if we can hold off that explosion until the bridge, and really get the thing you're looking for, I can handle it better.' Things like that, which is what making records is all about. It's all about emotion and dynamics, and the way in which you treat your artists."

Ramone says that Bacharach and David were "both very sweet to their people, and everybody around them. That makes a difference, and if Burt got a reputation of being tough, or a perfectionist, I don't think anybody around us wasn't. We all wanted to get it better. I try to make myself a perfectionist, but also an understanding human being – understanding the process and how the process takes time and sometimes it takes more time than you wanted it to. You're working for that artist – that's the big deal."

The Bacharach/David/Warwick team provided a model for the artist-producer dynamic that Ramone heeded in his own production career, which took flight spectacularly in the '70s, when Ramone produced hit records for Billy Joel, Paul Simon and many others.

"The hardest thing in the world is to try and maintain a consistency," says Ramone, "and (Burt and Hal) did for years with (Dionne). I learned that working with Billy Joel or Paul Simon, for 10 years with each artist. I think it's a lot about understanding the writing process. I understood what Burt and Hal went through. I didn't sit with them while they wrote a song, but I saw things changing or being worked on – particularly in the theatre (working on the musical PROMISES, PROMISES)."

It's been said that in the studio, Burt – rather than the recording artist - was the star.

Singer B.J. Thomas, who recorded a number of Bacharach/David tracks in 1970-71, recalls Bacharach's glamorous appearance in the studio - "the flowing grey hair and the scarves, the ascots. He was a very Hollywood kind of guy. Whereas Hal was a very down-home, unaffected person who, if you didn't know who he was, you would never guess that he was involved in major music success."

Bacharach and David's choice of session musicians was a key element in the success of their records. Their songs were challenging not only to vocalists, but also to the instrumentalists behind them. Familiarity with their style was helpful, and Burt and Hal tended to work regularly with a core group of players.

"There was the basic rhythm section we worked with," recalls Hal. "We worked with (trumpet player) Clark Terry a lot. Basically, we had the same people, to the extent that they were available. And most times they were. We used two groups of background singers. There were the people who were involved with Dionne – her sister Dee Dee, Cissy Houston and a couple of other singers. And then there was another group that were more pop singers. We had a mixture of gospel and pop. We had about eight background singers."

After sessions at A&R, the studio team would retire to Jim & Andy's lounge and review their latest recordings.

"We'd all sit around," recalls Tyrell. "Florence, Burt, Hal, myself, Dionne, Paul Cantor, Dionne's manager. And we would talk about what should be the next record that we were gonna put out. We'd usually make a decision right after the session."

Chapter 9: The Look Of Love

Following the success of their theme for WHAT'S NEW PUSSYCAT?, Bacharach and David were asked to pen the title song for another Peter Sellers film, AFTER THE FOX, with Bacharach supplying the score. This time out, Sellers appeared on the theme song, delivering spoken contributions in his character from the movie, an Italian criminal mastermind. (The film also starred Victor Mature and Britt Ekland.) Handling the musical vocal parts on *After The Fox* were the Hollies, whose harmonies perfectly counterpointed Sellers' comic ranting.

The *After The Fox* session was an all-star affair, with the legendary George Martin on hand to produce Sellers and Ron Richards there for the Hollies. Still, it was reportedly Bacharach who oversaw most of the production. In addition, the composer contributed harpsichord and an ingenious 'vocal percussion' part. *After The Fox* was not a hit, but remains one of Bacharach and David's more memorable recordings. The song has rarely been covered, since its lyrics are so specific to the movie, but Losers Lounge did a groovy cover version on the late-'90s Hollies tribute album SING HOLLIES IN REVERSE.

In late 1966, Burt signed a deal with Liberty Records. The first release from this short-lived association was the single *Nikki*, a lovely instrumental named after, and written for, the composer's four-month-old daughter. Dionne Warwick ended the year with another pairing of Bacharach/David numbers, *Another Night* b/w *Go With Love* (peak position: No. 49).

ON THE FLIP SIDE CD

December 7, 1966 was the airdate for one of Bacharach and David's most ambitious projects yet – an original television musical entitled ON THE FLIP SIDE, which has been called "the first rock opera." The show – aired as part of the STAGE 67 SERIES on the ABC network – starred Ricky Nelson as a down-on-his-luck singer coming to terms with the "flip side" of music business success. Nelson's co-star was Joannie Sommers, best known for the hit *Johnny Get Angry*, for which Hal had penned the lyrics. Although few of the FLIP SIDE songs rank among Burt and Hal's best work, the show did contain a few musical gems – *Take A Broken Heart*, *It Doesn't Matter Anymore* and a majestic waltz entitled *They Don't Give Medals To Yesterday's Heroes*.

"I think *They Don't Give Medals* is a great song," says Hal. "That has a great meaning to me." From a lyrical standpoint, David used the song as a vehicle for his sympathy for overnight sensations that fall on hard times after a brush with chart success, something he observed many times over the years.

Although ON THE FLIP SIDE wasn't a hit, it did yield certain culinary fringe benefits for the lyricist.

"I used to drive to the Vitaphone studios in Brooklyn," he recalls. "That was the studio in New York where they did motion pictures, TV specials and so on. It was near Coney Island, and I remember getting off the parkway – I got off an exit too soon and suddenly I saw Nathan's, the famous Coney Island hot dog stand. And memories came back to me (Hal grew up near Coney Island), and I got myself a hot dog and an ear of corn. And then I went back every day and did the same thing."

"And that's my memory of ON THE FLIP SIDE," Hal says, laughing. "And it was fun working with Ricky."

Scepter Records declared March 1967 "Dionne Warwick Month." This promotional campaign was tied in with the release of a new Dionne album that, according to a report in BILLBOARD, was to be titled GREAT SHOWS THAT MADE GREAT MOVIES. (By the time the album came out, it had been retitled ON STAGE AND IN THE MOVIES.) Special promotional LPs were sent out to radio stations for Dionne Warwick month, and the singer's profile remained very high thanks to spots on the Ed Sullivan Show and a performance of *Alfie* at the 39th Academy Awards show.

POSTER FOR THE FILM CASINO ROYALE

Oddly, the Warwick LP, released as ON STAGE AND IN THE MOVIES, didn't feature any Bacharach/David numbers, although Burt did do the arrangements for Dionne's interpretations of various showtunes.

In 1967, Bacharach was eager to pursue more film scoring work, saying that he hoped to work on three pictures per year. For the first part of 1967, the composer had two projects lined up – the Jack Lemmon-Elaine May comedy LUV and a spoofy James Bond instalment called CASINO ROYALE. It soon became clear that Burt's schedule could not accommodate both projects. After starting work on the LUV score, he pulled out of the picture, whose music was instead supplied by Irving Joseph and Gerry Mulligan.

Having done so well with the soundtrack to WHAT'S NEW PUSSYCAT?, the film's producer Charles Feldman was eager to get Burt and Hal on board for his next venture, CASINO ROYALE. This comedic instalment in the Bond series starred David Niven as the super-spy. Despite its all-star cast – including Ursula Andress, Peters Sellers, Orson Welles, John Huston and Charles Boyer (who later starred as the High Lama in LOST HORIZON) – the film was weak. The only truly memorable thing about CASINO ROYALE was the soundtrack.

"It takes 3:03 for Dusty's new single to become an instant hit!!!" boasted an ad in BILLBOARD in June 1967. The record in question was *Give Me Time*, Dusty Springfield's latest 45 on the Philips label. In tiny print at the bottom of the ad was the name of the instant hit's flip side, *The Look Of Love*. *Give Me Time* proved to be an instant flop, peaking at No. 76 in early June. Later in the month, a Seattle disc jockey flipped the record over, and the Bacharach/David B-side soon climbed to No. 22.

VIDEO RELEASE FOR CASINO ROYALE

Springfield recorded two versions of *The Look Of Love*. The first was the soundtrack version, arranged by Burt and produced by Phil Ramone. The track was subsequently redone by Dusty Springfield's regular producer, essentially copying Bacharach's arrangement.

"One was right for the movie," Bacharach says. "And then they made a more commercial record after that, built around what I had done."

The Look Of Love subsequently became one of Burt and Hal's most enduring songs, most recently covered by Canadian jazz chanteuse Diana Krall. Although Springfield's is the best-remembered version, the biggest hit was a version by A&M artists Sergio Mendes and Brasil '66, which reached the No. 4 spot in 1967.

Although *The Look Of Love* became a huge hit, Bacharach and David weren't aiming for the charts when they wrote it.

Burt Bacharach & Hal David

NOT A BAD SPRING SO FAR!

CASINO ROYALE HERB ALPERT & THE TIJUANA BRASS ·850·
SUNSHINE GIRL THE PARADE ·841·
GLASS THE SANDPIPERS ·851·
LITTLE GIRL LOST AND FOUND THE GARDEN CLUB ·848·
HELLO-HELLO CLAUDINE LONGET ·846·
LIVE THE MERRY-GO-ROUND ·834·

A&M RECORDS AD

"You don't write songs to be hits when you're scoring a movie," Bacharach explains. "You write what's going to serve the movie."

With Bacharach's CASINO ROYALE score more or less finished, he and David travelled to London to finish work on the picture. They had already written at least one vocal number for the film (probably *Let Your Love Come Through*), but changes made to the picture during production called for a new song. David arrived in England after Bacharach and penned the lyrics for *The Look Of Love* based on a theme that the composer had already written for the film.

As with AFTER THE FOX and WHAT'S NEW PUSSYCAT?, the CASINO ROYALE soundtrack was recorded in London. The picture's main theme was performed by the hottest instrumental group of the mid-'60s, Herb Alpert and the Tijuana Brass.

"Burt Bacharach called me from London while he was doing the score for the movie CASINO ROYALE," recalled Alpert, "and asked if I would play the trumpet over the track that he had just recorded. He sent the tape and I put a couple of trumpets on, added some maracas and sent back a two-track stereo tape. It fit very nicely in the movie. Burt was happy. I was happy."

The CASINO ROYALE soundtrack was mostly instrumental, but the film itself did feature a goofy vocal version of the title theme, which played over the end credits. That vocal version of *Casino Royale* was (probably wisely) not included on the soundtrack LP.

In early 1967, Bacharach released a single pairing *Alfie* with *Bond Street*. The record was the first release with his new label A&M Records.

A&M had been founded in 1962, initially as a vehicle to release Herb Alpert's single *The Lonely Bull*. Alpert had teamed up with Jerry Moss and named the label using the initials of their surnames. Recorded with his group, the Tijuana Brass, *The Lonely Bull* was the first of many Latin-flavoured, easy-on-the-ears instrumental hits for Alpert, and A&M grew into a force to be reckoned with.

A&M Records Ad

By the time Bacharach came aboard, A&M had a solid roster of artists – including Claudine Longet, the Baja Marimba Band, Sergio Mendes and the Sandpipers – whose sophisticated easy listening sounds gave the label a clear identity. Although A&M later had success with such rock acts as Supertramp, Peter Frampton, the Police and Bryan Adams, the label's mid-'60s line-up was all about smooth, adult sounds. Bacharach fit in perfectly, especially since his own records were largely instrumental, with vocals mostly by session singers. Burt's deal with A&M lasted more than a decade and produced his most popular and best work as a recording artist.

At A&M, Burt hit his stride as a recording artist, creating records that transcended the easy listening style of his Kapp LP. His recordings were often instrumentals on which session vocalists – or Burt himself – would sing just part of the vocal line. It was an unusual but effective technique.

"It was intentional," Bacharach said of this approach in an interview with PULSE magazine. "I would only sing part of a song. I was afraid to do more. Then the girls would sing the rest. Or I wouldn't have a whole instrumental. If there were key lines I'd use vocal dramatically." These tracks were essentially instrumentals that featured lyrics - whereby the vocal was almost part of the instrumental score.

On the rare occasions when Bacharach sang an entire song himself, the result was stunning. Although a million miles from Dionne Warwick in technical terms, Burt's voice was, in its own way, just as expressive and touching.

"We all know his voice is not great," Herb Alpert said on TV's BIOGRAPHY, "but, man, it's *real*. And he's expressing himself and he's expressing the lyric."

When Burt sang on one of his own records, it was always special. What his voice lacked in technical ability it more than made up for in its vulnerable, sincere delivery.

Dionne Warwick's next single, *The Windows Of The World*, was one of her finest efforts, and proof that Hal David was quite capable of conveying a political theme in his lyrics. The song contained a subtle anti-war message, a theme that would be expanded upon several years later, on the LOST HORIZON soundtrack.

"*Windows Of The World* is a song I felt very keenly about," recalls David. "We were going through the Vietnam War and I had two sons – and still have them. So I pictured my sons getting involved, particularly my older son who was (soon) going to be of age. And that was my feeling. I wrote that, I guess, as a political song from a father's perspective."

"There are many message songs being written," David wrote in the late '60s. "More and more of them are violent. I tend to take a gentler approach in my protest. I have a feeling that in the final analysis, the gentler approach will reach more people."

Despite his gentler approach, the lyricist was nonetheless "sympathetic to the discontent" expressed in the protest songs of the era, and cited "Blowin' In The Wind" and "Where Have All The Flowers Gone" as two of his favourites.

Dionne Warwick also felt strongly about *The Windows Of The World* and pointed to it as an example of Hal's approach to lyric writing.

"Hal doesn't just write songs," she said. "He writes himself. There's nothing contrived in what he does. He goes by feeling. *The Windows Of The World* has become one of our biggest hits, yet Hal didn't even think of it as a song to be written but as something that had to be said. Other people have been thinking it, and one day he just found a way to say it. It's about the kind of world we live in, and the way we feel about it, and again he tells it simply in just the way we'd like to say it ourselves."

Today, asked what her favourite Bacharach and David song is, Warwick doesn't hesitate before answering, "*The Windows Of The World*."

"I love that song," she says. "It's so meaningful. It was written and recorded during a period of time when it really needed to be heard. And the words that were written needed to be said."

Bacharach – ever the perfectionist – was less than satisfied with the *Windows Of The World* single.

"I didn't do a good production and arrangement on that," he says. "I missed that record a little bit."

To the rest of the world, the record was faultless. *The Windows Of The World* reached No. 32 in August 1967. It was followed three months later by another Bacharach/David/Warwick classic. After the thoughtful *Windows* 45, the trio returned with a more straightforward love song, yet with a typically sophisticated and dynamic musical backing. An instant classic, *I Say A Little Prayer* rose quickly to the No. 4 position, one of the biggest hits of Warwick's career. The other side of *I Say A Little Prayer* – the Andre and Dory Previn-penned theme from the movie adaptation of Jacqueline Susann's trashy classic VALLEY OF THE DOLLS – was actually a bigger success.

As with *Windows Of The World*, Burt feels he missed the mark with Dionne's version of *I Say A Little Prayer*.

"I didn't like Dionne's record," he explains. "I didn't like the record we made. I though the tempo was too fast. It was too rushed, too nervous. I even tried not to have the record come out."

Both *The Windows Of The World* and *I Say A Little Prayer*" showed up on Warwick's next LP, THE WINDOWS OF THE WORLD, in August 1967. It was followed three months later by the first of many Warwick compilation albums, DIONNE WARWICK'S GOLDEN HITS, PART ONE. Not surprisingly, Bacharach and David penned every track on that collection.

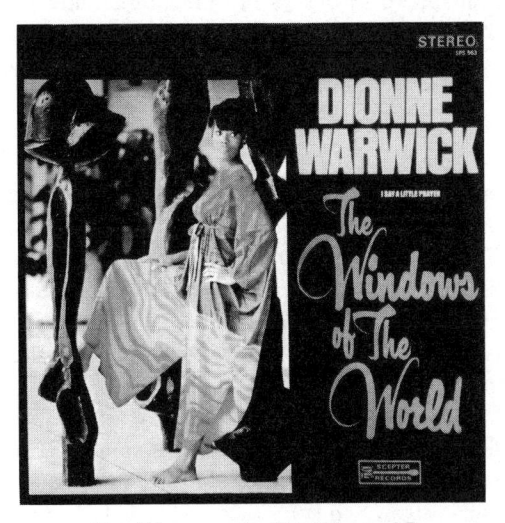

THE WINDOWS OF THE WORLD LP

In November 1967, Burt released his second A&M single *Reach Out For Me* b/w *The Look Of Love*, both sides extracted from REACH OUT, his first album for A&M.

April 1968 saw the release of yet another classic Dionne Warwick single – *Do You Know The Way To San Jose?* – whose lyrical theme was reminiscent of *Message To Michael*. The song featured one of Hal David's best lyrics ever, with such lines as "L.A. is a great big freeway" being great examples of his unmatched ability to capture the essence of something big in a simple, straightforward line.

"'L.A. is a great big freeway' is probably how I saw L.A. the first time I came out here to go to work," said David in a 2001 BBC Radio interview.

Although the song has become a standard, Dionne has said that she didn't care for "San Jose" when Burt and Hal first played it for her. She subsequently learned to love it, and the song remains in her repertoire to this day.

"I just didn't get it," Warwick says. "You know – 'whoa-whoa-whoa-whoa-whoa.' It was like, 'What is *that*?' But Hal David had a deep affinity for San Jose. Apparently he was stationed there in the navy and wrote a song about it. Time has a wonderful way of making people understand things that they don't, and I finally got the complete picture, living in Los Angeles for as long as I did. And it *is* a great big freeway, you know, and people are pumping gas or waiting tables while they're waiting for that opportunity."

Do You Know The Way To San Jose? was one of the last recordings Bacharach and David did with engineer Eddie Smith at Bell Sound, since the duo increasingly favoured recording with Phil Ramone at A&R. The record turned out to be another double-sided hit, with *San Jose* reaching No. 10 and the flip – *Let Me Be Lonely* – making it to No. 71. *San Jose* also won Dionne her first Grammy award, for Best Contemporary Pop Vocal.

Scepter included *Do You Know The Way To San Jose?* on Warwick's next LP, VALLEY OF THE DOLLS. Warwick's previous album, THE MAGIC OF BELIEVING, had seen the singer taking a breather from the Bacharach/David sound to revisit her Gospel roots. In early 1969, she released another LP that seemed designed to show that she was about more than just the sophisticated pop of Bacharach and David. That album, SOULFUL, didn't include any Bacharach and David songs. In the late '60s, Bacharach and David's records with Warwick had less of an R&B sound, with the emphasis moving to a sophisticated pop style.

The change in style of the Bacharach/David/Warwick trio wasn't a rejection of R&B, but the natural evolution of Dionne's collaboration with Burt and Hal. In the mid-to-late '60s, many artists' styles were evolving rapidly and Bacharach and David were no exception. Before getting into R&B in the early '60s, they had written in other styles and they had continued to do so even through the early years of their success with Warwick. In the late '60s, they moved into a style that was in some respects lighter and more "adult." Latin sounds increasingly came to bear in the music, inspired no doubt by Bacharach's fondness for Jobim and the influence of Herb Alpert and the A&M style. The R&B instrumentation that Burt had learned about from Leiber and Stoller was less evident as the years passed, in its place marimbas and Alpert-style trumpets.

Warwick rejects the idea that she and Bacharach and David were ever working specifically within the R&B genre.

"Basically we were doing exactly the same thing that we're doing today," she says. "None of my songs were considered R&B. They were borderline pop. Nobody really understood or knew how to categorize it, which was the wonderful part of recording their music. They were considered R&B because I happened to be a black woman. R&B stations were not really playing my music. They were played more in the pop arena than they were in the R&B arena."

"We were so different musically from anything that was being recorded and/or written in that period of time that we kind of carved our own little niche out," Warwick says. "Although I showed up on the pop charts, I was still working some of the black clubs. I was colourless."

By 1968, Bacharach and David had written plenty of big hit records – among them some of the most memorable songs of the '60s – but they had not yet written a song that had reached the coveted No. 1 spot in America. It finally happened in May 1968. It was a million miles away from Tijuana Brass fare like *Spanish Flea* and *Tijuana Taxi*, but Bacharach and David's *This Guy's In Love With You* turned out to be Herb Alpert's biggest hit ever, sitting at No. 1 for four weeks.

Initially included on the Tijuana Brass LP THE BEAT OF THE BRASS, the song was performed by Alpert in the group's TV special of the same name, dedicated to his wife. Viewer reaction to Herb's vocal spot was so strong that A&M decided to put the song out as a single.

Although Alpert was not known as a vocalist, the TV special's director, Jack Haley Jr., wanted the TJB frontman to put down his trumpet and sing on the program. Alpert agreed, if he could find an appropriate song.

HERB ALBERT – BEAT OF THE BRASS LP

"I was in the habit of asking all great songwriters if there was a melody that haunted them that they had written or that had been recorded and felt should have been a hit," said Alpert. "When I asked this question of my friend Burt Bacharach, he gave me a song titled *This Girl's In Love With You*. I fell in love with the melody and called Hal David to ask if he would consider doing some modifications on the lyrics in order to suit my appearance on the television special. He graciously agreed, and I flew to New York to be with him while he made the changes in the lyric which suited me and the show perfectly."

"We had written the song," says Bacharach. "And then we made some changes in the song for Herb. It was a pretty ideal song for him. And I was close to Herb and close to Jerry Moss, because of being signed to the label."

"He wanted to do that song on a TV special he was doing," says Hal David. "It was song he was going to sing to his wife. And (the original lyric) was not quite appropriate for what he wanted to say. He asked us whether we could change (the lyric) so it would fit what he needed. And I did. And he did it on the show, and got a terrific reaction, and recorded it. And it turned out to be a stunning hit."

The original song was titled *That Guy's In Love With You* and featured a different lyrical perspective ("he looks at you the way I do/when he smiles, I can tell/ you know each other very well," etc.).

"The song dealt with someone else and he thought it should deal with him," said David.

This Guy's In Love With You was billed as a solo effort by Alpert, since the Tijuana Brass didn't appear on the track. Since Alpert was known for his instrumental hits with the TJB, most listeners assumed that the song was Herb's vocal debut. In fact, he had cut two vocal singles in 1962, prior to *The Lonely Bull*, under the name Dore Alpert.

Burt Bacharach & Hal David

Opening with a gently swinging electric piano, adding Alpert's distinctive lead vocal and slowly building to the dynamic peak of the chorus, *This Guy* became a radio staple and was, inevitably, widely covered. Alpert's version was recorded at Goldstar Studios in Los Angeles, produced by Alpert and Jerry Moss, with Bacharach conducting his own arrangement.

The single's chart ascent was aided in no small part by the massive exposure it received on the TV special. THE BEAT OF THE BRASS had the top national Nielson rating for the two-week period ending May 5, 1968, and was seen in over 17 million homes.

Despite the success of *This Guy's In Love With You*, Alpert had no desire to be a full-time singer.

"There are no plans to develop Herb as a vocalist," noted A&M's general manager Gil Friesen in 1968. Nevertheless, Alpert charted again in August 1968 with another Bacharach/David ballad, *To Wait For Love* (previously recorded by Jay and the Americans, Jackie DeShannon, Tom Jones and Tony Orlando), which climbed to No. 51.

The same month saw Aretha Franklin hit No. 10 with a record that proved – as the Love version of *My Little Red Book* had done – that Bacharach and David's productions of their songs were not always the definitive versions.

At a session for another song, Franklin and her back-up singers had been fooling around, doing an impromptu rendition of *I Say A Little Prayer* between takes. So convincing was their off-the-cuff performance, that a full arrangement was worked up – a slower, more soulful interpretation than the Bacharach/David/Warwick recording, with Aretha and her singers trading lines.

"When Aretha recorded *Say A Little Prayer*, she changed the melody a bit, some other things, and I thought, 'Hmmmm.'" Burt told the LOS ANGELES TIMES. "But when I got used to it – and she's incredible – I was fine with it. Those kind of things give your tune an existence beyond its original self."

In August, Dionne Warwick scored another double-sided hit with *Who Is Gonna Love Me* (which reached No. 33) and *(There's) Always Something There To Remind Me* (which peaked at No. 65).

Chapter 10: Promises, Promises

By 1966, David Merrick had made his mark as one of the most successful American stage producers of the 20th century. Nicknamed "The Abominable Showman," Merrick had achieved his greatest success with such Broadway musicals as HELLO, DOLLY!, 42ND STREET and GYPSY. At a lunch meeting in 1966, Merrick pitched his latest idea to playwright Neil Simon. Simon was at the top of his game, having wowed Broadway audiences with BAREFOOT IN THE PARK, THE ODD COUPLE and COME BLOW YOUR HORN. Among Simon's other credits was the screenplay for the Bacharach-scored film AFTER THE FOX.

At the lunch meeting, Merrick asked Simon if he was interested in collaborating on a Broadway musical. Although Simon had recently enjoyed success with SWEET CHARITY, the playwright was not interested in penning another musical at that point. Merrick, who clearly knew how to get what he wanted, then asked Simon that if he *were* to do another musical, who would he choose to write the songs? Bacharach and David, Simon replied. A perfect fit, as it happened, since Merrick had already been pitching ideas to Burt and Hal. Merrick continued, asking that, were Bacharach and David to be recruited, what type of show might Simon want to do. An adaptation of Billy Wilder's film THE APARTMENT, said Simon.

Before he knew it, Simon was agreeing to Merrick's proposal, and the seeds of PROMISES, PROMISES were sown.

"David Merrick had been wanting us to do a show," Hal David recalls. "And he had brought a couple of projects to us, neither of which seemed right for us. And he said to us one day, 'I think I've got something for you. Just don't make any commitments to anybody for the next...' – whatever it was – 'I think I have something you're going to love.'

"I was out in Los Angeles," David continues, "either for ASCAP or for the Academy Awards – staying at the Beverly Hills Hotel. David Merrick called me in my room – I didn't know he was out there. He said, 'Do you have a minute for me? I've got something of interest to tell you'."

"(Merrick) came over, and he said, 'How would you like to do a show based on *The Apartment*, with Neil Simon doing the book and Bob Fosse directing?' I said, 'That sounds fantastic.' So he said, 'Do you think Burt'll like it?' I said, 'I'm sure Burt'll love it. Let's call him now.' So we put a call in, and Burt was there. I said, 'David Merrick is here, and he has a wonderful idea for us. Let me have him tell you.' So I put Merrick on the phone, and Burt reacted the same way I did. And we agreed to do the show."

The storyline of the musical – which came to be titled PROMISES, PROMISES - was faithful to that of THE APARTMENT: Chuck Baxter tries to get ahead by loaning out his apartment to his bosses for their romantic dalliances. One of his bosses' lovers, Fran Kubelik, attempts suicide in Chuck's apartment. Chuck helps her sort things out and they fall in love.

"We started writing the show in California," says David. "We didn't start immediately, because Neil (first had to do his first draft of the book.) And when he wrote the first draft – which was great – we went to work. The first song we wrote was *She Likes Basketball*."

She Likes Basketball wasn't one of the show's highlights, but it didn't matter. Bacharach and David found it easier to get into a big project by starting off with a song that wasn't necessarily going to be the cornerstone of the project. Breaking the ice with a lesser number was a good way for them to get past the daunting nature of such a big piece of work.

After completing *She Likes Basketball*, Burt and Hal wrote the show's opening number, *Half As Big As Life*. Armed with their first two songs, Bacharach and David invited Simon and Fosse to Bacharach's house to play them the songs.

"They both liked them a lot," David recalls. "Bob Fosse didn't end up directing the show. At that time, he was in the process of directing the show. Shortly after that, Fosse got the opportunity to direct a movie (SWEET CHARITY). He had never directed a film before and it was something he very much wanted to do. He came to us and asked us if we would release him from his commitment to us – he had already been signed by Merrick – and of course we did."

"We kept writing songs, without a director, based on Neil Simon's script," David continues. "And we had to go out and find somebody to replace Bob Fosse. We wound up finding two people to do the job – Bob Moore, the director, who had done THE BOYS IN THE BAND – he'd just had a big hit in New York with that. Neil suggested we go see the show and we did. David Merrick retained him. And Michael Bennett – we had heard great reports about his work and then Merrick signed Michael Bennett."

In June 1968, with the songs for the show completed, Bacharach and David recorded demos of their PROMISES, PROMISES songs. On these recordings, Bacharach's piano accompanied Bernie Nee, Rose Marie Jun and several other singers.

Bernie Nee was no stranger to Bacharach and David's music. Nee – known as the "king of the demo singers" – sang on various Bacharach and David demos, including *Blue On Blue*. His multi-tracked voice had masqueraded as 'The Five Blobs' on the Bacharach-Mack David-penned single *The Blob* and he had released Bacharach and David's *Country Music Holiday* as a single in 1958.

The numbers recorded in the PROMISES, PROMISES demo sessions were supposed to be the finished line-up of songs for the show: *Half As Big As Life, Upstairs, You'll Think Of Someone, She Likes Basketball, Wanting Things, Whoever You Are, Christmas Day, A Young Pretty Girl Like You, Promises, Promises, What Am I Doing Here, Let's Pretend We're Grown Up*, and *Tick Tock Goes The Clock*.

Whoever You Are, I Love You Music Sheet

The purpose of the sessions was to drum up cover versions of the songs.

"They would use these demos to show them to big-name singers," says Jun, "to try to get them to record the songs. Not so much the cast, because they'd be rehearsing with the cast all the time."

"You didn't get the music ahead of time," Jun recalls. "You'd walk into the studio and get it handed to you. I had a masters degree in music, and the other people were good at picking things up quickly. And with Burt it was hard - it was difficult stuff he wrote, with all kinds of different time signatures and switches in time. Every other bar, it was like 2/4, 3/4, 6/8... You had to be on your toes all the time. But it was a lot of fun."

Jun recalls that, in the studio, Bacharach was in "total control, all the time. He knew absolutely what he wanted. He knew the phrasing he wanted, he knew the way he wanted the words to go. He knew exactly the way he wanted it performed, and we did it pretty much the way he wanted it."

Like other singers who have worked with Bacharach, Jun says that Bacharach's own renditions of the songs were a big influence.

"The phrasing – he'd have certain little ways of saying the words himself," Jun says, "and he wanted you to do it that way. He knew exactly what he wanted. Richard Rodgers was the same way – he wanted it exactly the way it was written – no changes, not a dot different. Whereas other people... I remember Jerry Herman would say, 'Let me hear how you would do it,' and he'd let you have much more freedom. With Burt, you could say, 'Well, couldn't I do it this way?' He'd give it some thought but generally you did it the way he wanted it done."

As on his recording dates with Dionne Warwick and other artists, Bacharach's piano playing on the demo sessions was a source of inspiration.

"He was good at the piano," recalls Jun. "He was really good to sing with, because he played very strong. If you listen to the album, you can hear how strong he plays. It pushed you and it was good to sing with."

Even on those demo sessions, Hal David was in the control booth, co-producing in his low-key style.

"Hal was the quiet one," Jun adds. "When he had something to say he would say it quietly, but it was still very definite. He was more concerned with the lyrics, needless to say. He commanded a lot of respect – a lovely, lovely, lovely man."

With the songs completed and demos recorded, rehearsals began with the cast, which included Jerry Orbach and Jill O'Hara in the lead roles of Chuck and Fran. Burt and Hal assumed their work as songwriters was essentially finished at that point. As rehearsals began, they quickly realized that wasn't the case.

"In the first week of rehearsals I learned that what I had thought was a completed score was only the first draft," wrote Hal in his book WHAT THE WORLD NEEDS NOW.

The first casualty was a song originally intended to close the first act. When the number proved too difficult to choreograph, Michael Bennett asked Bacharach and David for a replacement. They replaced the troublesome tune with the new *Turkey Lurkey Time*. Then, during rehearsals, Hal found that the second act opener wasn't working because the lyrics didn't ring true for the characters. So that song was cut and a replacement, *A Fact Can Be A Beautiful Thing*, was substituted. Other numbers – *Upstairs* and the newly added *Where Can You Take A Girl?* – were shortened during the rehearsal process.

When rehearsals came to an end, the *Promises, Promises* company moved to Boston for their first public performances. In Boston, further changes were made to the show, including changes to the song line-up. After the Boston opening, Bacharach and David realized that one of the songs in the second act, *Wouldn't That Be A Stroke Of Luck*, wasn't working. Four executives performed the song who "had found a way to get back at Chuck for denying them the use of his bachelor pad," David recalled. Although *Wouldn't That Be A Stroke Of Luck* had worked well in rehearsals, it didn't get any response from the Boston audience.

"The song revolved around four tired old men," said David. "It should have been about one young pretty girl who was just recovering from a disastrous love affair and hopefully on the verge of a new and happy relationship."

To that end, he and Bacharach penned one of their most enduring songs, *I'll Never Fall In Love Again*. After very little rehearsal, the new song made its debut on the last night in Boston. Despite being under-rehearsed, *I'll Never Fall In Love Again* was an immediate hit with the audience.

After Boston, PROMISES, PROMISES moved to Washington for a four-week run. Here, final changes were made in preparation for the New York opening. One last song was cut in Washington, replaced by *Our Little Secret*, and Bacharach and David "froze" the show. After months of fine-tuning, PROMISES, PROMISES was ready for Broadway.

Merrick had booked the Schubert Theater for the show's run but, upon inspecting the venue, Bacharach decided that the Schubert was acoustically "dead." Having gone to such lengths to capture sonically perfect versions of his and Hal's songs over the years, Burt wasn't about to make his Broadway debut with substandard acoustics. So he and Phil Ramone devised a sound system for the theatre that would bring the music to life.

"A special semi-enclosed orchestra pit was constructed," reported CURRENT BIOGRAPHY, "with celotex covering on the floors, walls and ceiling to limit sound leakage, and into the pit were put 17 microphones, an electric bass, an electric organ, two electric guitars, and four girl singers."

AD FOR *I'LL NEVER FALL IN LOVE AGAIN* SINGLE

It was the first time in Broadway's history that a vocal chorus had been installed in the pit. The pit singers sang into microphones and their voices were processed through an echo chamber. To achieve the perfect mix of instruments and voices, the sound was tweaked on an 11-channel mixing board at the back of the theatre. Although primitive by today's standards, the set-up was groundbreaking at the time and many of the show's firsts have now become standard procedures on Broadway.

"I set it all up," says Phil Ramone of the PROMISES sound system. "They let me design it. The producer was not sure that what I had in mind was ever going to work. And we built a studio underneath the stage, with separation and stuff, so we could control certain elements of the orchestra. And then we soundproofed the booth that was under the stage so it didn't act like a hollow echo chamber. Then we added echo, and I put stuff in there that had not been done in the theatre prior to that."

In addition to the complex set-up, it was also important for Burt to get the appropriate musicians. "I tried to get the right musicians who could play my kind of pop music," said Bacharach, "instead of the usual pit orchestra."

PROMISES, PROMISES made its Broadway debut on December 1, 1968. The show was a huge success, running for 1281 performances (it closed in January 1972). Weekly profits were as much as $35,000, a record at the time.

Burt Bacharach & Hal David

Audiences loved the show, and so did the critics.

"It is an absolutely marvellous musical and... all two hundred million of my fellow-citizens should make plans to go and see it as quickly as possible," raved the NEW YORKER'S theatre reviewer, who added, "I sat watching it in a daze of pleasure from start to finish."

WOMEN'S WEAR DAILY hailed the show as "easily the most satisfying and successful musical in a very long time." VARIETY praised Orbach's Chuck – "half slickie, half schlemiel, but always endearing."

With the New York production a runaway success, productions of *Promises, Promises* opened in other cities around the world. In October 1969, the show opened at the Prince of Wales theatre in London, where it enjoyed a run of 560 performances. The British version starred Betty Buckley and Anthony Roberts.

Cast recordings of PROMISES, PROMISES were made from not only the Broadway version (recorded at A&R) but also the incarnations from London and Italy. The Broadway recording is regarded as the best version, although the BLACKWELL GUIDE TO THE MUSICAL THEATER ON RECORD contended that "the prize for charm... goes hands down to the Italian disc, a truncated recording featuring only the 10 numbers in which Johnny Dorelli and Catherine Spaak were involved."

PROMISES, PROMISES spawned several of Bacharach and David's most enduring compositions, the first of which appeared as a Dionne Warwick 45 in late '68. The title song *Promises, Promises* was musically tricky – darting between 3/4, 4/4 and 5/4 time – but also possessed a strong commercial appeal. Warwick, naturally, made it sound easy, and her version charted at No. 19. Warwick's version was recorded before the show opened, and cast members were given copies of her version, to help them get to grips with the complex number.

"*Promises, Promises* was a tough song," Burt recalled years later in an interview with the LOS ANGELES TIMES. "When I wrote it out, I realized that it was changing time signatures nearly every bar. The reason it was written like that was because of the urgency of what was happening on stage. But when I wrote it out it felt natural and good to me."

As with their motion picture assignments, Bacharach and David's songs for PROMISES, PROMISES were not written with the charts in mind, but merely to serve the show.

"Every song was meant to do something in the show," says David. "*I'll Never Fall In Love Again*, which became a big hit, was written for a given situation in the show. The fact that it became a hit afterwards was gravy."

PROMISES, PROMISES won a Grammy award, for Best Original Soundtrack Recording Of A Musical Play, and Jerry Orbach won a Tony for his portrayal of Chuck.

After the experience was over, Burt confessed that, despite the success of PROMISES, PROMISES, he had no desire to do another Broadway show. In an interview with the SATURDAY EVENING POST, the composer revealed his frustration with the Broadway process.

"If you do a good job in a recording studio, or if you write a movie score, it's that way forever," Bacharach said. "But if you come back the next night and hear what's happening in a Broadway musical, you'll rush to the corner bar for a quick drink. It changes too much and I can't stand it."

Bacharach was used to producing his own recordings and to conducting live performances. But staging a Broadway show meant relinquishing some of that control. A show's performances inevitably change to some extent during the course of a run, not necessarily through any inadequacy on the performers' part. But Burt didn't like to see this happening to his and Hal's songs.

"Both Burt and Hal went crazy, because every night it was slightly different – the tempos were not quite the same," recalls Phil Ramone. "When we were doing the show, the emotional way in which this conductor would conduct the show just didn't have any kind of magic and power. And so Burt made a change. The show went through a few changes, but boy was it fun to do."

"It was intense," Bacharach recalls. "I felt real bad out on the road most of the time. I got pneumonia in Boston. Trying to rewrite songs when you're just getting out of the hospital is not so great, you know? It's a different kind of thing. You don't have the control. You have the control when you conduct the orchestra in the pit every night for the run of the show. 'What are you doing tonight?' 'I can't have dinner with you because I'm conducting the pit orchestra.' You don't want that. So you have somebody else conducting. You have different subs in the orchestra, and my music's not the easiest to play. But I was delighted it was a hit, delighted that it created the stir that it created."

"I enjoyed that experience, I believe, more than Burt did," says David. "There were many opportunities after that (to do Broadway shows) and we didn't do them. At that time in his life, Burt didn't enjoy the process as much as I did. I loved it. I had a great time. I could've gone on in that direction for the rest of my life."

September 1968 saw the publication of Hal David's book WHAT THE WORLD NEEDS NOW AND OTHER LOVE LYRICS, a collection of his lyrics, selected and annotated by him, with a foreword by Dionne. A second edition, expanded to include the lyrics from PROMISES PROMISES, was published in 1970.

Bacharach saw out 1968 with a catchy seasonal 45, *The Bell That Couldn't Jingle* (previously cut by Bobby Vinton), backed with *What The World Needs Now Is Love*. December 1968 also saw the release of Dionne Warwick's PROMISES, PROMISES LP, featuring her versions of several numbers from the Broadway show, including of course the title song.

In February, 1969 – just eight months after Herb Alpert had topped the charts with *This Guy's In Love With You* – Dionne Warwick reached No. 7 with her own *This Girl's In Love With You*, extracted from her PROMISES, PROMISES LP.

Warwick was reportedly not keen on recording the song but, since she needed one more number for the album, Steve Tyrell suggested she give it a shot. Scepter pulled *This Girl's In Love With You* as a single and, to everyone's surprise, it made the Top 10. B.J. Thomas also cut the song, with a backing that sounded similar to the Warwick version. In fact, Scepter reportedly sometimes re-used the same backing tracks with different vocalists, and this was likely what they did for Thomas' version.

In May, Warwick followed *This Girl's In Love With You* with the Bacharach and David-composed movie theme, *The April Fools*, which peaked at No. 37. 1969 saw Warwick make her debut as a movie actor, starring in SLAVES, for which she also recorded the theme song. May 1969 saw another Bacharach solo 45 – a great version of *I'll Never Fall In Love Again*, taken from his second A&M album MAKE IT EASY ON YOURSELF.

MAKE IT EASY ON YOURSELF LP

Like Burt's other LPs, MAKE IT EASY ON YOURSELF mixed instrumental versions of Bacharach/David tunes with the occasional appearance of unnamed session vocalists. Burt himself delivered a touching vocal performance on the album's title track. Though not technically a great singer, Bacharach's voice gives the track an aching beauty that makes the song his own.

As the '60s drew to a close, the Bacharach and David songbook continued to attract an amazing variety of interpreters. The latter months of 1969 found Engelbert Humperdinck at No. 38 with *I'm A Better Man* and Isaac Hayes at No. 30 with his version of *Walk On By*, the first of several Bacharach-David tunes recorded by the *Shaft*-man.

In 1970, 13 years after they wrote their first song together, Burt and Hal were at the top of their game. It was reported that Dionne Warwick had sold 12,500,000 singles of Bacharach and David numbers, and more hits were on the way. As 1969 drew to a close, Warwick reached No. 6 with her version – probably the definitive recording - of *I'll Never Fall In Love Again*.

Warwick's *I'll Never Fall In Love Again* – like her *Message To Michael* – was a record that only came out after another determined effort by Steve Tyrell. "I called Burt and said,

'Let's put this record out at Christmas' – which was usually a bad time," he recalls, "because people play Christmas records."

I'll Never Fall In Love Again was done at a typically productive Warwick/Bacharach/David session towards the end of 1969. The studio, as usual, was packed – Bacharach, David and Phil Ramone in the control booth; Dionne at the mike, backed by thirty players, including the usual team of guitarist Bill Suyker, bassist Russ Savakus and drummer Gary Chester. Chester was there from the beginning of the Bacharach/David/Warwick partnership, laying down the beat to many hits, including *Don't Make Me Over, Walk On By, I Say A Little Prayer* and *Promises, Promises.*" Bacharach and David relied upon the skills of these players and used them whenever they were available. Other regulars on their dates included percussionist George Devens and pianist/keyboard player Paul Griffin.

Like so many Bacharach/David/Warwick dates, the *I'll Never Fall In Love Again* session went into overtime, but the results were worth every cent. No B-sides, but three hit A-sides were made that night: *I'll Never Fall In Love Again, Paper Maché* and *Let Me Go To Him* - a cache of tracks that would keep Dionne in the charts through the summer of 1970.

As always, Burt in particular was demanding of the musicians.

"He's possessed," Russ Savakus told NEWSWEEK. "And a little of each man's flesh is left in the session." But the musicians adored Bacharach and the results of those severe sessions speak for themselves.

Chapter 11: Nothing's Worrying Me

"Hey, man, you see these records?" Dionne called to Burt.

The singer and songwriter were in the 54th Street offices of Scepter Records in New York City, when a delivery arrived from the RIAA. Noticing the two gold record plaques being carried in, Warwick had walked into the room where Bacharach was.

"B.J.'s got two million sellers," she told him. "You'd better write this guy something!"

"B.J." was Scepter artist B.J. Thomas who had, by that point, racked up a total of four gold discs for the label. In 1966, not long after signing to Scepter, Thomas had scored a Top 10 version of Hank Williams's *I'm So Lonesome I Could Cry.* In the intervening years, his success had continued with such hits as *The Eyes Of A New York Woman* and the massive *Hooked On A Feeling.* Being on the same label as Bacharach and David mainstay Dionne Warwick certainly made him a logical candidate for a song from the duo.

"I was kind of in the back of (Burt's) mind," Thomas recalls. "He was possibly going

Burt Bacharach & Hal David

to write me something. We had kind of been politicking him and trying to get him to do a session with me, really, ever since I got with the record label. Steve Tyrell had been working on it and so had Paul Cantor – he was Dionne's personal manager and he was my personal manager at the time, too."

An offer eventually came while Thomas was on the road, doing a three-week tour of the Midwest.

"I got word from Paul Cantor that, when I finished that string of dates, I was going to California and that I was going to get a session with Burt Bacharach," says Thomas. "He said, 'We've got this song in this Paul Newman movie.'"

Raindrops Keep Falling On My Head Sheet Music

As soon as the tour was over, Thomas was on a plane to Los Angeles.

Bacharach and David had been tapped for the soundtrack of a new Paul Newman film called BUTCH CASSIDY AND THE SUNDANCE KID, a light-hearted western that also featured the soon-to-be-famous Robert Redford.

Burt and Hal were asked to write two songs for the picture, with Burt also providing the score. They viewed a rough cut of the film, to which director George Roy Hill had already added music to aid in the editing process. Hill had used classical music in place of an original score and, for the famous Paul Newman-Katherine Ross bicycle sequence, had inserted Simon and Garfunkel's *59th Street Bridge Song (Feelin' Groovy)*.

Bacharach and David were very impressed by the film, and set to work on a song to take the place of *Feelin' Groovy*.

"I just kept watching that (bicycle) scene on my moviola machine," Bacharach recalled, "and I got this theme."

Burt and Hal came up with the title *Raindrops Keep Fallin' On My Head*, and wrote the song to capture the essence of Butch Cassidy.

"We wrote the song with Paul Newman in mind," David says. "With Butch Cassidy in mind. In writing for a film, you don't write for the singer who's going to sing over the scene, you should be writing it for the character. And that's exactly why and how the song was written."

"*Raindrops* really came out of the scene where Paul Newman and Katharine Ross were on the bike having a wonderful time in the sunshine on a beautiful day," Hal told filmscore.org. "All the while you knew that he was the original loser and everything went wrong for him, so writing the song against the look of the scene seemed like a great idea. Burt's melody was so terrific and writing the lyric a little down, I thought, gave the juxtaposition that made an interesting song for the scene."

Armed with a tape of Bacharach's melody, David wrote the words in a suite at the Beverly Wilshire Hotel. Hal wrote two different sets of lyrics then used elements from both in the finished song.

AD FOR *RAINDROPS KEEP FALLING ON MY HEAD*

Raindrops Keep Fallin' On My Head has become synonymous with B.J. Thomas, who recorded it for the film, but he wasn't Bacharach and David's first choice. The duo first asked Ray Stevens.

"Ray Stevens came out to California to see the movie and hear the song," Bacharach says. "And he didn't like the movie and he didn't like the song."

"It wasn't that I didn't like it," says Stevens. "The timing was bad. I had just spent weeks in the studio, working on what I thought was a wonderful record of a wonderful song. The song was called *Sunday Mornin' Comin' Down*, written by Kris Kristofferson. I had so much confidence in that record that I just didn't want to wait to put it out. And I liked the song *Raindrops Keep Fallin' On My Head*. I flew to L.A., went to Burt's house and he sang the song for me at the piano. I was very flattered to have been asked to do the song. Obviously hindsight is 20/20 and, if I had the chance again, I'd shelve *Sunday Morning* and do *Raindrops* instead!"

It has been suggested that *Raindrops* was written with Bob Dylan in mind. Although a folksinger may seem an unlikely candidate for a Bacharach/David tune, consider that just three years later the duo tapped Shawn Phillips to sing the theme for their ill-fated movie LOST HORIZON.

"I'm not sure that they pitched the song to Dylan," says Thomas. "But I know that

Burt Bacharach & Hal David

Burt wrote the melody — and he wrote a lot of his melodies — with Bob Dylan in mind. I'm not sure if it's because of Dylan's phrasing or whatever. Burt is a real genius in the way he phrases the melody and the way he fits the lyrics in there. There's a possibility that they did offer the song to Bob Dylan. You know, that 'fallin' on my *head*' kind of thing," says Thomas, emphasizing the line's Dylan-esque phrasing.

"I tended to sing it, in its original form, sort of like Dylan-esque thing," Bacharach says. "And B.J. acquired a little of that."

Indeed, there is a similarity between the singing styles of Dylan and Bacharach. Neither possesses a great range, but both can convey a great deal of emotion. Thomas agrees. "You know, I think that's why Burt always liked him, because Dylan's not really a singer, but he really makes it work. Burt really admired him for that."

Thomas arrived in Los Angeles late one night in 1969, caught a taxi at the airport and was soon heading up Mulholland Drive to Bacharach's house. Although a celebrity in his own right, the Texan found himself a little out of his element.

"It was dark and it was late at night and I couldn't find the doorbell," he recalls. "I pushed this button and the garage door went up. And then, out of the kitchen door, came Angie Dickinson, just looking every inch a movie star. She brought me in the back and I went down to the basement music room that he had and rehearsed with him. I'll never forget that."

Bacharach sat down at the piano in his music room, and sang *Raindrops* for the singer. Thomas had a distinctive singing style, which had brought him plenty of success, but he found that Bacharach was not much interested in any reinterpretation of his and Hal David's work.

"I have some vocal tricks that I do, running around the notes and doing those things," says Thomas. "And he just told me straight out. He said, 'B.J., after you do this song and all the notes exactly like I've written them, if you have any space to do that, well, feel free.' So really the only place where I could kind of play with the melody was at the end, where I did the (sings) 'me-e-e-e-e-ee...' And when I did that in the studio, he was conducting the orchestra and he kind of looked over his shoulder at me, and kind of looked and he said, 'Oh, okay, that works'. So, he didn't allow me to use much of my style. Basically I just sang his notes."

Raindrops was recorded twice. The first version was recorded in Los Angeles, to meet the film's production deadline.

"I was a little under the weather when I did the (soundtrack version)," says Thomas. "You know, back in those days I kind of burned the candle at both ends. By the time I finished that tour, my voice was really shot." This somewhat hoarse version appeared in the movie, underscoring the famous bicycle riding sequence. It also appeared on the soundtrack album, as *On A Bicycle Built For Joy*.

A few weeks later, a re-make of the song was cut in New York. This version was not included in the movie but was released as a single and is the familiar hit version.

"Burt had written the tag on the end, so we went into Columbia studios on Broadway in Manhattan and re-cut it," Thomas recalls. "And that's the single version. However, the kind of scratchy version is the one in the movie."

On his first session with Bacharach and David, Thomas was acutely aware that he was now in the big leagues. Thomas sang the song and the musicians played live, as the famous bicycle sequence rolled on a big screen in front of them.

"There was a lot of tension in it and, really, self-imposed pressure for me," he says. "Just a few years previous to that I was just singing with basically a garage band in Texas. It was really an exciting session. We did the song against the bicycle scene where Paul has Katherine Ross on the handlebars. It was a big band, a huge orchestra; back in those days you used all live musicians. So it was a real exciting thing."

AD FOR BURT BACHARACH LPS ON A&M

The contrast between Burt and Hal's respective styles was quite apparent in the studio.

"Burt was more demonstrative in his production techniques," says Thomas. "Hal is a very quiet mild-mannered person, but he had lots of input in their productions, too, but he had it in a quieter – maybe less showy – way. They worked great together."

Raindrops was naturally selected as a single. After the first batch of 45s was pressed and shipped, Bacharach had a last-minute idea. Listening to the record in England, he decided that the beginning of the track was too fast, and had the first pressing recalled. Twentieth Century Fox protested, but the composer insisted, immediately flying back to New York to replace the first part of the track with an earlier, more laid-back take.

"If it's off a percent and a half, that looms large," Bacharach explained to NEWSWEEK. "It's my life. And I felt the beginning was too fast."

Burt Bacharach & Hal David

"We had done *Raindrops*, and we'd made an edit and put the mix out," recalls Phil Ramone. "And it was climbing the charts, into the Top 40 somewhere. And Hal and Burt and I were in England, and we heard it on the radio, and he said, 'You know, I think you were right: maybe the edit from seven to four is better if we just stick with four all the way.' We came back and remastered it. And it's not about ego or craziness or anything. It was just that, in the fast judgement of getting the record out, we had made an edit."

"They used to tease me because I have one of those steel-trap minds about remembering intros and exits from a verse into a chorus, things like that," says Ramone. "Remembering take numbers, and how I edited and why. It was the day and age of making the mix work as great as you could, right off the bat. Remixing was kind of simplistic, and these guys made their deadlines."

BUTCH CASSIDY AND THE SUNDANCE KID LP

The revamped *Raindrops* reached the No. 1 spot, where it spent four weeks. The BUTCH CASSIDY soundtrack also garnered a few awards to add to Bacharach and David's growing collection. In addition to another Grammy (for Best Soundtrack), the soundtrack also scored big at the Oscars. After three previous nominations (for *The Look Of Love*, *Alfie* and *What's New Pussycat?*), Burt and Hal finally won for Best Original Song (*Raindrops*). BUTCH CASSIDY won a second musical Oscar, for Best Original Score.

Although they had originally been tapped to write two songs for BUTCH CASSIDY AND THE SUNDANCE KID, *Raindrops* was the only one included in the film. The potential second song was *Where There's A Heartache (There Must Be A Heart)*, a lovely number based on one of Burt's melodies from the film's score.

"It was a melody from BUTCH CASSIDY, and I wrote that lyric for it," says Hal. "I loved the melody."

Following the huge success of *Raindrops*, B.J. Thomas got first refusal of several new Bacharach/David numbers.

"A lot of times they would give me a tape of the song, for me to kind of go over and listen to before we would rehearse, because I didn't read music," Thomas recalls. "And that was one thing that me and Burt kind of butted heads on. He wanted me to learn how to read music, and I told him I didn't really want to be any more technical with my singing. I've always had kind of a free style that just is more about feeling. And I didn't want to do it, and so we always kind of disagreed on that. I would go to his apartment, after I'd learned the melody as well as I could. I'd go in and we'd work and sing it down a few times. And he would tell me what he wanted."

The singer's vocal performances on his first two Bacharach and David-penned numbers (*Raindrops* and *Everybody's Out Of Town*) sound closer to Bacharach's own vocal style than to B.J.'s usual delivery.

"When he would sing the song down to me, he pretty much wanted me to sing the song the way he sang it," Thomas recalls. "So, yeah, it did have something to do with it. I couldn't really sound like him – he was a little more scratchy and a little less tonal. But I would try to sing it back to him just like he sang it to me. That's the way he wanted it."

"Back in those days, when you did a Burt Bacharach/Hal David song, it was not about you," says Thomas. "It was all about them. Especially me having only a few hit records and those guys being long-time mainstays of music, they didn't really look for a lot of input from me, other than just bring the vocal messenger, you know?"

"It was just a big thrill to work with them," says Thomas. "In my opinion, when they broke up, I think it was a real kind of a tragedy in music, because together, you know – even next to the Beatles, next to John Lennon and Paul McCartney – Hal David was maybe the greatest lyricist that our country has ever produced. And Burt of course was kind of like the Beethoven of pop music and probably still is."

Chapter 12: Close To You

The 1970s began with yet another hit recording of *(There's) Always Something There To Remind Me*. This time out, the artist was R.B. Greaves – following up his big hit *Take A Letter, Maria*. The excellent Greaves version reached No. 27 in February 1970. Dionne Warwick began her second decade of hitmaking with *Let Me Go To Him*, which ascended to No. 32 in May 1970.

In March 1970, B.J. Thomas released *Everybody's Out Of Town*, his Bacharach and David-penned follow-up to *Raindrops Keep Fallin' On My Head*. While Bacharach, David and Thomas seem to have been trying to recapture some of the magic of the earlier hit, the similarities between the two songs are largely superficial and *Everybody's Out Of Town* has its own distinct charm. It did recapture the musical feel of *Raindrops*, with lyrics offering a gentle social comment typical of Hal David's work from this period. Given the success of *Raindrops*, the song sounds like it could have been written specifically for Thomas.

"I don't think they wrote it with me in mind," says Thomas. "They were trying to come up with a song for the follow-up record to *Raindrops*. I think that *Everybody's*

Burt Bacharach & Hal David

Out Of Town had already been written. But they went through their songs and came up with that for the follow up record. And it was a huge record in South America, but it wasn't a big record here – it did probably about 800,000 copies. But in South America it was a big record for me and when I go down to Brazil and those places, I still get lots of requests to do it down there."

It didn't match the huge success of *Raindrops*, but *Everybody's Out Of Town* was a modest hit, charting at No. 26 in April. The charming track showed that years of success hadn't lessened Bacharach's desire to experiment: *Everybody's Out Of Town*: featured some decidedly odd-sounding, almost avant-garde horn parts.

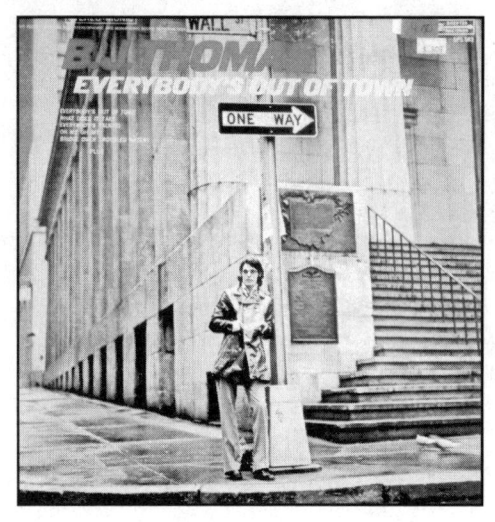

BJ THOMAS – EVERYBODY'S OUT OF TOWN LP

"They wrote just the most unique and different-sounding things," Thomas points out. "When we did *Everybody's Out Of Town*, after the first or second take, Burt left the studio and went to the bathroom or something. And the musicians were just laughing, like 'What is this?' They just didn't get it, you know? But I always thought his stuff was just great."

The next number Bacharach and David offered Thomas was *Send My Picture To Scranton, PA.* – a superb song, although not as immediately accessible as *Raindrops*.

"They really thought it was a hit record," recalls Thomas. "They tried to get Scepter to put it out. I always thought it was a hit record, too." Unfortunately, Scepter Records relegated *Scranton* to the B-side of *I Just Can't Help Believing* and it remains a "lost" Bacharach/David classic.

SEND MY PICTURE TO SCRANTON, PA 45

In 1968, Herb Alpert had asked Burt if there was a song that he's written that hadn't been a hit, but which still haunted him. Burt had chosen *This Guy's In Love With You* and given Alpert a huge hit. At that time, while consulting with Hal about modifications to the lyrics of *This Guy*, Alpert asked Hal David if there was a song that haunted him and that he felt deserved another chance. Hal's choice was *(They Long To Be) Close To You*.

"When I arrived back in Los Angeles there was a copy of *Close To You* waiting at my home," Alpert recalled. "I recorded it, but it didn't suit me, so I gave it to Richard and Karen Carpenter and the song ignited their career."

In June 1970, seven years after the song was written, *(They Long To Be) Close To You* reached the No. 1 spot where – like *This Guy's In Love With You* and *Raindrops Keep Fallin' On My Head* before it – it stayed for four weeks.

CARPENTERS – CLOSE TO YOU LP

"It was a dead horse that suddenly got up and won the race to the wire," Bacharach told BILLBOARD.

In the hands of the Carpenters, a brother-sister duo recently signed to A&M, the song was reborn. Richard Carpenter gave the song's arrangement a complete overhaul, reviving it with a gently swinging tempo and lush vocal harmonies. In fact, Carpenter's arrangement sounded more "Bacharach-esque" than Burt's original arrangement did. With Karen Carpenter's pure, faultless vocal and multi-tracked harmonies, *Close To You* was a classic pop record, and very different from Bacharach's own production.

"When we recorded the song (in 1964), it didn't feel like a hit at that time," recalls David. "But we always liked the song. That's why we sent it over to Herb Alpert. We had faith in the song, but we didn't feel we had the right rendition. When I first heard (the Carpenters' version), I didn't have the same enthusiasm as Burt did. I think Herb Alpert or Jerry Moss sent it over to Burt's house in California and we played it. And I liked it, but I didn't jump up and down. Burt thought it was a great record. I learned to fall in love with it very quickly but, on first hearing, I wasn't bowled over."

The Carpenters revisited the Bacharach/David catalogue several times, recording a great medley (including *Knowing When To Leave* and other songs) and *I'll Never Fall In Love Again*.

In July 1970, Dionne Warwick hit No. 43 with Bacharach and David's *Paper Maché*, a swipe at the increasing superficiality of consumer culture. Where the social commentary of *Windows Of The World* had been gentle, *Paper Maché* was much more direct in its approach: "There's a sale on Happiness/ You buy two and it costs less," crooned Dionne to Bacharach's lovely melody and stripped-down marimba backdrop. David's lyrics depict a shallow modern world with a shallow remedy for everything:

Burt Bacharach & Hal David

AN AD FOR DIONNE WARWICK'S *PAPER MACHÉ*

ONE LESS BELL TO ANSWER SHEET MUSIC

"Spray it with cologne and the whole world smells sweet..."

In October, 1970 – eight years after she accused Bacharach and David of 'making her over' by giving the song to someone else – Dionne Warwick released her own version of *Make It Easy On Yourself* as a single and saw it reach No. 37. On the flipside was a superb version of *Knowing When To Leave*, from the musical PROMISES, PROMISES.

In November, Hal and Burt almost chalked up another No. 1 hit, with the 5th Dimension's *One Less Bell To Answer*. The song had been written in 1967 and was originally recorded by Keely Smith, whose version didn't chart.

The inspiration for *One Less Bell To Answer* was a random comment that caught Hal David's ear, and struck him as a great song title.

"I was in London... and I was invited somewhere for a weekend," David recalled, "and the hostess said, 'When you get here, don't ring the bell. Just walk in – it'll just be one less bell for me to answer.' And the phrase took a hold of me and wouldn't let go."

Although the 5th Dimension's *One Less Bell To Answer* spent two weeks in the No. 2 position, it was kept from the top spot by George Harrison's mega-hit *My Sweet Lord*.

November 1970 saw the release of one of Dionne Warwick's finest Bacharach and David-penned singles, *The Green Grass Starts To Grow*, backed with *They Don't Give Medals (To Yesterday's Heroes)*, a song originally featured in the TV musical ON THE FLIP SIDE. That single climbed to No. 43 in January of the following year.

In 1970, Bacharach began his concert career. After spending his early years as a conductor and accompanist for other performers, the composer was now successful enough to stage his own shows. Concert appearances quickly became a staple of Bacharach's career and to this day he keeps up a steady schedule of live performances.

Bacharach has said that, as with his recording career, his solo concert career was not something he sought out for himself. It was something he was asked to do and, as natural as he seemed in the role, he had his doubts at first.

"I found it a hard transition moving to the centre of the stage," he said in an interview with the NME. "A lot of my musical life had been spent in the back or conducting for singers, and suddenly I was doing concerts by myself as the star, as the attraction. I had to talk to the audience but I could hardly get a word out because I was so nervous. It was tough... And still I couldn't really understand why people were paying me so much to go and play concerts in Paris or Las Vegas, just to see me conduct my music. I mean, I didn't tap dance, I sang with a very, very limited voice ... I was sure I'd better not sing too much otherwise people would see how bad I really sounded."

Bacharach began his concert career with dates at Harrah's in Lake Tahoe in early 1970. In May, he sold out five shows at the Westbury Music Fair in New York.

The Westbury shows were an especially rewarding experience for Burt, who grew up not far from the venue. After a 30-minute opening set from the Carpenters, the MC announced "Ladies and gentlemen, Mister Burt Bacharach!" The composer strolled down the aisle – pausing to shake a few hands – and wowed the hometown crowd with an evening of hits, including *The Look Of Love, Anyone Who Had A Heart, This Guy's In Love With You* and *Do You Know The Way To San Jose*. Onstage, Bacharach gave his all – as usual – supported by twenty-eight musicians and four singers.

"If the music reflects the man," wrote BILLBOARD reviewer Robert Sobel of the Westbury shows, "Burt Bacharach is a romantic visionary who views the world through love-coloured glasses tinged with whimsy and wonderment... He sang and played piano with refreshing truthfulness, conducted the spirited 28-piece orchestra with fiery tenderness, and directed the four girl singers with professionalism born from instinct.

Two months later, Bacharach broke box office records at the Greek Theater in Los Angeles, grossing $176,636 for a week's worth of performances.

"The money is fantastic," Burt told the NEW YORK TIMES. "But it's not the primary thing. The real charge is being out there on the stage with all those people around you."

Burt Bacharach & Hal David

As with the PROMISES, PROMISES stage show, Bacharach was eager to have his own concerts sound as good as possible. To that end, he recruited Phil Ramone to join him on the road.

"I used to go out on the road and get those sounds," recalls Ramone. "We'd keep redesigning the sound system, so that you could hear the orchestra right in person."

"When we went on the road, a couple of times Burt would say, 'Why don't you go rehearse the string section?'" says Ramone. "I'd be telling them how to bow, what to do. 'Who is this nut case up here?' 'I think he's the engineer.'"

Bacharach's profile was also raised by a series of successful TV variety specials, including THE BURT BACHARACH SPECIAL, ANOTHER EVENING WITH BURT BACHARACH and BURT BACHARACH IN SHANGRI-LA. At the 1971 Emmy Awards, two Bacharach specials were nominated for the Best Variety Special award, with THE BURT BACHARACH SPECIAL winning out.

Meanwhile, Hal David had been doing some moonlighting of his own, penning two songs with composer John Barry for the 1969 James Bond film ON HER MAJESTY'S SECRET SERVICE. Hal penned the lyrics for two songs used in the film, *Do You Know How Christmas Trees Are Grown?* and *We Have All The Time In The World*. The former was recorded by Jackie DeShannon, and the latter number, delivered beautifully by Louis Armstrong, ranks as one of Hal's very best non-Bacharach songs.

During this period, Hal collaborated with Barry on another classic song, *The Good Times Are Comin'*, which became a modest hit for Mama Cass Elliott in 1970. That same year Hal wrote the movie theme *The Man Who Had Power Over Women* with Johnny Mandel.

Chapter 13: Long Ago Tomorrow

Through 1970 and 1971, Burt Bacharach kept up a hectic pace of live dates, TV specials, studio work and songwriting. Unfortunately the latter pursuit was getting less and less of Burt's time and his output of new material was slim compared to the bumper crops of previous years.

"When he was busy recording Burt Bacharach, he wasn't available to be recording Dionne Warwick," Hal David points out. "Nor was he available to be writing songs."

With the success of his concerts and TV specials, 1970 was Bacharach's biggest year as a recording artist. He released a superb self-titled LP and two 45s, *All Kinds Of People* b/w *She's Gone Away* and *Freefall* b/w *One Less Bell To Answer*.

The excellent BURT BACHARACH LP, featuring one of the composer's increasingly assured vocals on the charming *Hasbrook Heights*, is generally regarded as his best work as a recording artist.

Although the Carpenters' *Close To You* and the 5th Dimension's *One Less Bell To Answer* were massive hits in 1970, both were revivals of songs written several years earlier.

Compared to the years that preceded it, 1971 saw little in the way of new Bacharach/David material. And what new songs Burt and Hal did produce – although generally excellent – didn't storm the charts as easily as their previous efforts.

BURT BACHARACH'S SELF-TITLED 1970 LP

As the '60s gave way to the '70s, the music scene was changing rapidly. The Brill Building scene was on its last legs as the singer-songwriter era began in earnest. More and more artists were writing their own material, and those acts who still used outside writers tended to favour simple, sugary pop songs. At the same time, Bacharach and David's new material was ever more sophisticated and challenging. They were, clearly, still writing to please themselves, rather than trying to keep up with the latest chart trends. Hence, great new songs like *Long Ago Tomorrow* and *Paper Maché* got short shrift on the charts.

Bacharach and David's newer material was possibly too challenging for pop charts dominated by such lightweight pop fare as *Sugar Sugar* and *Knock Three Times*. Dionne Warwick's excellent *Who Gets The Guy* single failed to climb higher than No. 57 on the charts, while the B.J. Thomas-sung movie theme *Long Ago Tomorrow* peaked at No. 61.

"*Long Ago Tomorrow* was a song out of a movie by the same name that starred Malcolm McDowell," Thomas explains. "It was a story about a guy who had injured himself playing soccer and became a paraplegic. And then it dealt with their love story. A lot of the things that Bacharach and David did were ahead of their time. And I think that movie was kind of ahead of its time. People weren't ready to deal with that in a movie theatre situation. So it really wasn't a big record. But, you know, that song was a huge record for me in South America. When I go down there I have to perform it – sometimes two or three times during a show – the people just go nuts."

Long Ago Tomorrow was the last Bacharach/David number Thomas recorded. The songwriters were busy writing the songs for the movie musical LOST HORIZON, and Thomas left Scepter in October 1972 for a new deal with Paramount.

In the summer of 1971, Bacharach decided it was time to slow down a little.

"I'd never had a more frenetic year," he told the NEW YORK TIMES. "Concert appearances in cities clear across the country, TV shows, all-night recording sessions, travelling all the way to Japan. I just thought, 'Wait a minute! You're doing too much. You're not writing enough.' Principally, I believe I'm supposed to write more than I perform."

VERY DIONNE LP

Burt's lack of writing output was evident in Dionne Warwick's 1970 LP VERY DIONNE. Of the album's 10 songs, a mere three – The Green Grass Starts To Grow, Check Out Time and Walk The Way You Talk – were new Bacharach and David compositions, while the two other Bacharach/David contributions were from their back catalogue. The two oldies were Make It Easy On Yourself (a live recording, which scored on the singles charts) and a superb revival of They Don't Give Medals To Yesterday's Heroes, from ON THE FLIP SIDE. Most of Dionne's '60s albums had included at least five new songs by Burt and Hal but, as the '70s began, the songwriters had less time, wrote fewer songs and had less to offer Dionne.

Complicating Bacharach and David's situation with Warwick was the fact that the duo's Blue Jac Production Company was involved in a dispute with Scepter Records, which hit the press in March 1971. The dispute, reportedly over accounting of record sales as far back as 1963, resulted in a settlement whereby Scepter paid Blue Jac $339,000. With Warwick's contract with Scepter up for renewal, the timing of the dispute almost inevitably meant the end of Bacharach/David/Warwick's tenure at the label. In May it was announced that Warwick was leaving Scepter and, in conjunction with Blue Jac, was shopping around for a new label. Before the year was out a deal was struck with Warner Bros Records, reportedly the biggest deal ever signed with a female artist at that point.

"The important Miss Dionne Warwicke (with friends Bacharach and David) now has her first album on Warner Bros. Records, where she belongs," said a 1972 ad for the DIONNE LP. The DIONNE album was generally very strong, including such underrated classics as The Balance Of Nature and Hasbrook Heights. However, like the VERY DIONNE record before it, the new LP featured just a few new

Bacharach/David songs, making up the numbers with Dionne's take on *One Less Bell To Answer* and a new recording of *Close To You*.

The spelling in the Warners ad was not a typo. At the suggestion of noted psychic Linda Goodman, Dionne had added an 'e' to her surname "for vibratory reasons." Although Warwick was strongly influenced by astrology and numerology at this time, she eventually decided that adding the 'e' to Warwick had brought her anything but good luck. (In this book, I have stuck with the e-less spelling.)

Chapter 14: Lost Investments

"At last – A picture for everyone!" proclaimed the ad campaign.

How wrong they were.

Bacharach and David spent much of 1972 working on their most demanding project yet. After the success of their work on BUTCH CASSIDY AND THE SUNDANCE KID and PROMISES, PROMISES, and given Bacharach's lack of interest in doing another Broadway show, the natural next step was for Burt and Hal to write a movie musical.

The project they chose was a musical remake of the classic 1937 Frank Capra film LOST HORIZON, about a group of plane crash survivors who discover the mythical city of Shangri-La in the Himalayas and are torn between returning to the material world and embracing the spiritual paradise.

It was not the first time LOST HORIZON had been adapted as a musical. In 1956, an attempt entitled SHANGRI-LA had flopped on Broadway and was revived four years later on television, to no greater success. Although SHANGRI-LA was quickly forgotten, Burt and Hal's trip to the Himalayas was a flop of huge proportions and left an indelible mark on a partnership that had previously seen little failure.

LOST HORIZON was produced by Ross Hunter, who had scored at the box office with PILLOW TALK and THAT TOUCH OF MINK, as well as the musical FLOWER DRUM SONG. In 1971-72, Hunter was riding high on the success of his 1970 blockbuster AIRPORT. LOST HORIZON was Hunter's first film for Columbia Pictures and was a major priority for the studio. No cost was spared in putting together a sure-fire smash.

To direct the film, Hunter signed Carol Reed (the uncle of actor Oliver Reed), who had recently helmed the hit musical film OLIVER! Reed withdrew before filming started and was replaced by PATTON director Franklin Schaffner, who also quit. Undaunted, Hunter hired Canadian director Charles Jarrott, who had previously achieved acclaim as director of MARY, QUEEN OF SCOTS and ANNE OF A

Burt Bacharach & Hal David

THOUSAND DAYS. The film's dance numbers were staged by the talented Hermes Pan, the choreographer of such movie musical classics as FLOWER DRUM SONG, CAN-CAN and MY FAIR LADY. Hunter assembled a seemingly bullet-proof cast that included Michael York, John Gielgud, Sally Kellerman Peter Finch, Olivia Hussey and Bobby Van.

With Jarrott, Pan, Bacharach and David on board, an all-star cast and a story that had already proven successful at the box office, LOST HORIZON had all the elements for a hit picture.

The eventual failure of LOST HORIZON was compounded by the enormity of the promotion for the movie and its soundtrack. The film was Columbia's number one project for 1973, and Bell Records initiated its biggest promotional push ever for the accompanying soundtrack album.

Gordon Bossin, Bell's marketing VP told BILLBOARD, "Because of the scope of this project, the songwriters, the story, cast and producer... it required a major push of great proportion." Bell even ran a contest for its sales staff, to encourage retailers to create impressive window displays for the record, the winner getting "a trip to the 'Shangri-La of his choice, or a comparable cash compensation," according to a story in BILLBOARD.

LOST HORIZON SOUNDTRACK LP

Bell released the LOST HORIZON soundtrack LP in February 1973, packaged in a lavish fold out sleeve. The previous month, Bell had released as a single the picture's theme song, *Lost Horizon*, beautifully sung by folk singer Shawn Phillips. ("Burt was very high on him," recalls Hal.) The lyrics echoed the anti-war sentiments of *The Windows Of The World*. A truly beautiful song, gentle yet musically complex, *Lost Horizon* climbed to the No. 63 position in February 1973.

So strong was the push behind the project that cover versions of LOST HORIZON songs began appearing several months before the film's March 1973 release. Tony Bennett was among the first, releasing a 45 of *Living Together, Growing Together* in December 1972. Bennett's record failed to crack the Top 100 and his slightly awkward-sounding rendition of the tune was a sign of things to come for the whole venture.

Initially, Bacharach seemed enthusiastic about the project.

Robin Platts

"The idea of the picture is very close to me," he told the NEW YORK TIMES. "Imagine! Somewhere in Tibet in the middle of those mountains, there is a place called Shangri-La. Where you can live forever – almost. And you can stay healthy! And there is love! And peace! It's exactly what everybody wants today."

"The picture deals with the hope for things wonderful and people getting along and finding a peaceful solution and a happy solution to life," says Hal David. "And that kind of philosophy has been very dear to me and very close to me all my life. So it was something I just loved doing."

LIVING TOGETHER, GROWING TOGETHER 45

David's passion for the project comes through in his typically thoughtful, optimistic lyrics. But his lyrics, and Bacharach's equally strong music, were not enough to make the venture successful. The story was appealing, the cast was strong, and the songs and score were solid. But the various elements just didn't gel. The musical numbers didn't fit comfortably with the rest of the film, often slotted awkwardly into the narrative. The musical sequences were further marred by dull choreography and vocalists who lacked Dionne Warwick's ability to navigate Bacharach and David's songs.

Hal David sums it up: "LOST HORIZON was a film that just didn't work. And the score suffered because of it, in my opinion."

Although several actors – Sally Kellerman, James Sigheta and Bobby Van – sang the songs themselves, the other LOST HORIZON leads had their vocals dubbed by singers: Andrea Willis provided the vocals for Olivia Hussey, Diana Lee for Liv Ullmann, and Jerry Hutman for Peter Finch. In spite of this, most of the vocals sold short songs that might have worked in other circumstances.

LOST HORIZON LP

85

LOST HORIZON does have its moments and certainly did not deserve the disastrous reception it was met with. Bobby Van's old-school song and dance showmanship in *Question Me An Answer* and *The World Is A Circle* is fun, and the theme song plays well against the snow-covered mountain peaks in the opening titles. Bacharach's score was very strong and *If I Could Go Back* and *Share the Joy* are as haunting as any melodies he has ever written. Most of the songs are quite strong when taken out of the context of the movie and it's likely that, if a singer with Warwick's ability had recorded them on their own, it would have made for a pretty strong album.

"As I look back on the work," says David. "I think we did some beautiful things for it. There are things in that score that are very dear to me. *Where Knowledge Ends, Faith Begins* is a song I always loved. *The World Is A Circle* is becoming a little bit of a standard. Many people now seem to think the score's rather good. But if the picture doesn't work, nothing works."

"There are some good songs that came out of LOST HORIZON," agrees Bacharach. "*If I Could Go Back* is a pretty terrific song. *Living Together* is okay. *The World Is A Circle* – that's a good one. On their own, these songs were very good, but when you saw the movie..."

"If you have a dog picture," says Bacharach. "The songs are not gonna fly."

While the Shawn Phillips *Lost Horizon* single was not a major hit, another song from the LOST HORIZON soundtrack did find its way into the Top 40. The record in question was not an original soundtrack recording, but the 5th Dimension's reworking of *Living Together, Growing Together*, which peaked at No. 32 in February 1973. Like the Carpenters' *Close To You*, the 5th Dimension's *Living Together* sounded more "Bacharach-esque" than the version Burt arranged for the soundtrack.

Guy Chandler covered the title song and an Ed Ames released an LP, SONGS FROM LOST HORIZON AND OTHER MOVIE THEMES, which included an entire side of numbers from the movie. A&M artists the Sandpipers recorded a version of one of the picture's catchier tunes, *The World Is a Circle*. In 1974, Herb Alpert covered *I Might Frighten Her Away* on the album YOU SMILE - THE SONG BEGINS, his version sporting a string arrangement by Bacharach.

A kitschy curio from the LOST HORIZON era is a Disneyland Records LP called THE WORLD IS A CIRCLE, which features a Disney chorus singing *Living Together, Growing Together*, *Question Me An Answer* and *The World Is A Circle*, plus several non-Bacharach/David numbers.

LOST HORIZON is a favourite of many Bacharach/David fans, but the movie's reception by the general public was unfavourable.

If the public was unenthusiastic, the critics were merciless. NEWSWEEK said "the songs are so pitifully pedestrian it's doubtful that they'd sound good even if the actors could sing, which they can't." NEWSWEEK was especially unkind about the *Living

DISNEY'S THE WORLD IS A CIRCLE LP

Together, Growing Together sequence, saying that it "may be indeed the silliest piece of choreography ever put on film."

"The narrative has no energy," said the NEW YORKER, "and the pauses for the pedagogic songs are so awkward you may feel that the director's wheelchair needs oiling."

The NEW YORKER's review suggested that the fundamental problem was the source material: "There's probably no way to rethink this material without throwing it all away."

In an apparent attempt to make the film more palatable, Columbia trimmed several minutes of footage from LOST HORIZON shortly after its release. *I Come To You, If I Could Go Back* and *Where Knowledge Ends* were all cut from the picture, as well as some other brief segments, including a fertility dance.

The cuts didn't help. LOST HORIZON was universally derided and now remains a kitschy cult classic, not even available on video or DVD.

The film – nicknamed "Lost Investments" by movie business insiders – did untold financial damage to Columbia. It was, significantly, the last motion picture Ross Hunter ever made.

Chapter 15: Knowing When To Leave

The 5th Dimension's *Living Together, Growing Together* was the last new Bacharach/David composition to reach the charts while Burt and Hal were still working together. The enormous pressure of working on the LOST HORIZON soundtrack, compounded by the film's lack of success, drove a wedge between the songwriters.

Bacharach later recalled that, after the movie's disastrous reception, "I just went down to the beach at Del Mar and sort of hid. It was such a giant bust. I didn't want to be seen walking around the community."

Asked if he feels that the failure of *Lost Horizon* was a significant reason for his split with David, Bacharach says it was the "overwhelming reason. I just kind of resented

BURT BACHARACH – LIVING TOGETHER LP

that the picture did so badly. I resented that I had to keep working on the movie, while Hal basically was done. I had to keep working with singers and the voices that we would use for Liv Ullman and Peter Finch. I just broke my ass on that, with the score. I felt like I put a year – maybe longer – than Hal did. And it didn't feel very equal to me. That's wrong. I mean, that's the role I assume, as composer. The musician takes it further. There are certain areas that Hal couldn't have done – he's not going to score a scene."

Although he has admitted that the whole project was ultimately "very disheartening," David doesn't see LOST HORIZON as the main cause of his split with Bacharach.

"I certainly didn't feel that way," says Hal. "Burt may have. I was dreadfully disappointed in the movie. That was the culmination, but it wasn't that. It was that we were suddenly not writing songs, except for that, which was a very big undertaking. And Burt's part of it was really very burdensome. And we were not recording Dionne. We were not writing songs for Dionne. And she was very unhappy. And when Burt went in to record, he was recording for himself (i.e. his own records), as opposed to recording with Dionne and me. That was where his interest was going, and where his career was going. And that led up to LOST HORIZON, where the tensions were kind of high."

"There were a lot of rumours as to what the reasons (for their split) were," says Warwick. "Some say it was because the producer of the film hated the music but loved the lyrics and Burt had to re-write all the music. But, whatever it was, it happened, and they split."

In spite of the stresses of working on LOST HORIZON, Bacharach and David did not make the decision to split until after the film had come out. In February 1973, the month before the release of LOST HORIZON, VARIETY reported that Bacharach and David were "clearing the decks" for another Broadway show with David Merrick. This report appears to have been erroneous. David says that, at that point, he had no plans to work on another show with Bacharach and Merrick. (The report may have been in reference to the 1974 musical BRAINCHILD, which Hal wrote the lyrics for).

The end of the Bacharach/David partnership was, inevitably, problematic for Dionne Warwick, who had come to depend on the duo for most of her material and almost all of her hits. The last Bacharach/David/Warwick collaboration was the 1972 album DIONNE, the first record of Dionne's new deal with Warner Bros Records. The album had plenty of strong moments, but Bacharach was disappointed with it.

Robin Platts

DIONNE WARWICK'S 1972 ALBUM

"I don't think we delivered," Bacharach says of the DIONNE LP. "I really don't think we delivered well on that. I don't think I ever felt right about that album. It was the first with Joe Smith and Mo Ostin at Warners. They were my friends. And I felt that we didn't give them an album like we'd been delivering at Scepter."

The DIONNE LP's cover seemed designed to reinforce the notion that the hit-making team of Bacharach, David and Warwick was still going strong. The back cover photo shows the trio smiling in a unified pose, but a closer look reveals that – in contrast with Dionne and Hal's chummy grins – Burt looks somewhat uneasy. A close inspection of the album's credits reveals that, although six of the 10 tracks are Bacharach/David tunes, only four were conducted and arranged by Burt. Two of the album's Bacharach-David numbers – Close To You and One Less Bell To Answer – were older songs, revived in the wake of their success for the Carpenters and the 5th Dimension. Like the VERY DIONNE album before it, Warwick's Warner Bros debut was less of a Bacharach/David/Warwick effort than it appeared.

This fact was not lost on Warwick. And when plans to collaborate with Burt and Hal on her second Warner Bros album fell through because the songwriters had stopped working together, her situation became intolerable.

Although she sensed that all was not well with Bacharach and David, even Warwick wasn't aware of their split until after it happened.

"Anyone who knew them as well as I did knew that there had to be something wrong," Warwick says. "And there were a lot of rumours flying around within the industry itself about the fact that they were thinking about splitting. I kind of took that with a grain of salt, because I felt that if that were really going to happen, I certainly would be one of the first people to know it. Unfortunately, that's not the way it happened. I read about it, like everybody else, in the papers."

Even Warwick was never clear on the exact reasons for the split.

"All I know is that they split and left me kind of in the lurch," she says.

Warwick was synonymous with Bacharach and David. When they failed to contribute any material to her 1973 sophomore effort for Warner Bros, JUST BEING MYSELF, and the album flopped, she blamed them.

Burt Bacharach & Hal David

Despite the record's commercial failure, the Holland-Dozier-Holland-produced JUST BEING MYSELF was critically well received. ROLLING STONE gave the album a generally positive review and observed that Warwick had been given "the first chance in a long while to feel her R&B roots again."

Such praise offered little consolation for the singer.

In August 1975, Warwick filed suit against Bacharach and David. VARIETY reported that "Warwicke, who claims she had an agreement with defendants for them to produce and deliver an album to Warners, which she said they did not do, asks $5,000,000 exemplary damages for breach of fiduciary duties, and $1,000,000 for alleged breach of contract."

"We were obligated to Warner Brothers and to Dionne to do X number of records a year," says David. "And we were not fulfilling that, so she sued us."

In fact, Warwick had felt pressure from Warner Bros, and feared that the label might take legal action against her if she couldn't resolve her situation with Bacharach and David.

"It had nothing to do with me," says Warwick. "(Warner Bros) understood that it was Bacharach and David who were having their problems. In fact, they flew me up to Tahoe to talk to Burt, to see if he would go into the studio. I basically was given an ultimatum: either we go into the studio and complete our contract or they'd have to sue me. And I said, 'Excuse me?' And Mo (Ostin) made it clear that either Warner Bros would have to sue me for breach of contract or I would have to sue Bacharach and David for breach of contract."

"I was signed to Bacharach and David," says Warwick. "They were my producers. And they signed a contract with Warner Bros to produce me. And I finally came to a realization, and I said to Mo Ostin, 'Listen, there's no point in me asking them to go in the studio to write together when they don't even speak to each other. I mean, what do you expect to get out of them?' So, as a result of that, unfortunately I had to institute a suit and that was the end of that."

By the mid-'70s, the Bacharach, David and Warwick partnership was lost in the crossfire of legal actions from all concerned.

"When Hal David and I started to come apart, we weren't able to be there in the studio for Dionne," Bacharach said. "So she sued us and Hal sued me and I sued Hal. It was all very messy."

In a 1993 LOS ANGELES TIMES interview, Burt recalled that "I had a falling out with Dionne, then Hal got involved." In that interview, Bacharach expressed profound regret about the whole mess. "If I had to do it over again," he lamented. "I never, never would do it the same way."

Warwick's suit against Bacharach and David was settled out of court in 1979, for a reported $5.5 million, plus shared rights to their recordings.

Asked about the reason for her split with Bacharach and David, Warwick is unequivocal. "It was LOST HORIZON," she says. "That was the straw that kind of broke everybody's back. During the time when they were writing the songs for the film was apparently when they were having their differences."

Adding to the legal mayhem was an ongoing dispute over the recordings Burt and Hal had produced for Scepter Records.

In 1975, the songwriters filed for arbitration to get accounting of sales and payment information regarding the records they had made with Warwick and B.J. Thomas. The following year, the American Arbitration Association ordered Scepter to pay Burt and Hal $430,602 and to terminate their 1966 agreement with the songwriters. Bacharach and David were also awarded the rights to their Scepter recordings. Representing Burt and Hal in the arbitration action was lawyer Lee Eastman, father-in-law of another noted songwriter, Paul McCartney.

Scepter declared bankruptcy. With the label defunct, Warwick on Warner Bros. and Bacharach and David working with other writers, the hit-making days of the '60s seemed very far away. But, against the odds, Bacharach and David weren't quite through working together.

Chapter 16: I Took My Strength From You

After her first Warner Bros album, Dionne Warwick did a session with Burt Bacharach, presumably intended for the follow-up to DIONNE.

"I did three songs with Phil Ramone for Dionne," Bacharach recalls. "I don't know whatever happened to those songs."

Although specific details of that Warwick/Bacharach session are unknown, one of the tracks recorded was a new Bacharach and David composition entitled *I Took My Strength From You*.

Although Dionne's recording of *I Took My Strength From You* was consigned to the vaults, another vocalist soon recorded the song.

In 1975, Bacharach and David reunited long enough to write and produce an album by 15-year-old Stephanie Mills. Mills had made a name for herself starring as Dorothy in Broadway's THE WIZ and a recording career was a natural progression for her. After Jermaine Jackson recommended her to Berry Gordy, Mills inked a deal with Motown.

Burt Bacharach & Hal David

"Berry Gordy called me," Hal David recalls. "He was interested in me coming to work for Motown. I wasn't interested – not because of Motown, but I just wasn't interested in working for a record company, or working for anybody. And he said, 'Well, why don't you do an album for me? I've got this wonderful singer, Stephanie Mills. Who would you like to do it with?' I said, 'Well, let me call Burt and see how he feels about it.'"

Whatever tensions had come to the fore during the LOST HORIZON era didn't appear to hinder the project, which yielded Mills' first LP, FOR THE FIRST TIME.

"We had gotten past it," says David. "We had been together many years and had a very good relationship. And once we got past the discomfort of being on the outs, so to speak, once we got back together again, we were back together again. When we worked together, we were fine."

Phil Ramone, who engineered the album, remembers that David was more involved in the album than Bacharach.

"I did the album with Hal," he says. "I don't think Burt did too many songs on that album." Although Bacharach arranged just six of the 10 tracks on the LP, all but two of the songs on FOR THE FIRST TIME were new Bacharach/David compositions.

"There may have been an older song somewhere in the mix," David says, "but essentially they were all new songs."

STEPHANIE MILLS – FOR THE FIRST TIME LP

In addition to the eight new Bacharach/David songs, FOR THE FIRST TIME included two oldies – *Loneliness Remembers (What Happiness Forgets)* and a disco re-make of *This Empty Place*. The latter was issued as a single but, like the album, didn't meet with great enthusiasm. The record had some great moments, but is generally less distinguished than Burt and Hal's previous work together. They may have been trying to adapt their sound to the musical climate of the 70's, but Burt's music seemed less adventurous than before, closer to the style he would pursue in the late 70's and 80's. Perhaps the perceived failure of LOST HORIZON had lessened his confidence and his desire to take risks. Also, although she was a fine singer, Mills couldn't quite match Dionne Warwick's power in the vocal department.

"Stephanie was a very, very good singer," says David. "But I hope she won't be offended if I say Dionne Warwick is in a class by herself, in my opinion. But Stephanie was a terrific performer. She was very good to work with."

Warwick was not upset by the fact that, after failing to provide songs for her second Warner Bros LP, Bacharach and David had come up with almost an album's worth of new material for Mills.

"It was wonderful, as far as I was concerned," Warwick says. "I was doing what I was doing with other songwriters and getting a taste of what was happening musically outside of Bacharach/David. The unfortunate thing is that the album went nowhere for Stephanie."

After Bacharach and David's decade-long association with Warwick, it would have been tough for any other singer to fill her shoes, even someone as talented as Mills. "It is kind of hard for any other singer to decide they're going jump on in this pool," says Warwick, "because they don't know deep that water really is. And taking nothing away from Stephanie's talent - because she's a very, very talented young lady. It was just not her thing."

"As a matter of fact, Berry Gordy sent the album to me with a note," says Warwick. "He was very disappointed in the production. And he literally told me, in so many words, 'I hope you enjoy these – these had to be Bacharach/David rejects by you'."

Although FOR THE FIRST TIME flopped, Mills broke through when her *single Never Knew Love Like This Before* went Top 10 in 1980.

Bacharach feels that the Stephanie Mills album and Warwick's DIONNE LP were symptomatic of the fact that his partnership with Hal was on its last legs.

"I don't think either one of those two albums was our best - Dionne's first album on Warners or the Stephanie Mills album," says Bacharach. "We were running out of gas, you know? Maybe we just needed to regroup. And of course LOST HORIZON just killed us."

"Things happen with every group," reflects David. "Through it all, the fact that we, at a certain point, stopped writing together is just really a blip in our relationship. We really remained very good friends all the way through, as we are today. I think time erodes... You're together X number of years. Your mind goes one way and the other guy's mind goes the other way. I didn't think there was anything abnormal about it, in retrospect. Everybody changes and you just go where your life takes you."

Chapter 17: It Was Almost Like A Song

In February 1973, several years after Burt Bacharach began his concert career, Hal David stepped into the limelight with a show of his own. New York's Kaufman Concert Hall hosted two performances of "An Evening with Hal David," as part of the LYRICS & LYRICISTS series. The two-hour show saw Hal trace his career with the assistance of five singers - Cissy Houston, Bobbi Baird, Northern J. Calloway, Louis St. Louis and Bernie Nee.

HAL DAVID

Hal talked about how and why he wrote certain songs, then the singers performed them and helped illustrate certain aspects of the songs' creation. Along with a slew of Bacharach/David hits, there was a LOST HORIZON medley (*If I Could Go Back* and *Where Knowledge Ends*), a rejected number from PROMISES PROMISES (*Wouldn't That Be A Stroke Of Luck?*), *She Likes Basketball*, and a medley that included such early non-Bacharach hits as *The Four Winds And The Seven Seas*, *American Beauty Rose* and *My Heart Is An Open Book*. Hal closed the show with a spoken word performance of the song that encapsulates his message – *What The World Needs Now Is Love*.

Although he and Bacharach didn't collaborate in the immediate aftermath of LOST HORIZON, David co-wrote a pair of movie themes during 1973. With Frank DeVol, he wrote *A Man And A Train* for the movie EMPEROR OF THE NORTH POLE, and with Henry Mancini penned *Send A Little Love My Way* for the film OKLAHOMA CRUDE.

In the latter months of 1973, Hal collaborated with Michel LeGrand on songs for a new musical, BRAINCHILD. Unfortunately, the show was not a success. It never made it to Broadway, closing after a short run in Philadelphia in early 1974.

In 1974, David began a more fruitful songwriting collaboration, with English singer-songwriter Albert Hammond. Hammond had previously penned a number of hits, including the Hollies' smash *The Air That I Breathe*. He had also scored as a recording artist in the early '70s with several hits, the biggest being *It Never Rains In Southern California*.

In 1975, Hammond released the 99 MILES FROM L.A. album. Produced by Hammond and David (Phil Ramone was on board to engineer), the record included a number of the songs they had written together. Among the most memorable of their collaborations are the album's title track – covered by Art Garfunkel on his BREAKAWAY LP – and *To All The Girls I've Loved Before*, which achieved massive success a decade later as a duet between Willie Nelson and Julio Iglesias.

In the early '70s, Hal David had visited Nashville for the first time, to accept an ASCAP award for *Only Love Can Break A Heart*, which had enjoyed some success in the country market. Hal was impressed by the local scene and, in 1976, he made the city his part-time home.

In Nashville, David collaborated with a number of different writers, including Curley Putnam (best known for *The Green, Green Grass Of Home*), Rafe Vantley, Bobby Braddock, Buddy Killen and Archie Jordan. One of Hal's first Nashville successes was *It Was Almost Like A Song*, co-written with Jordan and a big hit for Ronnie Milsap in 1977.

The Nashville scene was a far cry from New York and the Brill Building, but it suited Hal perfectly.

"I feel comfortable here," he told BILLBOARD in 1976. "I had written many songs that came out in the country field – and I didn't even know I was writing country songs."

Examples of Hal's "unexpected" country songs had included *The Story Of My Life* and *My Heart Is An Open Book*. In 1984, David was inducted into the Nashville Songwriters Foundation's Hall of Fame.

Despite his talent for country songs, Hal continued to write in other genres. In 1979, he re-teamed with John Barry, co-writing the theme to the latest James Bond film, MOONRAKER. Shirley Bassey sang the number over the picture's opening credits.

Hal's biggest success of 1979 was the No. 1 Adult Contemporary hit *I Never Said I Love You*, recorded by Orsa Lia. The track came from Lia's self-titled album, which David wrote and produced with Archie Jordan. The record's best moments, including *I Never Said I Love You* and *No Walls, No Ceilings, No Floors*, were among Hal's best work and the latter would not have sounded out of place on a Dionne Warwick album circa 1970.

In 1980, David was elected President of the American Society of Composers, Authors and Publishers (ASCAP). He held the position until 1986. Hal had become a member of ASCAP's Board of Directors in 1974, and was made Vice President in 1979. When he was voted in as President in 1980, Hal was ASCAP's first new president in 20 years, Stanley Adams having held the post since 1959.

David's ASCAP duties occupied much of his time in the '80s, and his songwriting output lessened. The two worlds collided on one memorable occasion in the early '80s. Producer Richard Perry had decided to revive the David/Hammond number *To All the Girls I've Loved Before* for a session with Willie Nelson and Julio Iglesias. However, the backing track Perry had produced ran longer than Hammond's original. Not keen to simply have the singers repeat part of the lyric, Perry phoned David to ask for additional lyrics. David, who was just about to enter an ASCAP board meeting agreed, and discreetly penned an extra verse while helming the meeting.

In 1985, Hal and Joe Raposo wrote *America Is* the official song for the 1986 centenary of the Statue of Liberty. B.J. Thomas debuted the song on the MERV GRIFFIN SHOW in 1985.

Chapter 18: The Best That You Can Do

In April 1973, Burt Bacharach returned to the concert stage with a show at Harrah's in Tahoe. As well as his hits, the concert featured several LOST HORIZON numbers, with a chorus of 10 children singing on *The World Is A Circle* and *Question Me An Answer*, and singer Gene Merlino providing the vocals for *If I Could Go Back*. But with a few months, the colossal failure of LOST HORIZON caused the composer to temporarily retreat from the music scene.

"I took a year off," Burt says. "I was feeling defeated by the LOST HORIZON situation."

Bacharach's withdrawal from the music scene was short-lived. By the end of 1973, he was composing again.

"I tried to write a couple of songs with Bobby Russell," he says. With Russell — best known for penning *Little Green Apples* and *The Night The Lights Went Out In Georgia* — Bacharach wrote several songs, including *Charlie* (later recorded by Bobby Vinton) and *Us* (recorded by Tom Jones). Bacharach and Russell reportedly penned several other songs at the time, including *Everything I Need*, *Peaches Don't Grow On A Cherry Tree*, *Place With No Name* and *Plastic City*.

Bacharach's collaboration with Russell, his first major work with another lyricist since the early '60s, was a clear indicator that Bacharach and David were no longer a team. In March 1974, BILLBOARD reported that Bacharach was "back to full-time songwriting after a three-year period during which he was mainly occupied with TV specials, concerts and the score of a disappointing musical film, LOST HORIZON."

During this period Burt also wrote some songs with Neil Simon. The reason for their collaboration was another clear sign that Bacharach and David were through working together: Simon and Bacharach were writing songs for a planned movie adaptation of PROMISES, PROMISES, to be made by 20th Century Fox. The project never reached fruition, but at least two songs were completed — *And Then She Walked In The Room* and *Seconds*, the latter subsequently recorded by Gladys Knight.

Although Burt was back to writing, he was less interested in producing his songs than he had been previously. He told BILLBOARD, "I am determined that from now on I won't get into the trap of wanting to protect my song, so I write an arrangement and then get talked into producing the artist's album and get stuck six months in the studio. I don't want to get sidetracked away from my writing and my family."

Despite the failure of LOST HORIZON the previous year, Bacharach's next LP featured a number of songs from the picture and even took its name, LIVING TOGETHER, from one of them. Although the album was strong and generally on par with Bacharach's self-titled 1970 LP, LIVING TOGETHER faired poorly, peaking at No. 181 in the charts. The follow-up, BURT BACHARACH'S GREATEST HITS, also released in 1974, didn't do much better, peaking at No. 173 that December.

Robin Platts

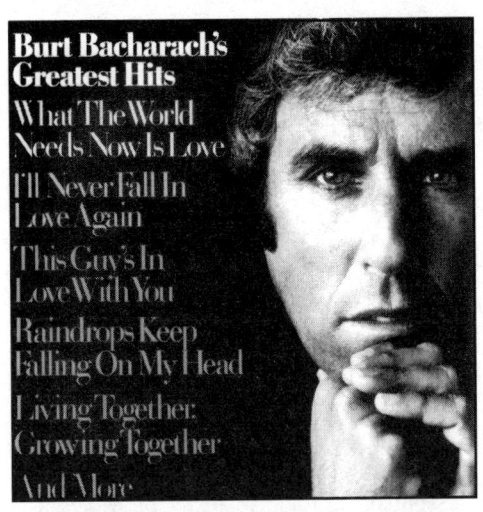

BURT BACHARACH – GREATEST HITS CD

BURT BACHARACH – FUTURES LP

Clearly, interest in Bacharach/David songs had fallen into a temporary slump in the wake of LOST HORIZON.

For the rest of the '70s, Bacharach worked with a number of different songwriting partners, but didn't find any chart success. In 1976, he wrote with Norman Gimbel (*Time And Tenderness* and *Where Are You*) and James Kavanaugh (*The Young Grow Younger* and *Night*). The results of those collaborations appearing on his next LP, FUTURES, along with two recent Bacharach/David songs (*I Took My Strength From You* and *No One Remembers My Name*) and *Seconds* from the aborted PROMISES, PROMISES movie.

Although not a commercial success, FUTURES proved that the Bacharach's muse had by no means deserted him. And, in the face of ambivalence from radio stations, the composer was as ambitious as ever. Bacharach's next album, WOMAN, was recorded live with the Houston Symphony at the Jones Hall. The entire record was completed in one two-and-a-half hour session.

"It was a great challenge," Bacharach told BILLBOARD, "and the result is hard to peg. It isn't classical, although it leans that way. It covers a wide range of feelings... It represents a free, different type of music people don't associate with me."

WOMAN was the first Burt Bacharach album that didn't feature any of Hal David's lyrics. The album included collaborations with Libby Titus (*Amnesia*, *Chicago Farewell* and *Single Girl*), Anthony Newley (*Dancing Fool*), Sally Stevens (*There Is Time*) and Carly Simon (*I Live In The Woods*).

In 1979, Bacharach collaborated with Paul Anka on the soundtrack for the film TOGETHER, featuring vocals by Jackie DeShannon. The project yielded a minor hit single, *I Don't Need You Anymore*.

97

Another Bacharach project reportedly in the works at that time was a Broadway musical based on the life of Charlie Chaplin. That show, to have been written in collaboration with Anthony Newley, never came about, although one Bacharach/Newley number, *The Dancing Fool*, appeared on the WOMAN LP.

The late '70s were a low point in Bacharach's career. He hadn't written a hit since parting ways with Hal David. The composer attributed the comparative commercial failure of his recent efforts to an image problem.

"The world tends to link me to the Henry Mancini school of music," he told BILLBOARD. "As a result, I get pigeonholed by radio stations and my records don't usually stand much of a chance for airplay."

As the decade drew to a close, Bacharach felt washed up, that his career as a composer was through. Although he could still pack in audiences for his shows (many of which were in Las Vegas), they were essentially coming to hear the oldies. The music scene had undergone huge changes and Bacharach's last hits were almost a decade behind him. As if that weren't enough, his marriage to Angie Dickinson was over. In 1979, however, Bacharach met a woman who would turn his career and his love life around.

By 1979, Carole Bayer Sager had already proven her worth as a songwriter and a singer. In addition to her own 1977 hit *You're Moving Out Today*, co-written with Bette Midler, she had penned many successful songs for other artists, including the Mindbenders' *A Groovy Kind Of Love*, Melissa Manchester's *Midnight Blue* and the James Bond theme *Nobody Does It Better*.

Burt and Carole met on an episode of THE MIKE DOUGLAS SHOW. They hit it off and soon began dating and writing songs together. Bacharach and Sager were married in 1982. As well as finding a new wife, Bacharach had found the songwriting partner who would put him back in the charts.

Sager's single *Stronger Than Before* was their first hit, reaching No. 30 in 1981. The track came from Sager's SOMETIMES LATE AT NIGHT LP, a concept album of sorts about Bacharach and Sager's love affair.

"I hope that there are four or five albums that will continue telling the story of the Bacharach/Sager love affair," said Neil Bogart, president of Sager's label Boardwalk Records president.

After the success of SOMETIMES LATE AT NIGHT, Bacharach and Sager began pitching their songs to other artists, yielding a string of hits that spanned the next five years: *Arthur's Theme* (performed by Christopher Cross in the hit Dudley Moore comedy ARTHUR), *Making Love* (Roberta Flack), *On My Own* (Patti Labelle and Michael McDonald) and *Love Always* (El DeBarge).

Robin Platts

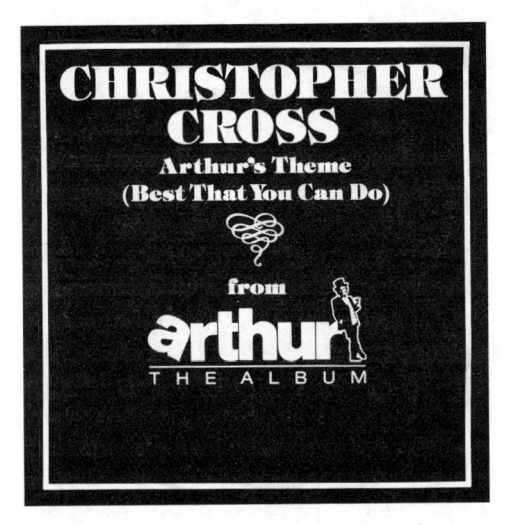

CHRISTOPHER CROSS – ARTHUR'S THEME SINGLE

One of Bacharach and Sager's biggest records was *Heartlight*, inspired by the movie *E.T.*, and written with and performed by one of the last big-name writers to come out of the Brill Building scene, Neil Diamond. Although he had started out in the mid-'60s penning hits for such artists as the Monkees and Jay and the Americans, Diamond quickly established himself as a performer and hit his stride as one of the biggest acts of the 1970's. Although he was quite a bit younger than Bacharach, the collaboration was a good match, and Neil penned several other numbers with Burt and Carole.

In the wake of their success with ARTHUR, Bacharach and Sager wrote songs for several other movies: TOUGH GUYS (*They Don't Make Them Like They Used To*, recorded by Kenny Rogers), BABY BOOM (*Everchanging Time*), NIGHT SHIFT and ARTHUR 2: ON THE ROCKS.

In September 1984, it was announced that Burt Bacharach and Dionne Warwick would be working together for the first time in twelve years.

Apart from a number one hit single (*Then Came You*, featuring the Spinners), the '70s had not been easy for Warwick. The singer's legal action against Bacharach and David, because of their failure to participate in her second Warner Bros album, was not without foundation. After her split with Burt and Hal, Dionne truly found that, in the eyes of the music business, Dionne Warwick was synonymous with Bacharach and David.

In a 1979 VARIETY interview, Warwick recalled that Warner Bros executives "were looking for something that wasn't there anymore, the Bacharach-David sound. Everyone wanted to write like Bacharach and David, instead of writing their own thing for the person who made that sound happen, Dionne Warwick."

By 1979, however, Warwick had a new deal, with Arista Records, and a label president, Clive Davis, who wasn't out to recreate Warwick's '60s sound. Instead, Davis cannily teamed her with a man who had the Midas touch in the '70s, singer-songwriter Barry Manilow. With Manilow producing, Warwick had immediate success on Arista with the hit single *I'll Never Love This Way Again*, and the album DIONNE which, oddly, had the same title as her Warner debut of seven years previous.

Although Bacharach and Warwick had both found their way back into the hit parade, many people felt that the composer and the singer should be making new hits together. Among them was Aaron Spelling, producer of the TV show FINDER OF LOST LOVES. After recruiting Bacharach and Sager to write the program's theme song, Spelling insisted that Bacharach call his estranged vocalist.

"Aaron Spelling felt nobody could sing the song but me. So (Burt) had to pick up the phone," says Warwick with a chuckle.

Inevitably, that first call was a little awkward.

"I hadn't spoken to him in almost a dozen years," says Warwick. "We were in two different worlds at that time. And he called and said he had a song he wanted to come over and play for me. And I told him to come on over."

"It was an amazing sort of a reunion," Warwick says, "based on the fact that I've always said that friendships prevail, regardless of what goes up or down – that's what makes a true friendship. And, after all that time had gone by, it was as if no time had passed at all."

Although Warwick made some great records with Bacharach and Sager in the '80s, a little bit of the magic was gone from the glory days of Bacharach, David and Warwick.

"Burt was still basically the producer," says Warwick. "But it was a different kind of feeling, you know. Bacharach and David – they were my friends, you know? And we relied upon each other in the studio very, very much. If I felt that I needed to change a note, I would, and it was okay. And if I needed to change a lyric to fit a note, I would. I did not really work with Carole that much. In fact, it was basically with Burt that I worked."

If Bacharach and Warwick's records from the '80s lack some other magic of their '60s work, it was partially due to the era's recording methods. Gone were the days of the singer and musicians performing together in the studio. Instead, Bacharach – like every other producer of the era – would record the backing tracks separately, then bring in Warwick to sing over them. Synthesizers took the place of the strings that were used in the '60s and records tended to lack the human touch that had produced so many classic sides in the '60s.

"All of a sudden, the music was done and you were standing at a microphone singing with earphones," says Warwick. "I truly miss live recording. There was something very special about recording with people in the studio, playing music with real instruments – not synthesizers and almost-strings, you know. It was quite different."

Although *Finder Of Lost Loves* didn't score on the charts, it paved the way for further Bacharach/Warwick sessions, one of which yielded a No. 1 hit in 1985.

Rod Stewart had previously recorded a Bacharach/Sager tune called *That's What Friends Are For* on the NIGHT SHIFT soundtrack, but the song didn't attract much attention. However, Warwick noticed the song while watching the film on TV and decided to record it herself.

The session was an all-star affair. Since the song was about friendship, Warwick called up some friends to sing with her. Elton John, Gladys Knight and Stevie Wonder joined Dionne on *That's What Friends Are For* and the result was, amazingly, the first ever Bacharach/Warwick chart topper. The record's success was for a very worthy cause. *That's What Friends Are For* was released as a benefit for the American Foundation for AIDS Research.

Less was heard from Bacharach and Sager towards the end of the '80s. Warwick charted with their song *Love Power* and the couple expressed a desire to do more production work. Burt told BILLBOARD that he wanted to make another solo album, but felt that his voice wasn't suited to the music scene of the time.

In 1991, another chapter of Burt Bacharach's life drew to a close. He and Carole Bayer Sager split, their songwriting partnership ending along with their marriage. Although another successful collaboration had come to an end, a new generation was discovering the songs Burt had written with Hal David.

Chapter 19: What the World Needs Now

"If I could write a song half as good as *This Guy's In Love With You* or *Anyone Who Had A Heart*," said Noel Gallagher. "I'd die a happy man."

Gallagher is the guitarist/songwriter of Oasis, one of the biggest British rock groups of the last decade and part of the so-called Britpop scene of the mid-'90s. He's also a huge Bacharach and David fan.

In June 1996, Gallagher joined Bacharach onstage at London's Royal Festival Hall. His unannounced appearance in Bacharach's show naturally attracted a great deal of media attention in Britain, where Oasis was the latest group canonized by the British music press in its ongoing quest for the New Beatles, New Stones, etc.

If the Britpop generation needed a validation of the Bacharach sound, then the sight of Noel Gallagher onstage with the maestro singing *This Guy's In Love With You* was it.

In a 1996 interview with VANITY FAIR, Bacharach seemed surprised by the revival of interest in his work, saying it was "kind of strange. At the Royal Festival Hall, I walked out and immediately got a standing ovation. Part of me is thinking, You're not dead. You don't have some incurable disease— or do you? Does the audience know something about me that I don't know?"

Gallagher was not the only recent artist with an affinity for the Bacharach and David songbook.

"People like Bacharach and Neil (Diamond) will probably be surprised to know how many people are now inspired by them," said Blackie Onassis of Urge Overkill in a 1995 interview with the L.A. Times, "It affected us as kids, it influences us now." Many other young artists expressed an affinity for the Bacharach and David songbook and their influence was heard on many recordings made since the mid-'90s.

"I like people rediscovering my songs," Burt told the LOS ANGELES TIMES. "It gives (the songs) renewed life. They were written with the concept that they were suitable for only one artist, made with (that artist) in mind. You hear Dionne singing in your head, and that's how you do the song. But (the covers) show the songs can be done another way."

In truth, Bacharach and David had never stayed away from the charts for long. Their songs had been revived numerous times in the '70s and '80s, and had made the charts on a number of those occasions. In 1973, in the wake of LOST HORIZON, the Stylistics had scored a big hit with a remake of *You'll Never Get To Heaven*, while Gloria Gaynor and the Average White Band both had moderate success with revamped versions of *Walk On By*, in 1975 and 1979, respectively. Naked Eyes went Top 10 with an electro-pop *Always Something There To Remind Me* in 1984, and *Don't Make Me Over* reached the charts courtesy of Jennifer Warnes (in 1979) and Sybil (in 1989). In 1990, the British group Deacon Blue issued an EP called FOUR BACHARACH AND DAVID SONGS and scored a No. 2 UK hit.

The Bacharach/David song catalogue was given a boost by a mid-'90s easy listening revival. Reissues of Burt's own recordings began to appear on CD, along with compilations of his hits with David and other writers. Suddenly, Bacharach's was the name to drop, both by young musicians and by critics looking for synonyms for "melodic." The British hipster magazine THE FACE called Bacharach "A genius long due for an irony-free re-evaluation."

Although Hal David characteristically kept a low profile, Bacharach was ready for the revival of interest – still as glamorous, charming and energetic as ever. In 1999, PEOPLE magazine deemed Burt one of its "50 Most Beautiful People in the World."

On April 8, 1998, a tribute concert in New York City brought the Bacharach revival straight into the pop culture mainstream. BURT BACHARACH: ONE AMAZING NIGHT was a star-studded event which proved once again that the Bacharach and David songbook was still as timely as ever. (Although the concert was a tribute to Burt, rather than Burt and Hal, most of the numbers performed were inevitably Bacharach/David collaborations.)

Sheryl Crow sang *One Less Bell To Answer*, All Saints did *Always Something There To Remind Me*, Elvis Costello sang *This House Is Empty Now* and *God Give Me Strength*, Wynonna Judd performed *Anyone Who Had A Heart*, the Ben Folds Five did *Raindrops Keep Fallin' On My Head* and Barenaked Ladies did *Close To You*. Mike Myers did a comical version of *What's New Pussycat?*, complete with Austin Powers dance moves.

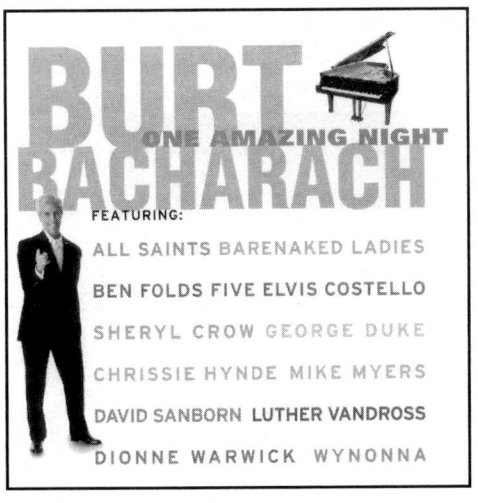

BURT BACHARACH – ONE AMAZING NIGHT CD

RHINO RECORD'S BACHARACH BOX SET

The master-stroke of Myers' version was the addition of the *Raindrops Keep Fallin' On My head* coda to the end of *Pussycat*. One of the show's high points was Chrissie Hynde's powerful medley of *Baby It's You* and *Message To Michael*.

Burt, who performed along with the other acts, did a few numbers on his own – *Alfie* and a medley of early hits, comprising *Magic Moments*, *The Story Of My Life* and *Tower Of Strength*. Dionne was also on hand, singing *Walk On By*, *I Say A Little Prayer*, *Do You Know The Way To San Jose* and *A House Is Not A Home*.

Later that year, Rhino Records issued THE LOOK OF LOVE: THE BURT BACHARACH COLLECTION. The superb, beautifully-packaged three-CD set was a dream come true for Bacharach fans, packing in just about every hit, along with a good assortment of rarities.

With the notable exception of LOST HORIZON, Bacharach and David had always fared well with movie songs. The use of their vintage numbers in hit movies was a key factor in their revival in the '90s.

MY BEST FRIEND'S WEDDING, a romantic comedy starring Julia Roberts, was another clear indicator that the Bacharach and David sound was mainstream once more. The movie's soundtrack was dominated by Burt and Hal's songs: *I Say A Little Prayer*, *Wishin' And Hopin* (sung by Ani DiFranco), *I Just Don't Know What To Do With Myself*, *What The World Needs Now Is Love*, and *I'll Never Fall In Love Again* (performed by Mary Chapin Carpenter).

Dionne's recording of *Wives And Lovers* was used in the movie FIRST WIVES CLUB,

Burt Bacharach & Hal David

Naked Eyes??' *Always Something There To Remind Me* featured in ROMY AND MICHELLE'S HIGH SCHOOL REUNION, ONE FINE DAY featured *This Guy's In Love With You* and the mega-hit FORREST GUMP included two Bacharach/David numbers.

The most prominent of all was Mike Myers' '60s spy spoof AUSTIN POWERS – INTERNATIONAL MAN OF MYSTERY. After an early cameo appearance by the BURT BACHARACH PLAYS HIS HITS LP – one of superspy Powers' most treasured possessions – Burt himself appeared in the film, singing *What The World Needs Now Is Love* atop a double-decker bus in Las Vegas. Burt's solo rendition segued into a version by Seattle rock group the Posies, and the soundtrack also featured a sultry version of *The Look Of Love* by Bangles singer Susanna Hoffs. Bacharach showed up in the film's sequel, THE SPY WHO SHAGGED ME (performing *I'll Never Fall In Love Again* with Elvis Costello) and the third instalment, *Goldmember*, featured Hoffs singing *Alfie*.

AUSTIN POWERS SOUNDTRACK CD

For most of the period between the late '70s and the early '90s, Burt Bacharach and Hal David had communicated with each other only through their respective attorneys. "It was a very messy situation—and a very unfortunate time," Burt said years later in THE LOS ANGELES TIMES.

In 1993, their legal battles behind them, Bacharach and David were reunited. Appropriately, the instigator of their reunion was Dionne Warwick.

"I got the two of them together to write a song for me," says Warwick.

"We finally made our settlement," Burt told the LA TIMES. "Dionne and I are touring again, and Hal and I found a touch of the old spark when we wrote *Sunny Weather Lover* for Dionne's new album. It was the first song we'd written together in 17 years."

Sunny Weather Lover was included on her Dionne's FRIENDS CAN BE LOVERS album. It was a decent song, but was undermined by its production.

"We thought it was good," says David. "But it just didn't work. I didn't think it was one of our great songs. I think, under certain circumstances, it could have happened."

"I guess because they hadn't been in the studio together for a length of time, it just didn't quite hit the mark," says Warwick. "It really wasn't what people expected of Bacharach and David."

DIONNE WARWICK – FRIENDS CAN BE LOVERS

The new collaboration didn't attract much attention and, in the years that followed, Burt and Hal continued to pursue their respective projects apart from each other.

The disappointment with *Sunny Weather Lover* was due in part to the fact that the song bore little resemblance to Bacharach and David's '60s work. A 1996 soundtrack assignment was the catalyst that spurred Bacharach to revisit his vintage composing style. The film was GRACE OF MY HEART, director Allison Anders' story of a songwriter who moves from the Brill Building era through the singer-songwriter era of the early '70s. The story – loosely based on the life of Carole King – required authentic-sounding period music, so Anders recruited songwriters of the era and teamed them up with contemporary artists whom they had influenced.

Burt was paired up with Elvis Costello, the bespectacled British singer-songwriter who had come out of the post-punk/new wave scene of the late '70s. At a glance, Costello might have seemed an unlikely partner for Bacharach. However, Costello had been influenced by Burt and had even covered *I Just Don't Know What To Do With Myself* many years earlier.

GRACE OF MY HEART SOUNDTRACK CD

Writing entirely by long distance – by phone, fax and answering machine – Costello and Bacharach penned a magnificent song called *God Give Me Strength*, featuring lyrics by Costello and music by both. Sung in the film by Kristen Vigard, *God Give Me Strength* was the musical high point of GRACE OF MY HEART, and was generally perceived as a return to form for Bacharach.

"It was in that 6/8, 12/8 thing I used to write in, that I hadn't done in years," Bacharach said in a VANITY FAIR interview. "Musically, I can't go back and say, I want to write something like *Don't Make Me Over*.

Burt Bacharach & Hal David

ELVIS COSTELLO & BURT BACHARACH

I just don't think that way. But this was for a movie about the Brill Building, so I thought, Great!"

Costello penned the lyrics for *God Give Me Strength*, as well as the melody for the verse but musically, the whole song sounds like pure, vintage Bacharach.

"I suggested a couple of new chords and changes, wrote the bridge, and did the orchestration," Burt told VANITY FAIR. "To me, the song has a certain timelessness. It works as a period piece, but it also works for the time the movie's being released in."

Burt and Elvis enjoyed the project so much that they subsequently turned out several more songs and made a fine album, PAINTED FROM MEMORY, in 1998.

Despite the success of the Costello project, Bacharach's perfect co-writer was still Hal David. In a 1996 conversation, David did not rule out the possibility of further collaborations, "if a project came along that was interesting. We talk from time to time about doing something. If a show came along or the right film, I think we would love to do it. At least, I would and I suspect he would, too."

Not long after that comment, a perfect opportunity presented itself. Neil Simon asked Bacharach and David to write a new song for a revival of PROMISES, PROMISES. The new collaboration, *You've Got It All Wrong*, was written in a manner that recalled their earlier collaborations. A duet by the characters of Fran and Peggy, *You've Got It All Wrong* appeared towards the end of the show's first act, in between *Wanting Things* and *Turkey Lurkey Time*. Hal wrote the lyric first and Burt was suitably impressed, thinking "Man, this guy is really a helluva writer."

You've Got It All Wrong certainly sounded closer to the vintage Bacharach/David style than *Sunny Weather Lover*. The fact that it was written for the show, rather than to pitch to an artist as a potential hit, took some of the pressure away and made the writing process more enjoyable. Burt and Hal simply had to run the song by Neil Simon.

"It's so different when it's not a marketplace kind of thing," said Bacharach.

You've Got It All Wrong was featured in two separate versions of *Promises, Promises*, both "semi-staged" versions of the show. This meant that the actors had scripts with them onstage and costumes changes and staging were minimal compared to the original production. The idea was that, by necessitating a minimal rehearsal period and a short run, these performances could attract TV and film stars who might not normally be willing to commit to the rigours of a full musical staging.

The first version, staged at New York's City Center as part of the "Encores!" series, ran for a limited run of five performances. Directed and choreographed by Rob Marshall, it starred Martin Short as Chuck, Kerry O'Malley as Fran and also featured the great comic actors Eugene Levy and Christine Baranski.

The second revival, in May, was also a limited run, at UCLA's 500-seat Freud Playhouse in Los Angeles. It featured SEINFELD star Jason Alexander as Chuck, as well as Alan Thicke, Fred Willard and Jean Smart. Directed by Stuart Ross, creator of FOREVER PLAID, the Los Angeles version's musical director was Peter Matz, who had worked on a number of projects with Bacharach, David and Warwick in the '60s.

The shows were met with positive reviews, especially Alexander's performance as Chuck.

"As the schlep accountant who loans his Manhattan flat to his bosses for their extramarital romps, (Alexander) looks properly self-effacing," said the LOS ANGELES TIMES, "yet he's a likeable dreamer, and he sings and dances with considerable charisma. He's supported by a number of other well-known actors – and the show sparkles... As the troubled love object, the Audrey Hepburn-esque Karen Fineman sings with controlled passion, and she and the tart-tongued Linda Hart get a driving duet, *You've Got It All Wrong*, that wasn't in the original show. Alan Thicke mixes the necessary oiliness of his cad character with the good looks and strong voice that make his seductive powers credible. A high-pitched and fluttery Jean Smart is an adorable drinking partner for the much shorter Alexander. Barney Martin employs his patented comic timing."

Having enjoyed that collaboration, Burt and Hal teamed up again to pen songs for the 1999 movie ISN'T SHE GREAT. The film, which starred Bette Midler and Nathan Lane, was based on the life of author Jacqueline Susann, best known for her novel VALLEY OF THE DOLLS, the movie version of which featured a hit theme song by Dionne Warwick. Burt scored ISN'T SHE GREAT and collaborated with Hal on two songs. The best of these, *On My Way*, was performed by Warwick.

"I think the producer of the film had an awful lot to do with that," says Warwick of her involvement with the project. "Due to the fact that I did do *Valley Of The Dolls*, they felt there was no way they could make the life of Susann without including me. Somebody would've said, 'What happened to Dionne?'"

The session with Dionne saw Burt and Hal return to their '60s recording set-up.

"It was wonderful," says Warwick of the *On My Way* session. "A studio full of musicians and singers – a normal session for us."

Although not quite on par with their best '60s collaborations, *On My Way* was a fine track, recreating much of the old magic. Vanessa Williams sang the film's end title number, Bacharach and David's *Open Your Heart*. The film was reportedly slated to feature another new song, *If I Should Ever Lose You*, performed by Chicago, but the song was cut at some point along the way.

In June 2000, the Nordoff-Robbins Music Therapy charity organization staged the all-star TRIBUTE TO BURT BACHARACH AND HAL DAVID at the Royal Albert Hall in London. Burt and Hal both took part, and saw their classics performed by such artists as Petula Clark, Elvis Costello, Sacha Distel, Edwin Starr and Dionne Warwick.

In January 2001, Burt was announced as the winner of the International Polar Music Prize for 2001. The prestigious Swedish award (previous recipients have included Paul McCartney, Dizzy Gillespie, Quincy Jones, Elton John, Joni Mitchell, Ray Charles, Ravi Shankar, Bob Dylan and Isaac Stern) was presented to the composer from His Majesty King Carl Gustaf XVI of Sweden in Stockholm on Monday, May 14.

ISN'T SHE GREAT VIDEO RELEASE

In recent years, Hal David has made his first public appearances as a singer. One of these was during a show called THE WRITER, THE SINGER, THE SONG, staged at the Mark Taper Forum in Los Angeles. The brainchild of Hal and wife Eunice, the evening featured a selection of songwriters (including Alan and Marilyn Bergman, Leiber and Stoller and Jimmy Webb) and singers (including Rosemary Clooney, Maureen McGovern and LOST HORIZON refugee Sally Kellerman).

Hal himself sang *I'll Never Fall In Love Again*, before being joined onstage by Dionne Warwick, who performed *Alfie*.

Chapter 20: Something Even Non-believers Can Believe In

Whether or not Hal David and Burt Bacharach ever choose to collaborate again, the contribution they have already made to popular music cannot be underestimated. Their work was rooted in the tradition of such great songwriting teams as Rodgers and Hart, as well as contemporaries like Goffin and King. Yet they took that tradition and carried it forward, their songs charting numerous times in the '60s and continuing to be covered in the '70s, '80s, '90s and beyond.

The reason for the enduring success of the songs of Bacharach and David is that they are simply great songs, from basic love songs to thoughtful philosophical reflections, pushing the boundaries of pop music whilst remaining commercial and accessible. Most of their work is truly timeless. Bacharach and David never paid much attention to current trends – they always seemed to be looking at the bigger picture, transcending the moment.

"I am a romanticist," Bacharach said. "And I like melody. I like songs that can be remembered but get to your heart at the same time."

It really all comes down to two things: Bacharach's melodies remain brilliant, beautiful and timeless, while Hal David's lyrics are sincere and universal. What the world needs now - as in the '60s - is love, sweet love. And anyone who had a heart could not help but be moved by a Bacharach and David song.

"The biggest thrill for me," said Bacharach in a BILLBOARD interview many years ago, "is being able to make a dent, even a small one, in somebody's life. The reward is when someone tells you one of your songs means something special to them. It might be the memory of a good time, or a love affair, or when their baby was born."

"I think we always tried to write up to the best of our ability," says David. "Not to what looked like it was going to be in the Top 10 on the charts because of what was happening at that moment, or what was the new fashion. We just tried to write with as much integrity as we could, tried to write the best we knew how."

Burt Bacharach & Hal David

The Songs:

(All chart positions are from BILLBOARD's Pop Chart unless otherwise indicated.)

In this section of the book, I have tried to provide a complete list of every song written by Burt Bacharach and Hal David, accompanied by information about the songs, when they were written and who recorded them. I haven't tried to list every artist who recorded each song, but to include the most interesting and important versions and to give an idea of the diversity of the artists who tackled the Bacharach/David songbook. Details on some of their more obscure collaborations are sketchy and some were probably not recorded at all.

Accept It
Tony Orlando recorded *Accept It* for the flipside of a 1964 single (The A-side was Bacharach and David's *To Wait For Love*).

Across The River, Round The Bend
This early Bacharach/David composition was recorded in 1960 by John Ashley.

After The Fox
The Hollies recorded *After The Fox* as the theme song for the 1966 Peter Sellers movie of the same title. In fact, Sellers himself appears on the record, in character, as "The Fox." Though just as strong as Burt and Hal's previous Sellers theme, *What's New Pussycat?*, *After The Fox* was much less successful in the charts. The Pied Pipers, Ferrante and Teicher, Oranj Symphonette and the Magistrates recorded cover versions. A recent version, by Losers Lounge, appeared on the Hollies tribute CD SING HOLLIES IN REVERSE.

Alfie
Both Bacharach and David have cited this as their favourite of all the songs they've written. *Alfie* was written for the Michael Caine movie of the same name, but not featured in some versions of the film (which was scored by Sonny Rollins).

Bacharach conducted Cilla Black's recording of the song, produced by George Martin for the film. Cher (whose recording featured in the American version of the film), Dionne Warwick, and Eivets Rednow (AKA Stevie Wonder) all charted with the song. Among the many artists who have tackled *Alfie* are Tony Bennett, Barbra Streisand, Dee Dee Warwick (Dionne's sister), Everything But the Girl and Jack Jones.

All Kinds Of People
This Sly And The Family Stone-style number was recorded by the Fifth Dimension (on

the INDIVIDUALLY AND COLLECTIVELY album), Jerry Butler, John Rowles, Burt Bacharach (on his self-titled LP) and Dionne Warwick. Warwick's version was part of a medley, with *Reach Out And Touch*, on the FROM WITHIN album, although she recorded a full version three decades later on the DIONNE SINGS DIONNE CD.

All The Way To Paradise (And Back Again)
Stephanie Mills performed this song on her 1975 album FOR THE FIRST TIME, produced by Burt and Hal.

Along Came Joe
This composition from 1961 was recorded by Merv Griffin, best known for his popular talk show THE MERV GRIFFIN SHOW.

(There's) Always Something There To Remind Me
Lou Johnson made the first recording of this Bacharach/David classic, achieving modest chart success. In Britain, it was cut by Sandie Shaw, who had great success with her version. Dionne Warwick eventually recorded it in the late '60s. It returned to the charts in the early '80s, courtesy of synth-pop duo Naked Eyes, whose make-over of the song went Top 10. Recorded by many other acts, including the Troggs, Lou Christie and Johnny Mathis.

And So Goodbye My Love
Burt himself recorded this number as the B-side of his 1963 Kapp single *Saturday Sunshine*.

And This Is Mine
Connie Stevens recorded this composition for a 1961 single. Ginny Arnell recorded a version in 1963.

Anonymous Phone Call
Bobby Vee recorded this for a 1962 single release, although the other side of that record, *The Night Has A Thousand Eyes*, turned out to be the hit. In Britain, *Anonymous Phone Call* was covered by Frank (*I Remember You*) Ifield.

Another Night
Dionne Warwick - who tended to get first refusal of any Bacharach/David songs – recorded this tune as a single in 1966. Dionne's recording can also be found on the Columbia House double ALBUM GO WITH LOVE: DIONNE WARWICK SINGS THE SONGS OF BURT BACHARACH AND HAL DAVID. Dusty Springfield covered the song on the album DUSTY... DEFINITELY.

Another Tear Falls
Gene McDaniels was the first artist to record this song, for the 1962 British film RING-A-DING RHYTHM (also known as IT'S TRAD, DAD!) and for a single release. The song subsequently provided a hit for the Walker Brothers in 1966. On the easy listening front, the London Symphonic Orchestra And Singers recorded a version for the three-record set THE COMPOSERS SERIES VOL. 1: BURT BACHARACH AND HAL DAVID.

Anyone Who Had A Heart
Dionne Warwick recorded this song on the same day she recorded *Walk On By*. The musical backing for both songs incorporated two grand pianos played simultaneously.

"We had done both those songs at the same session," recalls Hal David. "And we couldn't make up our minds which record to go with first. We went back and forth and finally elected to come out with *Anyone Who Had A Heart*."

At the end of 1963, the Beatles' manager Brian Epstein heard Warwick's version while on a trip to America. Convinced the song would be perfect for one of his artists – Cilla Black – Epstein brought a copy of the Warwick single back to England and played it for Cilla's producer, George Martin. Martin reportedly felt that that Cilla wasn't up to the song and suggested that Shirley Bassey could do a better job. Epstein insisted, Cilla recorded the track and proved that she was more than capable of delivering it.

In Britain, Black had a much bigger hit with the song than Warwick did. Dionne was not pleased by this and apparently felt that Cilla's version was little more than an imitation of her own recording. To further confuse matters, the song simultaneously provided Mary May with a minor British hit. Maureen McGovern revived the song in 1992, on her album BABY I'M YOURS.

Any Old Time Of Day
Dionne Warwick recorded this number for the flipside of *Walk On By*. It also showed up on the album DIONNE WARWICK'S GOLDEN HITS, PART ONE. One of Bacharach's most compelling melodies, navigated by Warwick as only she could.

The April Fools
Dionne Warwick recorded this lovely composition for the 1969 movie of the same name, a romantic comedy starring Jack Lemmon and Catherine Deneuve.

Are You There (With Another Girl)

A 1966 single by Dionne Warwick. The Buckinghams, best known for their hit *Kind Of A Drag*, recorded a version (with the lyrics changed from "girl" to "boy") on their 1968 album IN ONE EAR AND GONE TOMORROW.

As Long As There's An Apple Tree
Dionne Warwick's recording of this song appeared on her VALLEY OF THE DOLLS LP.

The Balance Of Nature
Bacharach's A&M albums of the late 60's and early 70's usually featured one or two vocal performances by the composer. On his 1973 LIVING TOGETHER LP, Bacharach sang *The Balance Of Nature*, which Dionne Warwick had recorded a year earlier on the DIONNE album.

Beads And Boots And A Green And Yellow Blanket
An unrecorded composition from 1970.

Be Aware
"Probably one of the finest lyrics that Hal David ever wrote," says Dionne Warwick of this song.

Warwick recorded this song for the 1972 DIONNE album, her first effort for Warner Bros. Barbra Streisand performed the song on a Bacharach TV special in 1971.

The Beginning Of Loneliness
This song first appeared as the flipside of Dionne Warwick's version of *Alfie* in 1967. It was subsequently included on the Warwick compilation album GO WITH LOVE.

Before You Leave Me
An unrecorded song from 1975, possibly a contender for the Stephanie Mills album FOR THE FIRST TIME.

Be True To Yourself
This number provided a Top 40 American hit for Bobby Vee in 1963.

Blue Guitar
An early 60's single by actor Richard Chamberlain, then best known as television's Dr. Kildare.

Blue On Blue
One of the few mid-60's numbers not offered to Dionne Warwick.

"We didn't play that for Dionne," Hal David recalls. "It didn't sound like Dionne at all."

Blue On Blue was instead given to Bobby Vinton, whose 1963 recording was a Top 10 hit in America. Burt conducted the Vinton track and also played piano on the session. Paul Anka also recorded this song, on his 1963 album SONGS I WISH I'D WRITTEN.

The Boss Is Not Here

Probably *not* a Bacharach/David song. This composition from 1965 appears to be an English-language re-write of a German song, *Der Boss Ist Nicht Hier* with lyrics by Hal David. The German version was written by Lothar Olias, but what's not clear is whether Bacharach was involved. Some sources credit this as a Bacharach/David song, but Hal David says he doesn't remember it as something he wrote with Burt. In any event, *The Boss Is Not Here* was recorded in 1965 by German singer Freddy Quinn.

A Bottomless Cup
An early collaboration, from 1957, co-written with Lou Melamed at Famous Music.

Boys Were Made For Girls
Everit Herter recorded this 1960 composition.

The Breaking Point
Chuck Jackson recorded this song for a 1963 album ANY DAY NOW.

Building Walls
An unrecorded composition from 1963.

Call Off The Wedding (Without A Groom There Can't Be A Bride)
A 1963 single by Babs Tino. Hailed by BILLBOARD as "a mighty attractive outing for this lass. The side is nicely sung and smart backing really makes it go."

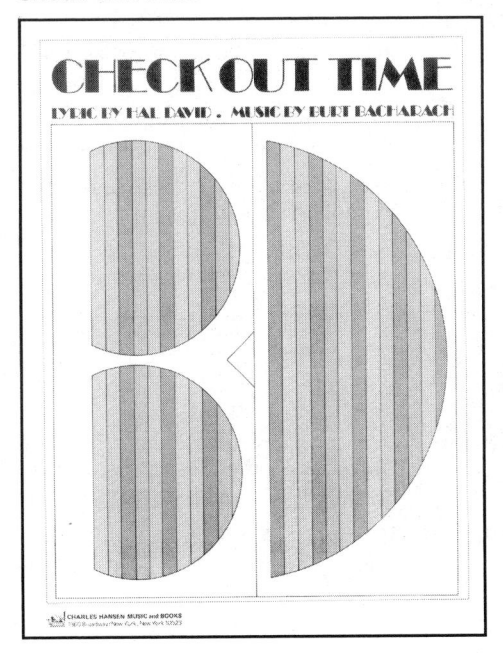

Check Out Time
Dionne Warwick sang this number on the VERY DIONNE album, her final effort for Scepter Records.

Christmas Day
First recorded by Johnny Mathis in 1958, this seasonal number was subsequently used in the musical PROMISES, PROMISES. In the original Broadway production, Edward Winter, Kay Oslin, Rita O'Connor, Julane Stites and Neil Jones sang *Christmas Day*. Yuletide specialist Robert Goulet also recorded a version.

(They Long To Be) Close To You
Although the Carpenters version was a big hit in 1970, several other artists had previously recorded this song. *(They Long To Be) Close To You* was cut first by actor Richard Chamberlain, then by Dionne Warwick (as a B-side) and by Dusty Springfield on her 1967 album WHERE AM I GOING.

"I made the first few records of it with the wrong groove, wrong feel," Burt told author Paul Zollo. "Richard (Carpenter) came in and nailed it."

"When we recorded the song (with Chamberlain and Warwick), it didn't feel like a big hit at that time," says Hal David. "We always liked the song and that's why we sent it over to Herb Alpert. We didn't feel that we had the right rendition. Herb Alpert liked it and played it for the Carpenters. I heard the record – Her Alpert or Jerry Moss sent it over to Burt's house in California. And we played it. And I liked it, but I

Burt Bacharach & Hal David

didn't jump up and down. Burt thought it was a great record. I learnt to fall in love with it very quickly. On first hearing, I wasn't bowled over."

After the Carpenters' hit, the song was re-recorded by Warwick, Johnny Mathis, B.J. Thomas and numerous other artists.

Come And Get Me
Jackie DeShannon's second Bacharach/David-penned single was a great recording, but failed to match the commercial success of *What The World Needs Now Is Love*.

County Music Holiday
This 1958 number was written for the movie of the same title, the tale of a hillbilly singer, starring Ferlin Husky, June Carter Cash and Zsa Zsa Gabor. *Country Music Holiday* was recorded by Bernie Knee (who sang on many of Burt and Hal's demos) for a single release. The song was also recorded (and released as a single) by British singer Adam Faith.

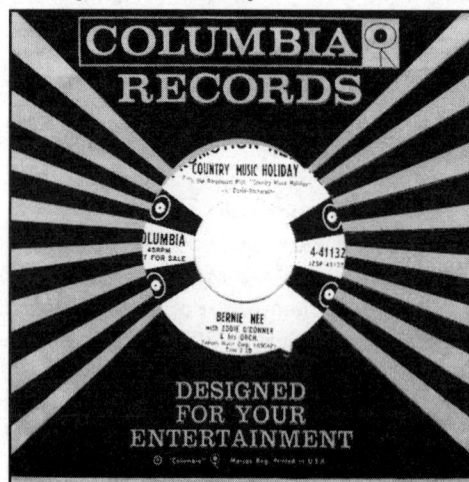

Cross Town Bus
This 1960 composition was recorded by the Swedish group Gals & Pals, on their 1968 LP SING SOMETHING FOR EVERYONE. Although a throwaway by Bacharach and David standards, the Gals and Pals track succeeds by virtue of a swingin' *Austin Powers*-esque arrangement.

Dance Mamma Dance Pappa
This song – a vocal version of the instrumental *Marriage French Style* (from the WHAT'S NEW PUSSYCAT score) – was recorded by Joanne & The Streamliners. A German version, entitled *Dans Je De Hele Nacht Met Mij* was recorded by Karin Kent.

Do I Have To Say More
An unrecorded composition from 1962.

Do Not Speak To Me Of Love
Sylvaine Clair recorded this seldom-heard composition for a 1970 single.

Don't Count The Days

A collaboration written in 1961 at Famous Music. This was recorded by Marilyn Michael and, in 1968, by Sandi and Salli.

Don't Do Anything Dangerous

An unrecorded composition from 1961.

Don't Envy Me

This 1961 composition was recorded by George Hamilton in 1963, and was also covered by Joey Powers.

Don't Go Breaking My Heart

The first recording of this song was by Bacharach himself, released as a single in 1965. Two more versions showed up the following year. Dionne Warwick's rendition was the B-side of her single *Trains And Boats And Planes*, while Herb Alpert and the Tijuana Brass' lively instrumental version appeared on their S.R.O. album.

Don't Make Me Over

Dionne Warwick's first single, written specifically for her. The story goes that, after Dionne sang on the demo for *Make It Easy On Yourself*, she assumed that it was hers to record. When Bacharach and David gave the song to Jerry Butler, Warwick supposedly told them, "Don't make me over!" It's a great story, but it may just be a myth.

Hal David is non-committal on the subject. "Maybe that happened," he says. "I've heard that too."

Although Warwick's version didn't chart in Britain, the Swingin' Blue Jeans had a U.K. hit with it in 1966. Petula Clark turned it into a country-pop number on her 1976 album BLUE LADY. Tommy Hunt also recorded a version of this song.

Don't Make Me Over has proven to be one of Bacharach and David's most enduring compositions, with several different artists charting with cover versions in the '70s and '80s: Brenda and the Tabulations (in 1970), Jennifer Warnes (in 1979), and Sybil (a top 20 hit in 1989).

Don't Say I Didn't Tell You So
A Dionne Warwick B-side, the flip of her 1965 release *Who Can I Turn To?* Petula Clark also covered this song, in 1971.

Do You Know The Way To San Jose?
This Bacharach/David classic was first recorded by Dionne Warwick, who had a big hit with it in 1968. Although it's one of her most requested numbers, Dionne has made no secret of the fact that she initially didn't care for the song.

A wide assortment of artists have rendered this song, including Robert Goulet, Ramsey Lewis and Frankie Goes To Hollywood.

Dream Sweet Dreamer
One of Dionne Warwick's best B-sides, this gem was hidden on the flipside of her 1969 hit *This Girl's In Love With You.*

An Errand Of Mercy
Actor George Hamilton is more famous for his tan than his recording career, but among his musical efforts was this obscure Bacharach/David composition.

Everybody Knows The Way To Bethlehem
The title suggests that this is a Christmas song, but little else is known about this composition.

Everybody's Out Of Town
Written for B.J. Thomas as the follow-up to *Raindrops Keep Fallin' On My Head.* Easily as strong as *Raindrops* and with a similar feel, it was a moderate success. This underrated recording was first released as a single and then on the Thomas album of the same title. A rare cover version came courtesy of Robert Goulet, and Rex Harrison sang the song with Burt on a 1972 TV special.

Everyone Needs Someone To Love
Cliff Richard recorded this 1964 composition in 1965. Nick Palmer did a version in 1968.

Everything Is Nothing Without You
Probably another unrecorded number, although Dennis Lotis recorded a song with the same title.

The Eye Of The Needle
Cliff Richard recorded this song – a favourite of Hal David's – as the B-side to his 1965 single *Wind Me Up*. Another version was cut by Donna Marie.

A Fact Can Be A Beautiful Thing
Jerry Orbach and Marian Mercer sang this number in the original Broadway production of PROMISES, PROMISES.

Faker, Faker
A 1959 collaboration, written at Famous Music in New York, this was recorded by the Eligibles.

Fender Mender
Joannie Sommers sang this number in the TV musical ON THE FLIP SIDE, in which she co-starred with Rick Nelson.

(The) Fool Killer
Gene Pitney recorded this theme for the 1967 movie of the same title, which featured PSYCHO star Anthony Perkins. The song was not included in the film, and was probably written as an "exploitation song" to promote it.

For All Time
This 1962 composition was recorded by the Russells.

For Once In My Life
In ASCAP's database of song titles, no publisher is listed for this composition, which probably wasn't recorded.

Burt Bacharach & Hal David

Forever My Love
Dionne Warwick, Burt Bacharach and Jane Morgan all recorded this composition, originally written as the theme to the 1962 film of the same name, starring Romy Schneider.

Forever Yours I Remain
Bobby Vinton, who had a big hit with Bacharach and David's *Blue On Blue*, included this song on his 1964 album MR. LONELY.

Forgive Me (For Giving You Such A Bad Time)
Babs Tino recorded this as a single in 1962.

From Rocking Horse To Rocking Chair
Paul Anka's recording of this pleasant song was released as a single in 1964, but failed to chart.

Go With Love
Dionne Warwick recorded this as the B-side for her 1966 single *Another Night*. *Go With Love* was also the title track for a double album compilation, which collected many of her lesser-known Bacharach-David recordings.

Gotta Get A Girl
Frankie Avalon recorded this obscure Bacharach/David number for a 1961 single release.

Grapes Of Roth
This instrumental from PROMISES PROMISES is listed as a Bacharach/David composition. Unless Hal wrote lyrics that weren't used, this was probably written by Burt alone.

The Green Grass Starts To Grow
Dionne Warwick's version of this song came out as a single in 1970 and subsequently appeared on the VERY DIONNE album.

Half As Big As Life
This number from PROMISES, PROMISES was sung by Jerry Orbach in the original Broadway production.

The Hangman
An early collaboration, from the Famous Music era, this was written for the 1959 movie THE HANGMAN, a western starring Jack Lord. Recorded by John Ashley.

Hasbrook Heights
Burt sang this charming number on his self-titled 1970 LP. Dionne Warwick also recorded a version, for her Warner Bros debut DIONNE.

He Who Loves
Jerry Vale and Lenny Welch both recorded this early number. Welch's version was released in 1968. Perry Como is also rumoured to have recorded this song in 1967.

Here I Am
Dionne Warwick's contribution to the WHAT'S NEW PUSSYCAT? soundtrack, an overlooked Bacharach/David/Warwick classic. The swingin' Swedish vocal group Gals and Pals also covered *Here I Am*.

Here Where There Is Love
Dionne Warwick sang this on her album of the same title.

Hideaway Heart
Probably an unrecorded number, although Kitty Kallen recorded a song with the same title in 1957.

Hot Food
Written in 1968 for PROMISES, PROMISES, but cut from the finished production.

A House Is Not A Home
Written for the Shelley Winters movie of the same name. The first version was recorded by Brook Benton, known for such hits as *The Boll Weevil Song*, *It's Just A Matter Of Time*, and *Hotel Happiness*. Both Benton and Dionne Warwick charted with this song. Subsequent recordings by Burt himself, Georgie Fame, Della Reese (on her album ON STRINGS OF BLUE) and numerous other artists.

Burt Bacharach & Hal David

How Can I Hurt You?
Dionne Warwick included this song on her 1966 LP HERE I AM.

How Does A Man Become A Puppet?
This song, a vocal version of the Bacharach instrumental *She's Gone Away*, was recorded by Malcolm Roberts and Ed Ames, best known for his 1967 hit *My Cup Runneth Over*.

How Many Days Of Sadness
The 1965 LP THE SENSITIVE SOUND OF DIONNE WARWICK included this composition. Bacharach has said he feels this had the potential to be a hit, and Luther Vandross has cited it as one of his favourite Warwick recordings.

Humble Pie
Burt and Hal wrote this unrecorded song in 1957 at Famous Music in New York.

The Hurtin' Kind
This unrecorded number dates from 1970.

I Come To You
A duet from LOST HORIZON, sung by Diana Lee (who's singing voice was dubbed for Liv Ullmann), and Jerry Hutman (singing for Peter Finch).

I Could Kick Myself
An unrecorded composition from 1958.

I Could Make You Mine
Dionne Warwick recorded this for her 1963 LP ANYONE WHO HAD A HEART. It had previously been cut by the Wanderers in 1960.

I Cry Alone
Ruby And The Romantics (best known for the 1963 single *Our Day Will Come*) recorded this as the B-side to their 1964 hit *When You're Young And In Love*. Others who recorded *I Cry Alone* included Dionne Warwick, Betty Carter, Vicki Carr, Jack Jones, Maxine Brown and Jackie Lee.

I Cry More
Alan Dale, best known for the 1955 hit *Sweet And Gentle*, recorded this rockin' tune in 1956 for the movie DON'T KNOCK THE ROCK.

I'd Still Be A Fool
An unrecorded composition from 1975, possibly intended for the Stephanie Mills LP FOR THE FIRST TIME.

I Fell In Love With Your Picture
This 1964 composition was recorded the following year by Freddie and the Dreamers, the lively British group known for the hit *I'm Telling You Now* and for inventing a dance called The Freddie.

I Forgot What It Was Like
Ray Peterson – best known for the hits *Tell Laura I Love Her* and *Corinna, Corinna* – recorded this number in 1963, on the flip side of his *Missing You* single. Bobby Helms also recorded a version of *I Forgot What It Was Like*.

If I Could Go Back
Andy Williams, Dorothy Squires and Tony Bennett covered this song from the LOST HORIZON soundtrack, sung in the film by Jerry Hutman, who dubbed the vocals on Peter Finch's songs. Singing actor Richard Harris, best-known musically for the Jimmy Webb-penned *MacArthur Park*, sang *If I Could Go Back* on the 1973 TV special BURT BACHARACH IN SHANGRI-LA.

If I Ever Make You Cry
Dionne Warwick sang this number on her 1966 LP HERE I AM.

If I Never Get To Love You
Both Timi Yuro and Lou Johnson recorded this song in 1963. Marianne Faithfull also recorded a version.

If You Can Learn How To Cry
Burt and Hal wrote this song for the 1975 Stephanie Mills album FOR THE FIRST TIME.

If You Never Say Goodbye
This song appeared on the 1972 album DIONNE, Warwick's last collaboration with Bacharach and David (and her first album for Warner Bros).

Burt Bacharach & Hal David

I Just Have To Breathe
Another number from the 1972 DIONNE LP.

I Just Don't Know What To Do With Myself
Tommy Hunt, Dionne Warwick, Linda Ronstadt, Gary Puckett, Cissy Houston, Isaac Hayes and Elvis Costello are just some of the artists who have recorded this number. Dusty Springfield's version gave her a hit single in Britain, but only showed up Stateside as a track on the 1964 album DUSTY.

I Leave You All My Love
An unrecorded number.

I'll Kiss You Goodnight In The Morning
An unrecorded composition from 1957.

I'll Never Fall In Love Again
Written for (and featured in) the musical PROMISES, PROMISES, this song was finished very quickly as a last-minute replacement for *Wouldn't That Be A Stroke Of Luck*. At the time it was written, Burt was in the hospital with pneumonia, which inspired the lyric "What do you get when you kiss a girl/You get enough germs to catch pneumonia." In the original production of PROMISES, PROMISES, Jill O'Hara and Jerry Orbach performed this song.

I'll Never Fall In Love Again provided a hit for Dionne Warwick. Bobbie Gentry's version reached No. 1 in Britain, but wasn't a hit in the U.S.. This tune was also recorded by the Carpenters on their debut album CLOSE TO YOU, along with the Bacharach-David title song. Other artists who have covered this number include Patti Page, Johnny Mathis and Anne Murray (on her self-titled 1971 album). Bacharach performed the song with Elvis Costello in Mike Meyers' AUSTIN POWERS sequel THE SPY WHO SHAGGED ME.

I'll Never Forget 'What's Her Name'
An unrecorded composition from 1960.

I Looked For You
Charlie Gracie recorded *I Looked For You* for a 1960 single on Roulette Records.

I'm A Better Man (For Having Loved You)
Engelbert Humperdinck recorded this song for his self-titled 1969 album, produced

by Peter Sullivan. Humperdinck's recording was also released as a single and gave him a No. 15 hit in Britain.

I Might Frighten Her Away
Originally featured in the movie LOST HORIZON, this was also covered by Herb Alpert on the 1974 LP YOU SMILE - THE SONG BEGINS.

In Between The Heartaches
Both Dionne Warwick and Anita Kerr tackled this mid-60's composition. *In Between The Heartaches* was also covered by jazzman Stan Getz on the LP WHAT THE WORLD NEEDS NOW - STAN GETZ PLAYS BACHARACH AND DAVID.

In The Land Of Make Believe
One of Burt Bacharach's favourite Bacharach/David songs. The Drifters were the first act to record this song, as the B-side to their 1964 hit *Vaya Con Dios*. Dionne Warwick also recorded a version in 1964. Dusty Springfield included *In the Land Of Make Believe* on her legendary 1969 album DUSTY IN MEMPHIS. Springfield's version was also released as a single, but didn't chart.

In The Right Kind Of Light
One of several numbers written for, but cut from, the musical PROMISES, PROMISES.

In Times Like These
Written during the Famous Music period, this was recorded by Gene McDaniels as a single in 1964. It was revisited several years later by Stan Getz, on the album WHAT THE WORLD NEEDS NOW – STAN GETZ PLAYS BACHARACH AND DAVID. The Kingston Players also covered the song.

I Say A Little Prayer
One of Bacharach and David's best-known songs, this was first recorded by Dionne Warwick. "I never wanted that record of Dionne's to come out," Burt confessed in Paul Zollo's book SONGWRITERS ON SONGWRITING. "I thought I had blown it on the record, that I took it too fast. I was very happy that I was very wrong."

The song provided a hit for Dionne Warwick, Glen Campbell and Anne Murray and Aretha Franklin. Many others have covered this tune, including Anita Harris, Peter Nero, Sergio Mendes, Johnny Mathis, Isaac Hayes and Dionne Warwick (the latter two as a duet). *I Say A Little Prayer* showed up again in the 1997 Julia Roberts movie MY BEST FRIEND'S WEDDING, along with several other Bacharach-David numbers.

Burt Bacharach & Hal David

I See Things Differently Now
An unrecorded effort from 1975, this may have been intended for the Stephanie Mills album FOR THE FIRST TIME.

I See You For The First Time
Another number from Stephanie Mills' 1975 Motown LP FOR THE FIRST TIME, written and produced by Burt and Hal.

I Smiled Yesterday
The B-side of Dionne Warwick's first single, *Don't Make Me Over*, in 1962.

Is There Another Way To Love You
Another Dionne Warwick flipside, this one playing second fiddle to *Who Can I Turn To* in 1965. This song also appeared on the album THE SENSITIVE SOUND OF DIONNE WARWICK. Also covered by Tony Blackburn.

I Took My Strength From You
This number first appeared as the opening track on Stephanie Mills' album *For The First Time*, with an arrangement by Burt Bacharach. It was subsequently recorded by Burt himself on the FUTURES album and by disco star Sylvester. Dionne Warwick recorded this song in the early 70's for an album that was never released. Eyvind Kang covered the song on the Bacharach tribute album GREAT JEWISH MUSIC.

It Doesn't Matter Anymore
Rick Nelson recorded this overlooked gem for ON THE FLIP SIDE. *It Doesn't Matter Anymore* was covered in the '60s by the Cyrkle (best known for the Paul Simon-penned *Red Rubber Ball*) and, more recently, the BMX Bandits.

It Seemed So Right Last Night
An early composition from Burt and Hal's days at Famous Music in New York, "It Seemed So Right Last Night" was recorded by Mary Mayo in 1958.

It's Love That Really Counts
The first Bacharach/David song ever recorded by Dionne Warwick. Warwick didn't have a record contract but had asked Burt and Hal if she could sing on some of their demos, which led to her signing with Scepter Records. This was then recorded professionally by both the Shirelles and the Exciters (best known for the hit *Tell Him*). In Britain, the Merseybeats' recording was a No. 24 hit in 1963.

Robin Platts

It's Wonderful To Be Young
Cliff Richard sang this title song from the 1962 movie WONDERFUL TO BE YOUNG. Richard's version was also released as a single.

I Wake Up Crying
Recorded by Tom Jones on the TOM JONES FEVER ZONE LP, this was originally cut by Chuck Jackson. Others who lent their vocal stylings to this number include Gene Chandler, Ray Charles and Tyrone Davis.

Juanita's Place
Burt Bacharach recorded this for the B-side of his Liberty Records single *Nikki*. It was also featured in the TV musical ON THE FLIP SIDE, performed by the Celestials.

Kentucky Bluebird
See *Message To Michael*.

Knowing When To Leave
One of the strongest numbers from the PROMISES, PROMISES Broadway show, this song was recorded by Dionne Warwick, Edie Gormé, the Carpenters (as part of a Bacharach/David medley) and Hugo Montenegro. On Broadway, the song's vocalist was Jill O'Hara.

The Last One To Be Loved
One of Dionne Warwick's favourite Bacharach/David songs. Lou Johnson recorded this song in 1964, as the B-side to *Kentucky Bluebird (Send A Message To Martha)*. Burt himself also recorded a version.

The Last Time I Saw My Heart
Written at Famous Music, this was recorded by Marty Robbins in 1958 and included on the album MARTY'S GREATEST HITS.

Let Me Be Lonely
First recorded Dionne Warwick as the flipside of *Do You Know The Way To San Jose*, this song was later tackled by the 5th Dimension on their 1973 album LIVING TOGETHER, GROWING TOGETHER.

Let Me Go To Him
Dionne Warwick's first single release of the 70's, and one of her favourite Bacharach/David numbers. This also showed up on the LP I'LL NEVER FALL IN LOVE AGAIN.

Burt Bacharach & Hal David

Let's Pretend We're Grownup
Written for the musical PROMISES, PROMISES, this number was cut before the show opened. A demo recording was released on the CD BROADWAY FIRST TAKE, VOLUME 2.

Let The Music Play
See *Make The Music Play*.

Let Your Love Come Through
This song, which added lyrics to music from the CASINO ROYALE score, was recorded by Roland Shaw and his orchestra. Also recorded by Kapp artist Shani Wallis in 1967.

A Lifetime Of Loneliness
First recorded in 1963, by Steve Alaimo, this track is better known as the B-side of Jackie DeShannon's Bacharach and David-penned smash *What The World Needs Now Is Love*. The track was subsequently issued as an A-side and became a hit. BILLBOARD magazine said of *A Lifetime of Loneliness* that the "dramatic, moving Bacharach-David ballad will top the success of her *What the World Needs Now Is Love*."

Lisa
Burt Bacharach recorded this song for his 1967 LP REACH OUT, his first album for A&M.

Live Again
Recorded by Irma Thomas, best known for her 1964 U.S. hit *Wish Someone Would Care*.

Living On Plastic
Included on Stephanie Mills' FOR THE FIRST TIME LP, this song hints at the type of material Bacharach and David might have come up with had they continued working together after 1975. A great, overlooked number and a later example of Burt and Hal's "three-minute movie" song scenarios, almost like a cousin to *Do You Know the Way to San Jose?*

Living Together, Growing Together
This catchy number from the movie LOST HORIZON subsequently provided an even catchier hit single for the 5th Dimension. It also appeared on the group's album of the same name. Tony Bennett was the first to record this, in late 1972. Also covered by Ed Ames, Reunion and piano duo Ferrante and Teicher. Ferrante and Teicher's biggest hit was the theme from the movie THE APARTMENT, upon which PROMISES, PROMISES was based.

Living Without Love
An unrecorded number from 1963.

London Life
This charming number was recorded by British singer Anita Harris in 1965 for a British single.

Loneliness Or Happiness
The Drifters cut this number as the flipside to *Sweets For My Sweet* in 1961.

Loneliness Remembers (What Happiness Forgets)
Dionne Warwick was the first artist to record this song, on the B-side of her 1970 single *Let Me Go To Him*. In 1975, it was covered by Stephanie Mills on the Bacharach and David-produced album FOR THE FIRST TIME.

Long After Tonight Is All Over
First recorded by Irma Thomas in 1964, this was subsequently covered by Dusty Springfield on the EVERYTHING'S COMING UP DUSTY album. Jimmy Radcliffe's rendition is perhaps the most recognizable, a U.K. hit in early 1965.

Burt Bacharach & Hal David

Long Ago Last Summer
Long Ago Last Summer was recorded in 1963 by Diana Trask, an Australian singer who had relocated to the United States in the early '60s. Although she did chart with *Long Ago Last Summer*, Trask scored on the country charts in the late '60s and early '70s, with such hits as *Hold What You've Got* and *Lean It All On Me*.

Long Ago Tomorrow
The last of the four singles Burt and Hal wrote for B.J. Thomas and one of the most moving. Not as immediately accessible as, say, *Raindrops Keep Fallin' On My Head*, *Long Ago Tomorrow* is a fine example of how the duo's writing had evolved by 1971.

Like their first collaboration with Thomas, *Long Ago Tomorrow* was a motion picture theme, this time from a 1970 British drama starring Malcolm MacDowell as a paralysed soccer player. The film was released under two different titles – LONG AGO TOMORROW AND THE RAGING MOON.

Long Day, Short Night
A peppy Dionne Warwick album track, from her 1966 album HERE I AM. The Shirelles cut a version that same year, but it wasn't released.

Looking Back Over My Shoulder
This unrecorded number was copyrighted in 1978.

Looking With My Eyes, Seeing With My Heart
Dionne Warwick released this as a single in 1965, to moderate success on the American charts.

Look In My Eyes Maria
First recorded by Jay And The Americans in 1963 (on the flipside of *Come Dance With Me*), this song was covered by Cliff Richard the following year.

The Look Of Love
Written for the poorly received James Bond spoof CASINO ROYALE, the song was inspired by one of the movie's stars.

"It was written as a love theme, or a sexual theme, for Ursula Andress," Bacharach told author Paul Zollo in SONGWRITERS ON SONGWRITING. "It wasn't really a love theme as much as a kind of very understated sexual theme written for her body and her face." The movie version was sung by Dusty Springfield, who also had a hit with the song. (Oddly, neither Springfield's version nor any other was a hit in Britain.) The song also proved successful for Sergio Mendes and Brasil '66 and was covered by Dionne Warwick, Lesley Gore and Johnny Mathis. Ex-Bangle Susannah Hoffs sang a new version in the movie AUSTIN POWERS and a great mid-60's cover by the Zombies showed up on the box set ZOMBIE HEAVEN.

Lorna Doone
The Marty Gold Chorus and Orchestra recorded *Lorna Doone* for a 1959 Kapp Records single.

Lost Horizon
The title song from Bacharach and David's last project, an ambitious musical remake of the 1937 Frank Capra movie about a group of plane crash survivors who discover the lost world of Shangri La in the Himalayas. Though widely panned upon its original release, the film's Bacharach/David soundtrack includes some fine songs, this being one of them.

With lead vocals by Shawn Phillips and a typically dynamic and beautiful arrangement, *Lost Horizon* was released as a single in 1973, making a minor impact on the U.S. charts. The version on the LOST HORIZON soundtrack album differed slightly from the single release, adding an orchestral introduction based on the melody of *If I Could Go Back*.

Lost Little Girl
The Light Brothers recorded *Lost Little Girl* for a 1964 single.

Love Bank
Burt and Hal wrote *Love Bank* with Lou Melamed at Famous Music in 1957. Bob Manning's version of this rockin' little number, made that same year, was released as a single by RCA.

Love In A Goldfish Bowl
This song, recorded by Tommy Sands, was the theme from the 1961 film LOVE IN A GOLDFISH BOWL, starring Sands and Fabian. "You'll have crazy notions and oceans of fun!" promised the picture's tag line.

Love Lessons
Recorded by Louis Prima cohort Sam Butera in 1961.

The Love Of A Boy
Timi Yuro recorded *The Love Of A Boy* for a 1962 single release. Dionne Warwick – who had sung on the demo version, one of her first efforts with Burt and Hal –

released her own version the following year. Dionne's version appeared as an album track (on PRESENTING DIONNE WARWICK) and a B-side (to *Anyone Who Had A Heart*).

Love Was Here Before The Stars
Engelbert Humperdinck, Brian Foley, and Doc Severinsen all took a stab at this number.

Loving Is A Way Of Living
Steve Lawrence recorded this tune from the Famous Music era in 1959. It was also recorded by the London Symphonic Orchestra and Singers for the Bacharach and David volume of their GREAT COMPOSERS series.

Loyal, Resourceful And Cooperative
Hal and Burt wrote a number of songs for PROMISES, PROMISES that were dropped before the show opened. *Loyal, Resourceful And Cooperative* was one of them.

Made In Paris
"This is Ann-Margaret BEFORE she went to Paris...This is Ann-Margaret AFTER she got to Paris...AND what happens in between is what it's all about!" went the tagline.

Trini Lopez (best know for the hit singles *Lemon Tree* and *If I Had A Hammer*) sang this catchy theme song from a 1966 romantic comedy starring Ann-Margaret and Louis Jordan. With a catchy guitar figure reminiscent of the Jackie DeShannon-penned *Needles And Pins*, Lopez' version was also released as a single. The track was arranged and conducted by Bacharach.

Magic Moments
Perry Como recorded *Magic Moments*, Bacharach and David's second hit song, In Britain, Como's No. 1 hit version was joined in the charts by Ronnie Hilton's recording, which made it to No. 22.

Magic Potion
A 1963 Lou Johnson B-side, *Magic Potion* was also recorded by Johnny Sandon and the Remo Four, and by the Searchers.

Make It Easy On Yourself
The second Bacharach and David demo to feature Dionne Warwick's voice was *Make It Easy On Yourself*.

At the time, Dionne had not yet recorded her first single. "We were looking for the right person to sing it," Hal David recalls. "And Eddie Wolpin, who was the head of Famous Music, took it over to Jerry Butler. And Jerry did the song and it came out and started to become a big hit. And Dionne was much perturbed, because she thought that was her song. I think that's what prompted us to take Dionne to Florence Greenberg's Scepter Records and see if we could get her a contract – which we were able to do right away."

Bacharach arranged the version by Jerry Butler, whose biggest chart successes were *Only The Strong Survive* and *Let It Be Me*. Butler's recording was a Top 20 hit in America in 1962, but Dionne charted with her own version several years later.

Others who have tackled *Make It Easy On Yourself* include the Walker Brothers, Burt Bacharach (with his own lead vocal), Cilla Black, the Four Seasons, Steve Lawrence, Jerry Vale, Neil Sedaka, Johnny Mathis and Percy Faith.

Make Room For The Joy
A 1958 composition recorded by Jack Jones. 1959's *Make Room for the Joy* was featured in the movie JUKE BOX RHYTHM.

Make The Music Play
First recorded by the Drifters as *Let The Music Play* in early 1963, this song appeared several months later as a Dionne Warwick single entitled *Make The Music Play*.

The Man Who Shot Liberty Valance
Like *Wives And Lovers*, this was written as an 'exploitation song' to promote the movie of the same title. The song, recorded by Gene Pitney, was not featured in the film.

Me Japanese Boy I Love You
Bobby Goldsboro recorded this song in 1964 as a single and album track. Bacharach arranged Goldsboro's version and, although not officially credited as such, reportedly produced it as well. *Me Japanese Boy* was covered a few years later by Harper's Bizarre, and again in the '90s by the Pizzicato Five.

Message To Martha
See *Message To Michael*.

Message To Michael
It's generally accepted that the first versions of this song were recorded by male singers, Lou Johnson and Jerry Butler, as *Message To Martha*. Dionne Warwick wanted to record the song, but Hal David wasn't comfortable with changing the song to a female perspective. Warwick went ahead anyway, cutting the song with Another producer and having a big hit.

In an interview with author Paul Zollo, Bacharach recalled that the first version of *Message To Michael/Martha* was the one he recorded with Marlene Dietrich (sung in German and titled *Kleine Treue Nachtigall*). It's not clear, though, if he means, Dietrich's version was recorded before Johnson's and Butler's records, or just before Warwick's.

Others who have recorded this song include Jay and the Americans, the Marvelettes, Ramsey Lewis and Deacon Blue. Chrissie Hynde performed *Message To Michael* as part of a medley on the TV special BURT BACHARACH: ONE AMAZING NIGHT.

The Mission Bell By The Wishin' Well
An unrecorded composition from 1958.

Moon Guitar
Billy Vaughn, Tommy Garrett and the Rangoons each recorded this Bacharach/David rarity.

Moon Man
A song from Hal and Burt's stint at Famous Music, *Moon Man* was recorded by Gloria Lambert in 1959.

The Morning Mail
One of Burt and Hal's very first collaborations, penned at Famous Music in 1956. This was recorded by the Galahads.

Move Over And Make Room For Me
An unrecorded composition from 1963.

My Heart Is A Ball Of String
Recorded by the Rangoons in 1961, as the flip side of their *Moon Guitar* single.

My Little Red Book
Manfred Mann was the first group to record this standard. Their version, featuring Bacharach on piano, was commissioned for the movie WHAT'S NEW PUSSYCAT? A more successful version - commercially and artistically - was the version by Love. Others who have covered this tune include Bacharach (on his first LP), the Standells, Mel Torme, Toni Basil (on her 1981 LP WORD OF MOUTH), Ted Nugent and Greg Kihn.

My Rock And Foundation
Peggy Lee (of "Fever" fame) is the only artist known to have recorded this obscure Bacharach/David number, on her 1971 album WHERE DID THEY GO?

The Net
This 1959 composition was recorded by John Ashley. It appears to be a movie theme (possibly an exploitation song), perhaps for the 1959 Alan Ladd picture THE MAN IN THE NET.

The Night That Heaven Fell
This 1958 composition was recorded by Tony Bennett.

Nikki
Burt Bacharach recorded this as the A-side of his one-off single for Liberty Records in 1966. The tune was later re-recorded by Burt on his self-titled 1970 LP for A&M. Doc Severinsen and Vincent Bell also committed versions of *Nikki* to vinyl. Vocal versions were done by Ed Ames and also by Ted Baxter and his Orchestra and chorus on THE BURT BACHARACH/HAL DAVID TREASURY. *Nikki* was used by ABC Television, starting in 1969, as their MOVIE OF THE WEEK theme.

No One Remembers My Name
Stephanie Mills was the first to record this lovely composition, on her FOR THE FIRST TIME LP. Burt also cut a version, for his 1977 album FUTURES.

Odds And Ends (Of A Beautiful Love Affair)
Dionne Warwick enjoyed a moderately successful U.S. single with this composition. Johnny Mathis also did a version, featured on his RAINDROPS KEEP FALLIN' ON MY HEAD LP, along with *Alfie* and, of course, the Bacharach-David title track. A third version was recorded by Billy Vaughn.

Oh Wendy Wendy
See *Wendy, Wendy*.

On A Bicycle Built For Joy
This B.J. Thomas track is actually an alternate take of *Raindrops Keep Fallin On My Head*, featuring an instrumental break in the middle of the song. It was this version, not the hit recording, that was featured in the movie BUTCH CASSIDY AND THE SUNDANCE KID. Both variations appear on the soundtrack album.

On My Way
Burt and Hal wrote this song in 1999 for the movie ISN'T SHE GREAT. It was performed on the soundtrack by Dionne Warwick.

On The Flip Side
Rick Nelson recorded this number for the TV musical of the same name.

One Less Bell To Answer
Although first recorded by Keely Smith in 1967, the best-known version of this song was the 5th Dimension's recording, which reached No. 2 in 1970. Gladys Knight and the Pips, Shirley Bassey, Barbra Streisand and Burt himself all recorded the song in the wake of the hit version.

Only Love Can Break A Heart
Gene Pitney's version of this tune was arranged and conducted by Burt, but produced by Aaron Schroeder and Wally Gold. Pitney's version reached the American Top 10 in 1962, but the song also provided minor U.S. hits for Margaret Whiting (in 1967) and Bobby Vinton (in 1977).

Only The Strong, Only The Brave
This track appeared on the 1965 album THE SENSITIVE SOUND OF DIONNE WARWICK. It was also released as the flipside of Warwick's *Looking With My Eyes* single.

Oooh, My Love
Vic Damone – best known for his 1958 hit *On The Street Where You Live* – recorded this song from Burt and Hal's Famous Music period. Bacharach was Damone's musical director during the '50s.

Open Your Heart
Former Miss America Vanessa Williams recorded this number Burt and Hal wrote for the movie ISN'T SHE GREAT.

Our Little Secret
Jerry Orbach and Edward Winter sang this number in the Broadway production of PROMISES, PROMISES.

Paper Maché
This great 1970 Dionne Warwick single didn't quite make the American Top Forty.

Paradise Island
Burt and Hal wrote this with Paul Hampton at Famous Music in 1959. It was recorded by the Four Aces.

Peggy's In The Pantry
This 1956 composition, recorded by Sherry Parsons, has also been referred to as *Peggy's Pantry* or *Peggy's In The Party*. An article in the PHOENIX NEW TIMES described the track as "a bizarre Sherry Parsons B-side from 1957 in which a jilted girl threatens to scratch her rival Peggy's eyes out for stealing her date."

Peggy's in the Pantry was recently aired during CBS' profile of Bacharach on the SUNDAY MORNING program. "A dog is a dog," commented Bacharach, upon hearing the song for the first time in many years. "You know, you try to forget it."

Phone Calls
Written for PROMISES, PROMISES, but dropped during rehearsals.

Please Let Go
Another number Stephanie Mills' 1975 LP FOR THE FIRST TIME.

Please Make Him Love Me
The B-side of Dionne Warwick's 1963 single *Make The Music Play*. The song was also recorded by Ray Lynn in 1966, as *Please Make Her Love Me*.

Presents From The Past
Burt and Hal came up with this number in their office at Famous Music in New York, in 1957. It was recorded by Cathy Carr, best known for the 1956 hit *Ivory Tower*.

Promise Her Anything
Tom Jones sang this theme for the 1966 comedy starring Warren Beatty. Despite its driving arrangement and typically energetic Jones vocal, this only achieved moderate success in America. In Britain, the song was relegated to a B-side.

Promises, Promises
The title song for Hal and Burt's first (and only) Broadway musical. Since the songs had to fit in with Neil Simon's book (i.e. script) for the show, the lyrics for the project tended to be written before the music, which wasn't usually the case with Bacharach and David. Although not an easy song to sing, there were several cover versions of *Promises, Promises*, the most successful by Dionne Warwick. Sung in the show by Jerry Orbach, it was also recorded by Gary Puckett and the Union Gap, Peter Paul and Mary, Herb Alpert (on the 1974 LP YOU SMILE - THE SONG BEGINS) and Percy Faith.

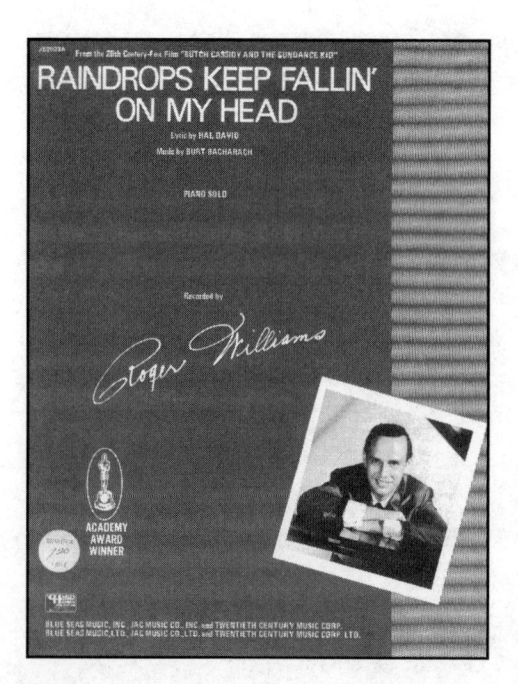

Question Me An Answer
Ed Ames was among the artists who covered this whimsical tune from LOST HORIZON, sung in the movie by Bobby Van.

Rain From The Skies
A 1962 composition, recorded by Peter Lemengello. Also cut by Adam Wade in 1963.

Raindrops Keep Fallin' On My Head
B.J. Thomas scored a huge hit with this song from the movie BUTCH CASSIDY AND THE SUNDANCE KID. Others who have recorded this standard include Dionne Warwick, Percy Faith, Peter Nero, Mel Torme,

Robert Goulet and Lawrence Welk. In Britain, Thomas' version was overtaken in the charts by another recording: while B.J.'s version only reached No. 38, a recording by French singer Sacha Distel made it to No. 10. The song also provided another U.K. hit for Bobbie Gentry, whose version reached No. 40.

Reach Out For Me
Lou Johnson was the first artist to record *Reach Out For Me*, for a 1963 single release. Johnson's version was a minor hit, but Dionne Warwick released a much more successful rendition the following year. Nancy Wilson recorded a superb version, Burt cut a version for his REACH OUT LP, and Olivia Newton-John did her own version in the '70s.

Reflections
This was written for the movie LOST HORIZON, in which it was sung by Sally Kellerman.

The Right To Love You
An unrecorded 1963 collaboration.

Rome Will Never Leave You
Actor Richard Chamberlain recorded this song for a 1964 single, which briefly edged its way into the U.S. Top 100.

Sad Sack
Burt and Hal wrote this for the 1957 movie of the same name. The song was recorded (and released as a single) by the film's star, Jerry Lewis.

Saturday Night In Tia Juana
The Five Blobs, who also cut the Burt Bacharach-Mack David theme from the movie THE BLOB, recorded this 1959 composition. Another version was recorded by Cindy and Lindy.

Saturday Sunshine
Burt Bacharach recorded this pleasant tune as a single for Kapp Records in 1963. Two recordings exist – one with vocals, the other mostly instrumental. Johnny Mathis also committed a version to vinyl, as did Petula Clark (on the flipside of *True Love Never Runs Smooth*).

Burt Bacharach & Hal David

Say Goodbye
Pat Boone sang this, on the B-side of his 1965 single *Baby Elephant Walk* (the Henry Mancini composition, which featured lyrics by Hal David). New Zealand's John Rowles recorded a version, on the flip side of his 1969 single *M'lady*.

The Secret Of Staying Young
An unrecorded collaboration dated 1957 - although the title suggests a LOST HORIZON reject.

Send A Message To Martha
See *Message To Michael*.

Send Me No Flowers
Doris Day sang this movie theme, from a comedy in which she starred with Rock Hudson and Tony Randall. The version released as a single is a different recording from the one featured in the movie.

Send My Picture To Scranton, PA.
Musically reminiscent of the BUTCH CASSIDY score, this was released B-side of B.J. Thomas' hit *I Just Can't Help Believing*. It was also included on his album EVERYBODY'S OUT OF TOWN.

Share the Joy
One of Burt's most haunting melodies, somewhat overlooked due to its inclusion in the much-maligned LOST HORIZON.

She Likes Basketball
Another number from PROMISES, PROMISES, performed in the show by Jerry Orbach.

Sing For The Children
Written with John Bettis in 1993, and recorded by James Ingram.

Sittin' In A Tree House
Marty Robbins recorded this song in 1958, as the B-side of *She Was Only Seventeen*. Not really a hit, *Sittin' In A Tree House* was nonetheless included on the album MARTY'S GREATEST HITS.

So Long Johnny
A great Jackie DeShannon B-side, discovered by flipping over the *Windows And Doors* 45. *So Long Johnny* also showed up on Jackie's ARE YOU READY FOR THIS? album.

Somebody Else's Sweetheart
A 1961 composition, recorded by the Wanderers.

Something Big
Mark Lindsey (lead singer of Paul Revere and the Raiders) sang this theme from the 1971 western of the same title, which starred Dean Martin, Brian Keith and Honor Blackman.

"Everybody wants to do something big once in his life," read the poster. "It's just that most people don't have to hold up a stagecoach, steal a girl, and swap her for a gun to do it."

Lindsey's version of *Something Big* was released as a single, which didn't achieve much success. Burt himself took the lead vocal on a great version of *Something Big*, included on his LIVING TOGETHER LP.

The Story Behind My Tears
Recorded by Kenny Lynch in 1961, for a British single release. In the U.S., Vic Dana recorded the song.

The Story Of My Life
Bacharach and David's first hit, written in 1957. In America, Marty Robbins had a big hit with this number, with subsequent versions courtesy of Paul Anka and Frankie Laine. In Britain, the Marty Robbins version was not a hit, but the song proved chart worthy for three other artists: Michael Holliday (whose version made No. 1), Alma Cogan and Dave King.

Suddenly Last Summer
This 1959 composition was probably written for the Elizabeth Taylor movie of the same title, possibly as an exploitation song.

Sunny Weather Lover
Dionne Warwick, reunited with Burt and Hal after twenty years, recorded this song for her FRIENDS CAN BE LOVERS album. It was Bacharach and David's first collaboration for almost two decades, but didn't attract much attention.

"We thought it was good," recalls Hal. "It just didn't work. I didn't think it was one of

Burt Bacharach & Hal David

our great songs. It was a good song. I think, under certain circumstances, it could have happened."

Take A Broken Heart
Rick Nelson sang this number in the 1966 TV musical ON THE FLIP SIDE. Nelson's version was also released as a 45, but didn't chart.

Tell The Truth And Shame The Devil
During Burt and Hal's early days at Famous Music, staff writers were continually swapping writing partners and working in ever changing configurations. In 1956, both Burt and Hal collaborated with Margery S. Wolpin on this number (some sources credit the third writer as "Martita"). The Harry Carter Singers recorded *Tell The Truth And Shame The Devil* on their album THE FANTASTIC SOUNDS OF...

Ten Times Forever More
Johnny Mathis recorded this early Bacharach/David number on his 1971 LP LOVE STORY.

That Guy's In Love With You
See *This Guy's In Love With You*.

That Kind Of Woman
This 1958 movie theme was recorded by Joe Williams with the Count Basie Orchestra, and was also the title track on one of his albums.

That's Not The Answer
This song was included on the 1965 long player THE SENSITIVE SOUND OF DIONNE WARWICK.

That's The Way I'll Come To You
Jack Jones recorded this song in 1963. Also covered by Bobby Vee.

(There Goes The) Forgotten Man
Jimmy Radcliffe recorded this song in 1964, a year before scoring a U.K. hit with the Bacharach and David-penned *Long After Tonight Is All Over*. Also known as *(Here Comes) The Forgotten Man*.

They Don't Give Medals (To Yesterday's Heroes)
Rick Nelson was the first artist to record this great tune, for ON THE FLIP SIDE in

1966. It was also cut by Dionne Warwick (as the B-side to *The Green Grass Starts To Grow*) and by Chuck Jackson. The song was subsequently included on the three-record set THE COMPOSERS SERIES VOL. I: BURT BACHARACH AND HAL DAVID, performed by the London Symphonic Orchestra And Singers. Hal Frazier, Lainie Kazan and Ben E. King also recorded this lesser-known Bacharach/David gem.

They're Gonna Love It
Donna Jean Young sang this number in ON THE FLIP SIDE.

The Things I Will Not Miss
Another number from the poorly received LOST HORIZON project. This duet is probably one of the film's musical low-points, but was covered by Diana Ross and Marvin Gaye during the sessions for their 1973 LP DIANA AND MARVIN. That version was left off the album but reinstated, as a bonus track, on the 2001 CD reissue.

Third From The Left
An unrecorded composition from 1958.

This Empty Place
Dionne Warwick's second single for Scepter Records. *This Empty Place* and Dionne's third single *Make The Music Play* fared poorly on the charts, but the singer recalls them getting a lot of airplay at the time. "They were just turntable hits," she told GOLDMINE in 1990, "Records the DJ's liked, but nobody else bought." *This Empty Place* was later recorded by Stephanie Mills (on FOR THE FIRST TIME) and Cissy Houston.

This Guy's In Love With You
Herb Alpert recorded the first and best-known version of this song, a huge hit in 1968. Originally entitled *That Guy's In Love With You*, the song was not written with Herb in mind, but was altered to suit him, and became first vocal success for the artist previously known as the trumpet-blowing frontman of the Tijuana Brass. Many artists have covered this standard, including Dusty Springfield, Petula Clark, Dionne Warwick (whose version was a Top 10 hit), the Spiral Staircase and Salena Jones.

Three Friends, Two Lovers
The Turbans, who had their biggest success with the 1955 single *When You Dance*, recorded this obscure Bacharach/David number in 1961.

Burt Bacharach & Hal David

Three Important Things
An unrecorded number from 1970.

Tick Tock Goes the Clock
This is one of several songs written for, but cut from, PROMISES, PROMISES. A new version was recorded in 1994, and featured on one of the LOST IN BOSTON CDs, which feature rare Broadway tunes. The 1968 demo recording of this song (produced by Burt and Hal) was recently released on the CD BROADWAY FIRST TAKE, VOLUME 2.

The Timeless Tide
This composition from 1959 was recorded by Joe Arthur.

To Wait For Love
Although not a very well-known song, *To Wait For Love* has been recorded by a number of different artists. The most popular version was Herb Alpert's, released as the follow-up single to *This Guy's In Love With You*. Tom Jones had previously recorded it, on the B-side of his first hit *It's Not Unusual*, while Jackie DeShannon's version (arranged and conducted by Burt) turned up on her 1966 album ARE YOU READY FOR THIS? Jay and the Americans and Paul Anka also covered this song, in 1964 and 1965, respectively.

Too Late To Worry
Babs Tino recorded this rarity in early 1961. Also covered by Sophia Loren and Richard Anthony. The latter version is a French adaptation (translated by Andre Salvet), called *Donne-Moi Ma Chance*. The French version was also reportedly covered by the Classels and Rosita Salvador.

Trains And Boats And Planes
Billy J. Kramer and Dionne Warwick both enjoyed U.S. hits with this Bacharach and David standard. In Britain, Kramer's version shared the charts with Burt's own rendition, while Anita Harris' version didn't chart at all.

Trial By Jury
An unrecorded number from 1966.

True Love Never Runs Smooth
A U.S. hit for Gene Pitney in 1963, this tune never charted in Britain. However, Petula Clark's version was released as a single in Britain, paired with *Saturday Sunshine*. Another version was recorded in 1963 by Don and Juan, best known for their 1962 single *What's Your Name?*

Try To See It My Way
Rick Nelson and Joannie Sommers sang this number in the TV musical ON THE FLIP SIDE. Peggy March (best known for her massive hit *I Will Follow Him*) also recorded a great version, released as a 45 in 1969.

Turkey Lurkey Time
Donna McKechnie, Margo Sappington and Baayork Lee performed this song in the original Broadway production of PROMISES, PROMISES.

24 Hours From Tulsa
"I wrote that (lyric) to a melody that Burt wrote," recalls Hal David. "And that's what the melody said to me. Music speaks to a lyric writer – at least, it should speak to a lyric writer. And that's what the music said to me. And why it did, I don't know. I don't think I had ever been to Tulsa. I've been to Tulsa since. I've always liked what I call 'narrative songs' – story songs. When I hear music, very often I hear a story. The fact that it's Tulsa, as opposed to Dallas, I don't think is terribly meaningful. The sound of 'Tulsa' rang in my ear."

Gene Pitney was the first to record this song, with subsequent versions cut by Dusty Springfield and Jay and The Americans

Two Against The World
An unrecorded composition from 1957.

Underneath The Overpass
A 1957 composition, written at Famous Music in New York, recorded by Jo Stafford.

Upstairs
Jerry Orbach sang this composition in the original production of PROMISES, PROMISES.

The Very First Person I Met (In California)
An unrecorded 1970 composition.

W.E.E.P.
A 1966 composition, recorded by Peter Matz in 1967. Featured as a radio jingle in ON THE FLIP SIDE.

Burt Bacharach & Hal David

Walk Little Dolly
This Dionne Warwick track appeared in 1967, on the flipside of *The Windows Of The World* and on the WINDOWS OF THE WORLD album. Covered by Terry Baxter in 1971.

Walk On By
One of Bacharach and David's best, and best-known songs, first recorded by Dionne Warwick at the same recording date as *Anyone Who Had A Heart*.

"That song was the turning point in all our careers," Warwick told GOLDMINE in 1990. "We never looked back after it and for almost 10 years Burt and Hal supplied me with nothing but the best."

The Beach Boys recorded an unfinished version of "Walk On By" in the late '60s, eventually released as a CD bonus track. Others who have covered the song include Isaac Hayes, Gloria Gaynor, the Average White Band, Mel Torme, Sybil, D Train and the Stranglers.

Walk The Way You Talk
Dionne Warwick sang this number on the VERY DIONNE LP. Also covered by Sergio Mendes.

Walkin' Backwards Down The Road
Dionne Warwick recorded this number for her 1968 album VALLEY OF THE DOLLS.

Wanting Things
This number from PROMISES, PROMISES was performed in the original show by Edward Winter. Dionne Warwick, Astrud Gilberto and the Pointer Sisters subsequently recorded it.

Warm And Tender
Warm and Tender first appeared in the 1957 movie LIZZIE, sung by Johnny Mathis. Bobby Vinton also cut a version, which turned up on the flipside of his U.S. hit *My Heart Belongs To Only You*.

Wastin' Away For You
A 1961 composition, recorded in 1962 by the Russells.

The Way I Feel About You
Stephanie Mills recorded this tune for her 1975 album FOR THE FIRST TIME.

Wendy, Wendy
A song from the Famous Music era (1958), this was also known as *Oh Wendy, Wendy*. Recorded by the Four Coins.

What A Night
Another composition from the offices of Famous Music, this one written in 1959.

What Am I Doing Here?
Written for PROMISES, PROMISES, this song didn't make the final cut, but was recorded by Edie Gormé. It was later performed by Liz Callaway, on the album LOST IN BOSTON II. The original demo recording appeared on the CD BROADWAY FIRST TAKE, VOLUME 2.

What The World Needs Now Is Love

Reportedly written for Gene Pitney, an early version of this composition was offered to Dionne Warwick, who tended to get the first crack at any new Bacharach/David songs in the mid-'60s. When she turned it down, Burt and Hal almost abandoned the song.

"There wasn't great enthusiasm for it," recalls Hal. "(But) I had great enthusiasm for it. We were asked by Liberty Records to record Jackie (DeShannon), who was a great singer – and a good songwriter, too. I remember we were in an office in the RKO Building and played a number of songs for Jackie. And I suggested to Burt that we play *What The World Needs Now Is Love*. And we did and Jackie said, 'That's the one I want to do.' Jackie was the catalyst. She was excited about doing that song."

The resulting track was a big hit for DeShannon, the first of several singles Burt and Hal wrote for her. Dionne subsequently recorded the song, with a similar arrangement to the DeShannon version.

In 1997, Burt performed the song for his appearance in the movie AUSTIN POWERS. His version segued into (and then back out of) a version by the Posies. Tony Bennett and Tom Jones also each rendered the song in their own inimitable styles.

What's New Pussycat?
Burt and Hal wrote this number for the Peter Sellers film of the same title and recruited Tom Jones to sing it. It's hard to imagine anyone else daring to record this, but Burt gave it a try on his first solo album, with a lead vocal by CABARET star Joel Gray. Needless to say, Gray's vocal paled in comparison to Jones' rendition.

Where Can You Take A Girl?
Paul Reed, Norman Shelly, Vince O'Brien and Dick O'Neill were the actors who sang this ditty in the original production of PROMISES, PROMISES.

Where Knowledge Ends (Faith Begins)
Another song from the LOST HORIZON soundtrack, cited by Hal David as one of his favourites from that project. Also known as *Where Knowledge Ends (Trust Me)*.

Where There's A Heartache
Pat Boone recorded *Where There's A Heartache* in 1971, for the flip side of his single *C'mon, Give A Hand*. The Sandpipers, Oliver, Astrud Gilberto and Van McCoy also lent their talents to this lovely song, which is a vocal version of one of Bacharach's main themes from the BUTCH CASSIDY AND THE SUNDANCE KID score, used in *Not Goin' Home Anymore* and *Come Touch the Sun*.

Where Would I Go
Dionne Warwick's 1968 long player VALLEY OF THE DOLLS featured this song in its line-up.

Who Gets The Guy (AKA Who Gets The Girl)
This might just be Dionne Warwick's most underrated Bacharach/David single. A classic example of the duo's style, it only achieved moderate success in the States and didn't chart at all in Britain. The song is registered with ASCAP as *Who Gets The Girl*, suggesting that Bacharach and David had originally intended it for a male vocalist.

Who Is Gonna Love Me?
This 1968 Dionne Warwick offering made the lower reaches of the U.S. Top Forty. Although Bacharach cites this as one of his favourite lesser-known Bacharach/David compositions, *Who Is Gonna Love Me?* has rarely been covered, one exception being a version by Peter Nero.

Whoever You Are, I Love You
Jill O'Hara sang this in the original production of PROMISES, PROMISES. Dionne Warwick, Tony Bennett, Bobby Short and Anita Kerr also tried their hand at this number.

Who's Been Sleeping In My Bed?
Linda Scott, best known for the hit *I've Told Every Little Star*, recorded this for a 1963 single release.

Wild Honey
This 1957 composition – one of Burt and Hal's first collaborations – was recorded by Cathy Carr.

Window Wishin'
Dionne Warwick recorded this for her 1966 long player HERE I AM.

Windows And Doors
Recorded as a single by Jackie DeShannon, *Windows And Doors* revisited the lyrical theme of *A House Is Not A Home*. It also showed up on DeShannon's 1966 album ARE YOU READY FOR THIS?

The Windows Of Heaven
A 1962 composition recorded by the Four Coins.

The Windows Of The World
"*Windows Of The World* is a song I felt very keenly about," says Hal David. "We were going through the Vietnam war. And I had two sons. And so I pictured my sons getting involved. Thinking about my older son, who was going to be of age pretty soon at that time. And that was my feeling. I wrote that as a political song or as a father would do."

The Windows Of The World was first recorded by Dionne Warwick, who recently named it her favourite song. Also covered by Isaac Hayes and the Pretenders.

The Wine Is Young
Dionne Warwick recorded this song for the I'LL NEVER FALL IN LOVE AGAIN album in 1970. Warwick still cites this as one of her very favourite Bacharach/David songs.

Winter Warm
Burt and Hal penned this unrecorded number at Famous Music in 1957. Gale Storm recorded it in 1959 on her Dot album GALE STORM SINGS.

Wishin' And Hopin'
Dusty Springfield rescued this Dionne Warwick track from B-side obscurity and turned it into an American hit in 1964. In Britain, the Merseybeats did the same.

With Open Arms
Jane Morgan recorded *With Open Arms* in 1959, her version being one of Burt and Hal's first chart successes. In Britain, Adam Faith cut a version for a B-side.

Wives And Lovers

Jack Jones sang this unforgettable number. The song written for the 1963 movie comedy WIVES AND LOVERS, which starred Janet Leigh, Van Johnson and Shelley Winters.

"We were asked to write what was called an 'exploitation song'," Hal David recalls. "It was never meant to be in the film, but it was meant to come out and every time it got played the name of the film would be performed. It was really a promotion song - an exploitation song - which was very common in those days."

Jones recorded his version at an August 13, 1963 session, while Andy Williams, Julie London and Dionne Warwick were among the others vocalists who attempted this classic.

Wonderful To Be Young

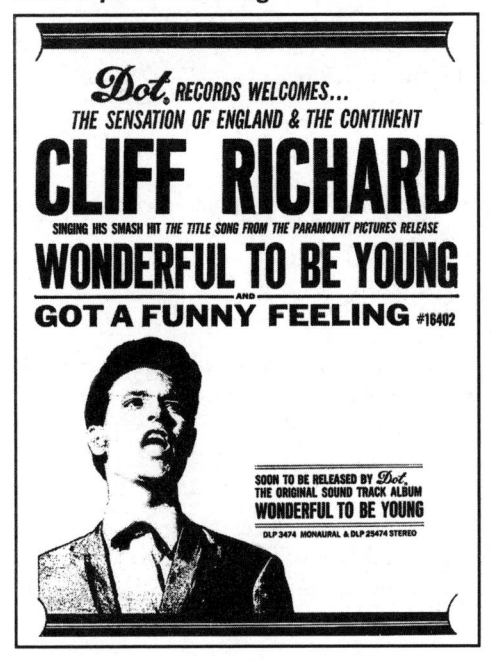

This song from the Famous era was written as the theme to the 1961 Cliff Richard film THE YOUNG ONES, which starred Richard, his group the Shadows and Robert Morley. (In America the film was released as WONDERFUL TO BE YOUNG.) Richard sang *Wonderful to Be Young* and released it as a single in 1962.

The World Is A Circle

From the LOST HORIZON soundtrack, this song has been described as being the "would-be hit" from the score. It was also the title track of a Disneyland Records album that included three songs from the movie. Andy Williams, Ed Ames, Frank Pourcel and the Sandpipers were among those who committed it to vinyl before the backlash hit.

Wouldn't That Be A Stroke Of Luck

Written for the musical PROMISES, PROMISES, this number was cut during the show's Boston run and replaced by *I'll Never Fall In Love Again*.

You Can't Buy Happiness

An unrecorded composition from 1967, also known as *You Can't Build Happiness*.

You Learn To Love By Loving

This unrecorded composition was copyrighted in 1978.

You'll Never Get To Heaven

Originally recorded by Dionne Warwick, this number was successfully revived by the Stylistics in the early 70's.

You'll Think Of Someone

Another number from PROMISES, PROMISES, this one a duet between Jerry Orbach and Jill O' Hara.

Burt Bacharach & Hal David

Young And Wild
From the Famous Music era (copyrighted 1959), this may have been written for the 1958 film of the same title. It was recorded by the Five Blobs for a 1960 single release.

A Young Pretty Girl Like You
Jerry Orbach and A. Larry Haines performed this in the original production of PROMISES, PROMISES.

Your Lips Are Warmer Than Your Heart
This 1956 composition was one of Burt and Hal's first collaborations. Singer Rose Marie Jun (billed as "Rosemary June") recorded it on a single for United Artists in 1960.

You're Telling Our Secrets
Dee Clark recorded this number in 1962, on the B-side of *Don't Walk Away From Me*. Not to be confused with Another song by the same name, recorded by Teresa Brewer in 1955.

You're The Dream
One of Burt and Hal's first collaborations, recorded in 1956 by the Marvellos.

You've Got It All Wrong
Burt and Hal's first collaboration since *Sunny Weather Lover* was a new song for a revival of PROMISES, PROMISES.

"Neil Simon asked us recently to write another song for a new Broadway production of Promises, which we did," Bacharach told Paul Zollo in the latter's book SONGWRITERS ON SONGWRITING. "It was kind of interesting, we did it in the same way we originally wrote the show: Hal brought in a lyric, and I got a general kind of first floor of the house built, you might say, and then started designating where I wanted to change musically from what's just been written."

Songs by Burt Bacharach and Hal David – Discography

This is a selected discography of recorded versions of Bacharach/David songs. A complete listing of every recorded version would probably fill an entire book, so I focused mostly on 'important' recordings, first recordings, those featuring the involvement of Burt and Hal, with some others included for the sake of interest. All songs listed here are Bacharach-David compositions, except for those which are in lower case and in parentheses. I have done this to clarify instances where the A-side was not by Bacharach and David, but the B-side was. Otherwise, if only one side of a single is listed, it is the A-side. Most of these are U.S. releases, except as indicated, although a few overseas titles may have slipped in undetected.

Singles:

Steve Alaimo:
A Lifetime Of Loneliness (Checker 1042, 1963)

Herb Alpert:
Casino Royale (A&M 850, 1967)
This Guy's In Love With You (A&M 929, 1968)
To Wait For Love (A&M 964, 1968)

Ed Ames:
Lost Horizon/Question Me An Answer (RCA 74-0800, 1972)
(butterflies are free)/The World Is A Circle (RCA 74-0883, 1973)

John Andrea:
Look In My Eyes Maria (MGM 13423, 1965)

Paul Anka:
From Rocking Horse To Rocking Chair (RCA Victor 47-8311, 1964)

Joe Arthur:
(when you care enough)/The Timeless Tide (Seeco 6050, 1960)

John Ashley:
The Hangman/The Net (Dot 15942, 1959)

Frankie Avalon:
Gotta Get A Girl (Chancellor 1077, 1961)

Burt Bacharach & Hal David

Tony Bennett:
The Night That Heaven Fell (Columbia 4-41237, 1958)
Living Together, Growing Together ((MGM/Verve 10690, 1972)
(tell her it's snowing)/If I Could Go Back (Verve 10714, 1973)

Brook Benton:
A House Is Not A Home (Mercury 7203, 1964)
(do your own thing)/I Just Don't Know What To Do With Myself (Cotillion 44007, 1968)

Cilla Black:
Alfie (Capitol 5674, 1966)
What The World Needs Now Is Love (DJM 70007, 1969)

Tony Blackburn:
Is There Another Way To Love You? (Fontana TF-601, 1965) (UK)

Pat Boone:
(c'mon, give a hand)/Where There's A Heartache (MGM 14282, 1971)

Bobby Brooks:
What's New Pussycat? (Hit 219, 1965)

Sam Butera:
(grasshopper, let him hop)/Love Lessons (Dot 16250, 1961)

Jerry Butler:
Make It Easy On Yourself (Vee Jay 451, 1962)

The Carpenters:
(They Long To Be) Close To You (A&M 1183, 1970)

Cathy Carr:
Wild Honey (Fraternity 765-2, 1957)
Presents From The Past (Fraternity 782, 1957)

Richard Chamberlain:
Blue Guitar/(They Long To Be) Close To You (MGM 13170, 1963)
Rome Will Never Leave You (MGM 13285, 1964)

Guy Chandler:
Lost Horizon (Oweman Records OM-2016, 1973)

Ray Charles:
(smack dab in the middle)/I Wake Up Crying (ABC 10588, 1964)

Cher:
Alfie (Imperial 66192, 1966)

Sylvaine Clair:
Do Not Speak To Me Of Love (Polydor 2457008, 1970)

Dee Clark:
You're Telling Our Secrets (Vee Jay 409, 1961)

Perry Como:
Magic Moments (RCA 7128, 1958)

The Cryan' Shames:
Please Stay/What's New Pussycat (London 1001, 1966)

Alan Dale:
I Cry More (Coral 61699, 1956)

Vic Damone:
Oooh My Love (Columbia 4-41245, 1958)

Billie Davis:
The Last One To Be Loved (Jerden 758, 1966)

Doris Day:
Send Me No Flowers (Columbia 43153, 1964)

The Delfonics:
Alfie (Philly Groove 177, 1973)

The Dells:
This Guy's In Love With You/Walk On By (Cadet 5691, 1972)

Jackie DeShannon:
What The World Needs Now Is Love/A Lifetime Of Loneliness (Imperial 66110, 1965)
A Lifetime Of Loneliness (Imperial 66132, 1965)
Come And Get Me (Imperial 66171, 1966)
Windows And Doors/So Long, Johnny (Imperial 66196, 1966)

Sacha Distel:
Raindrops Keep Fallin' On My Head (Warner 7345, 1969)

Don and Juan:
True Love Never Runs Smooth (Big Top 3145, 1963)

The Drifters:
(sweets for my sweet)/Loneliness Or Happiness (Atlantic 2117, 1961)
(on broadway)/Let The Music Play (Atlantic 2182, 1963)

Burt Bacharach & Hal David

In The Land Of Make Believe (Atlantic 2216, 1963)

The Eligibles:
Faker Faker (Capitol 4265, 1959)

Bobby Engemann:
Blue On Blue (Capitol P-2476, 1969)

The 5th Dimension:
One Less Bell To Answer (Bell 940, 1970)
Living Together, Growing Together (Bell 45310, 1973)

The Five Blobs:
(the blob)/Saturday Night In Tia Juana (Columbia 41250, 1958)
(juliet)/Young And Wild (Joy 230, 1959)

Brian Foley:
Love Was Here Before The Stars (Kapp 861, 1967)

The Four Aces:
Paradise Island (Decca 9-30874, 1959)

The Four Coins:
Wendy, Wendy (Epic 9286, 1958)
The Windows Of Heaven (Jubilee 5419, 1962)

Aretha Franklin:
I Say A Little Prayer (Atlantic 2546, 1968)
(Without Love)/Don't Go Breaking My Heart (Atlantic 3224, 1974)

Hal Frazier:
(spin, spin)/They Don't Give Medals To Yesterday's Heroes (Reprise 043, 1966)

The Gallahads:
The Morning Mail (Jubilee 5252, 1956)

Marty Gold:
Lorna Doone (Kapp Records, 1959)

Bobby Goldsboro:
Me Japanese Boy, I Love You (United Artists 742, 1964)

Charlie Gracie:
I Looked For You (Roulette 4255, 1960)

R.B. Greaves:
(There's) Always Something There To Remind Me (Atco 6726, 1970)

Merv Griffin:
Along Came Joe (Carlton 545, 1959)

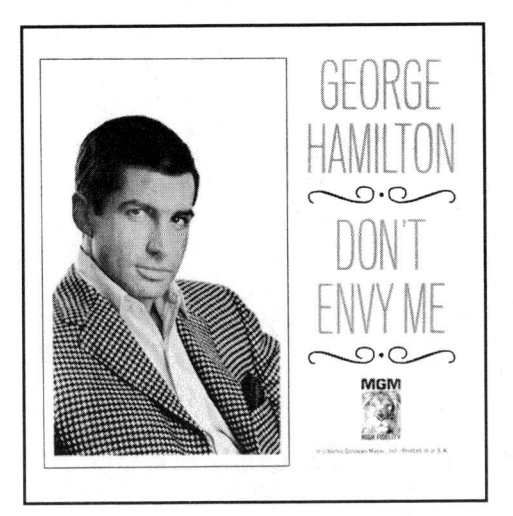

George Hamilton:
Don't Envy Me (MGM 13178, 1963)

Anita Harris:
London Life (Pye 7N15971, 1965) (UK release)
Trains And Boats And Planes (Warner 5638, 1965)

Isaac Hayes:
Walk On By (Enterprise 9003, 1969)
(I Stand Accused)/I Just Don't Know What To Do With Myself (Enterprise 9017, 1970)
The Look Of Love (Enterprise 9028, 1971)

Everit Herter:
(don't get serious)/Boys Were Made for Girls (Capitol 4383, 1960)

The Hollies (with Peter Sellers):
After The Fox (United Artists 50079, 1965)

Cissy Houston:
This Empty Place (Janus 131, 1970)

Engelbert Humperdinck:
I'm A Better Man (Parrot 40040, 1969)

Tommy Hunt:
I Just Don't Know What To Do With Myself (Scepter 1236, 1962)

Chuck Jackson:
I Wake Up Crying (Wand 110, 1961)
The Breaking Point (Wand 115, 1961)

Jay And The Americans:
Look In My Eyes, Maria (United Artists 669, 1963)
To Wait For Love (United Artists 693, 1964)

Lou Johnson:
If I Never Get To Love You (Big Top 3115, 1963)
Reach Out For Me/Magic Potion (Big Top 3153, 1963)

Burt Bacharach & Hal David

(There's) Always Something There To Remind Me/Magic Potion (Instrumental)
(Big Hill 552, 1964)
Kentucky Bluebird (Send A Message To Martha)/The Last One To Be Loved
(Big Hill 553, 1964)

Marv Johnson:
Another Tear Falls (United Artists 590, 1963)

Jack Jones:
That's The Way I'll Come To You (Kapp 534, 1963)
Wives And Lovers (Kapp 551, 1963)

Tom Jones:
(it's not unusual)/To Wait For Love (Parrot 9737, 1965)
What's New, Pussycat? (Parrot 9765, 1965)
Promise Her Anything (Parrot 9809, 1966)

Rosemary June (AKA Rose Marie Jun):
Your Lips Are Warmer Than Your Heart (United Artists 219. 1960)

Lainie Kazan:
They Don't Give Medals To Yesterday's Heroes (MGM 13943, 1968)

Anita Kerr:
Alfie/A House Is Not A Home (Dot 17210, 1969)

Ben E. King:
They Don't Give Medals To Yesterday's Heroes (Atco 6454, 1966)

Billy J Kramer with the Dakotas:
Trains And Boats And Planes (Imperial 66115, 1965)

Gloria Lambert:
Moon Man (Columbia 4-41402, 1959)

Steve Lawrence:
Loving Is A Way Of Living (ABC Paramount 10005, 1959)

The Lettermen:
Anyone Who Had A Heart (Capitol 2196, 1968)

Jerry Lewis:
Sad Sack (Decca 9-30503, 1956)

The Light Brothers:
Lost Little Girl (ABC-Paramount 10536, 1964)

Mark Lindsay:
Something Big (Columbia 45506, 1971)

Trini Lopez:
Made In Paris (Reprise 0435, 1965)

Love:
My Little Red Book (Elektra 45603, 1966)

Ray Lynn:
Please Make Her Love Me (Epic 10023, 1966)

Gene McDaniels:
In Times Like These (Liberty 55231, 1959)
(chip chip)/Another Tear Falls (Liberty 55405, 1962)
(There Goes) The Forgotten Man (Liberty 55752, 1964)

The Magistrates:
After The Fox (MGM 13980, 1968)

Manfred Mann:
My Little Red Book (Ascot 2184, 1965)

Bob Manning:
Love Bank (RCA, 1957)

Peggy March:
Try To See It My Way (RCA 47-9718, 1969)

The Marvellos:
You're The Dream (Theron 117, 1956)

Johnny Mathis:
Warm And Tender (Columbia 40851, 1957)
Don't Go Breaking My Heart (Columbia 44-4517, 1968)
Ten Times Forevermore (Columbia 4-45323, 1971)

Mary Mayo:
It Seemed So Right Last Night (Columbia 41190, 1958)

Sergio Mendes & Brasil '66:
The Look Of Love (A&M 924, 1968)

Marilyn Michaels:
Don't Count The Days (ABC 11098, 1968)

Stephanie Mills:

Burt Bacharach & Hal David

This Empty Place/I See You For the First Time (Motown 1382, 1976)

Hugo Montenegro:
Lost Horizon (RCA 74-0875, 1973)

Jane Morgan:
With Open Arms (Kapp 284, 1959)

Bernie Nee:
Country Music Holiday (Columbia 4-41132, 1958)

Rick Nelson:
Take A Broken Heart/They Don't Give Medals (To Yesterday's Heroes) (Decca 32055, 1966)

Jill O'Hara:
Knowing When To Leave/I'll Never Fall In Love Again (United Artists 50492, 1969)

Oliver:
(i can remember)/Where There's A Heartache (Crewe 346, 1970)

Tony Orlando:
To Wait For Love/Accept It (Epic 9715, 1964)

Nick Palmer:
Everyone Needs Someone To Love (RCA 47-9698, 1968)

Ray Peterson:
(missing you)/I Forgot What It Was Like (Dunes 2027, 1963)

Shawn Phillips:
Lost Horizon (A&M 1405, 1973)

Gene Pitney:
(The Man Who Shot) Liberty Valance (Musicor 1020, 1962)
Only Love Can Break A Heart (Musicor 1022, 1962)
True Love Never Runs Smooth (Musicor 1032, 1963)
24 Hours From Tulsa (Musicor 1034, 1963)

Frank Pourcel:
What's New Pussycat? (Imperial 66156, 1966)
The World Is A Circle (Paramount 0196, 1973)

Joey Powers:
Don't Envy Me (RCA 47-8119, 1962)

Jimmy Radcliffe:
There Goes The Forgotten Man (Musicor 1024, 1962)

Sue Raney:
Try To See It My Way (Imperial 66222, 1966)
Knowing When To Leave (Imperial 66340, 1968)

The Rangoons:
Moon Guitar/My Heart Is A Ball Of String (1961)

Eivets Rednow (Stevie Wonder):
Alfie (Gordy 7076, 1968)

Reunion:
(just say goodbye)/Living Together, Growing Together (Bell 45287, 1972)

Cliff Richard:
It's Wonderful To Be Young (Dot 16399, 1962)
Look In My Eyes, Maria (Epic 9737, 1964)

Marty Robbins:
The Story Of My Life (Columbia 41013, 1957)
The Last Time I Saw My Heart (Columbia 44182, 1958)
Sittin' In A Treehouse (Columbia 41208, 1958)

John Rowles:
(m'lady)/Say Goodbye (CBS BA 461218, 1969)
All Kinds Of People (Kapp 2131, 1971)
Blue On Blue (Kapp 2180, 1972)

Ruby and the Romantics:
(when you're young and in love)/ I Cry Alone (Kapp 615, 1964)

The Russells:
Wasting Away For You (ABC-Paramount 10319, 1962)

Sandi and Salli:
Don't Count The Days (Capitol 2089, 1968)

The Sandpipers:
(baby, I could be so good at lovin' you)/The World Is A Circle (A&M 1388, 1972)

Tommy Sands:
Love In A Goldfish Bowl (Capitol 4580, 1961)

Lalo Schifrin:
What's New Pussycat? (United Artists 50649, 1970)

Linda Scott:

Burt Bacharach & Hal David

Who's Been Sleeping In My Bed? (Congress 204, 1964)

Doc Severinsen:
(barbarella)/Knowing When To Leave (Command 4125, 1969)

Sandi Shaw:
(There's) Always Something There To Remind Me (Reprise 0320, 1964)

The Shirelles:
(stop the music)/It's Love That Really Counts (Scepter 1237, 1962)

Keely Smith:
One Less Bell To Answer (Atlantic 45-2429, 1967)

Joannie Sommers:
Alfie (Columbia 43731, 1966)

Soulful Strings:
Message To Michael (Cadet 5540, 1966)

Dusty Springfield:
Wishin' And Hopin' (Philips 40207, 1964)
I Just Don't Know What To Do With Myself (Philips 40319, 1965)
The Look Of Love (Philips 40465, 1967)
In The Land Of Make Believe (Atlantic 2673, 1969)

Dorothy Squires:
If I Could Go Back (Bell 45282, 1972)

Jo Stafford:
Underneath The Overpass (Columbia 4-40926, 1957)

Connie Stevens:
And This Is Mine (Warner Bros 5217, 1961)

The Stylistics:
You'll Never Get To Heaven (If You Break My Heart) (Avco 4618, 1973)

B.J. Thomas:
Raindrops Keep Fallin' On My Head (Scepter 12265, 1969)
Everybody's Out Of Town (Scepter 12277, 1970)
(I Just Can't Help Believing)/Send My Picture To Scranton, PA (Scepter 12283, 1970)
Long Ago Tomorrow (Scepter 12335, 1971)

Babs Tino:
Too Late To Worry (Kapp 458, 1962

Forgive Me (For Giving You Such A Bad Time) (Kapp 472, 1962)
Call Off The Wedding (Without A Groom There Can't Be A Bride)/Keep Away From Other Girls (Kapp 498, 1963)

Diana Trask:
Long Ago Last Summer (Columbia 441711, 1960)

Leslie Uggams:
In The Land Of Make Believe (Atlantic 2524, 1968)

Jerry Vale:
He Who Loves/Close To You (Columbia 44914, 1969)

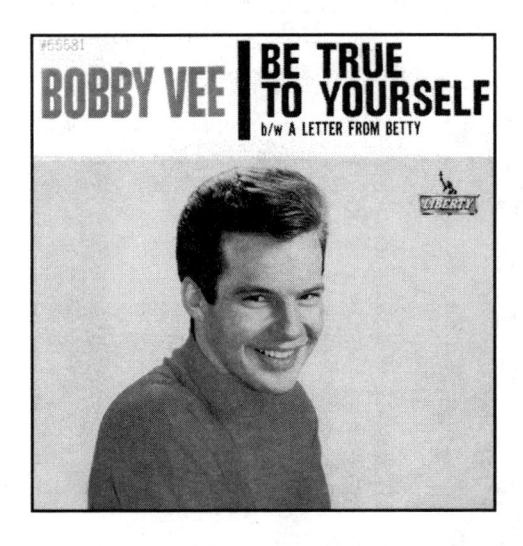

Bobby Vee:
Anonymous Phone Call (Liberty 55521, 1962)
Be True To Yourself (Liberty 55581, 1963)
The Story Of My Life (Liberty 55843, 1965)

Bobby Vinton:
Blue On Blue (Epic 9593, 1963)

Adam Wade:
Rain From The Skies (Epic 59566, 1963)

Shani Wallis:
The Look Of Love/Let Your Love Come Through (Kapp 817, 1967)

The Walker Brothers:
Make It Easy On Yourself (Smash 2000, 1965)
Another Tear Falls (Smash 2063, 1966)

The Wanderers:
I Could Make You Mine (Cub 9075, 1960)
Somebody Else's Sweetheart (Cub 9099, 1961)

Dee Dee Warwick:
Alfie (Mercury 72710, 1967)

Burt Bacharach & Hal David

Dionne Warwick:
Don't Make Me Over/I Smiled Yesterday (Scepter 1239, 1962)
This Empty Place/Wishin' And Hopin' (Scepter 1247, 1963)
Make The Music Play/Please Make Him Love Me (Scepter 1253, 1963)
Anyone Who Had A Heart/The Love Of A Boy (Scepter 1262, 1963)
Walk On By/Any Old Time Of The Day (Scepter 1274, 1964)
You'll Never Get To Heaven/A House Is Not A Home (Scepter 1282, 1964)
Reach Out For Me/How Many Days Of Sadness (Scepter 1285, 1964)
(you can have him)/Is There Another Way To Love You (Scepter 1294, 1965)
(who can I turn to)/Don't Say I Didn't Tell You So (Scepter 1298, 1965)
Here I Am/Close To You (Scepter 12104, 1965)
Looking With My Eyes/Only The Strong, Only The Brave (Scepter 12111, 1965)
Are You There (With Another Girl)/If I Ever Make You Cry (Scepter 12122, 1965)
Message To Michael/Here Where There Is Love (Scepter 12133, 1966)
Trains And Boats And Planes/Don't Go Breaking My Heart (Scepter 12153, 1966)
I Just Don't Know What To Do With Myself/In Between The Heartaches (Scepter 12167, 1966)
Another Night/Go With Love (Scepter 12181, 1966)
Alfie/The Beginning Of Loneliness (Scepter 12187, 1967)
The Windows Of The World/Walk Little Dolly (Scepter 12196, 1967)
I Say A Little Prayer/(valley of the dolls) (Scepter 12203, 1967)
Do You Know The Way To San Jose/Let Me Be Lonely (Scepter 12216, 1968)
Who Is Gonna Love Me?/Always Something There To Remind Me (Scepter 12226, 1968)
Promises, Promises/Whoever You Are, I Love You (Scepter 12231, 1968)

This Girl's In Love With You/Dream Sweet Dreamer (Scepter 12241, 1969)
The April Fools (Scepter 12249, 1969)
Odds And Ends/As Long As There's An Apple Tree (Scepter 12256, 1969)
(you've lost that lovin' feelin')/Window Wishing (Scepter 12262, 1969)
I'll Never Fall In Love Again/What The World Needs Now Is Love (Scepter 12273, 1969)
Let Me Go To Him/Loneliness Remembers (What Happiness Forgets) (Scepter 12276, 1970)
Paper Maché/The Wine Is Young (Scepter 12285, 1970)
Make It Easy On Yourself / Knowing When To Leave (Scepter 12294, 1970)
The Green Grass Starts To Grow / They Don't Give Medals To Yesterday's Heroes (Scepter 12300, 1970)
Who Gets The Guy (Scepter 12309, 1971)
(If We Only Have Love) / Close To You (Warner Bros. WB 7560, 1972)
Raindrops Keep Fallin' On My Head / Is There Another Way to Love You (Scepter 12346, 1972)

Lenny Welch:
He Who Loves You (Mercury 72811, 1968)

Joe Williams:
That Kind Of Woman (Roulette 4185, 1959)

Chip Wynn:
Everyone Needs Someone To Love (Scepter 12312, 1971)

Timi Yuro:
The Love Of A Boy (Liberty 55469, 1962)

Burt Bacharach & Hal David

LP Tracks:

(Bacharach-David compositions only)

Herb Alpert

S.R.O.
(A&M SP-4119, 1966)
Don't Go Breaking My Heart

SOUNDS LIKE...
(A&M SP-4124, 1967)
Casino Royale

WARM
(A&M SP 4190)
To Wait For Love

You Smile, The Song Begins
(A&M, 1974)
I Might Frighten Her Away
Promises, Promises

Ed Ames

WHEN THE SNOW IS ON THE ROSES
(RCA 3913, 1969)
Nikki

SINGS THE SONGS OF BACHARACH & DAVID
(RCA LSP 4453, 1969):
How Does A Man Become A Puppet
Nikki
What The World Needs Now Is Love
Do You Know The Way To San Jose
I Say A Little Prayer
Close To You
The Look Of Love
Wives And Lovers
Raindrops Keep Fallin' On My Head
Make It Easy On Yourself.

SONGS FROM LOST HORIZON AND OTHER MOVIE THEMES
(RCA LSP 4048, 1972):
The World Is A Circle
Reflections
Question Me An Answer
Lost Horizon
Living Together, Growing Together

Paul Anka

SONGS I WISH I'D WRITTEN
(RCA LPM 2744, 1963):
Blue On Blue

Tony Bennett

MORE... TONY'S GREATEST HITS
(Columbia CL 1535)
The Night That Heaven Fell

The Buckinghams

IN ONE EAR AND GONE TOMORROW
(Columbia CS9703, 1968):
Are You There (With Another Boy)

Adam Faith

ADAM FAITH
(Amy 8005, 1965):
Message To Martha

The 5th Dimension

INDIVIDUALLY AND COLLECTIVELY
(Bell 6073, 1972):
All Kinds Of People

LIVING TOGETHER, GROWING TOGETHER
(Bell 1116, 1973):
Living Together, Growing Together
Let Me Be Lonely.

The Fortunes

THE FORTUNES
(Press 73002, 1965):
This Empty Place

Bobby Goldsboro

LITTLE THINGS
(United Artists UAS 6425, 1964):
Me Japanese Boy, I Love You.

Engelbert Humperdinck

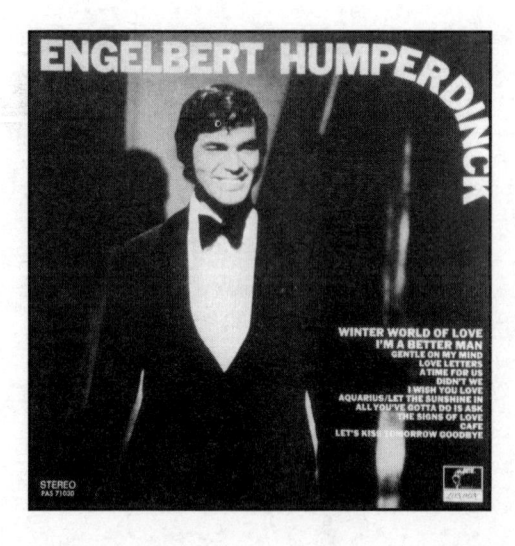

ENGELBERT
(Parrot PAS 71026, 1969):
Love Was Here Before The Stars.

ENGELBERT HUMPERDINCK
(Parrot PAS 71030, 1969):
I'm A Better Man.

Tommy Hunt

I JUST DON'T KNOW WHAT TO DO WITH MYSELF
(Scepter SRM-506, 1962):
I Just Don't Know What To Do With Myself

Chuck Jackson

MR. EVERYTHING
(Wand 667, 1965):
I Just Don't Know What To Do With Myself.

Tom Jones

WHAT'S NEW PUSSYCAT?
(Parrot, 1965):
What's New Pussycat?
To Wait For Love

LIVE! AT THE TALK OF THE TOWN
(Parrot PAS 71014, 1967):
What's New Pussycat? (live).

I (WHO HAVE NOTHING)
(Parrot XPAS 771039, 1970):
What The World Needs Now Is Love

Anita Kerr Singers

ALL YOU NEED IS LOVE
(Warner Bros 1724)
The Look Of Love

Johnny Mathis

JOHNNY MATHIS SINGS
(Mercury SR 61107)
Saturday Sunshine
(There's) Always Something There To Remind Me

RAINDROPS KEEP FALLIN' ON MY HEAD
(Columbia CS 1005, 1970):
Raindrops Keep Fallin' On My Head
Alfie
Odds And Ends.

LOVE STORY
(Columbia C 30499, 1971):
Ten Times Forever More

Stephanie Mills

FOR THE FIRST TIME
(Motown M6-859S1, 1975)
I Took My Strength From You
Living On Plastic
No One Remembers My Name
If You Can Learn How To Cry
Loneliness Remembers (What Happiness Forgets)
This Empty Place

Burt Bacharach & Hal David

The Way I Feel About You
I See You For The First Time
All the Way To Paradise
Please Let Go

Del Shannon

RUNAWAY WITH DEL SHANNON
(Big Top 12-1303, 1961):
I Wake Up Crying

B.J. Thomas

RAINDROPS KEEP FALLIN' ON MY HEAD
(Scepter SPS 580, 1970):
Raindrops Keep Fallin' On My Head
This Guy's In Love With You.

EVERYBODY'S OUT OF TOWN
(Scepter SPS 582, 1970)
Everybody's Out Of Town
Send My Picture To Scranton, PA

Jerry Vale

THIS GUY'S IN LOVE WITH YOU
(Columbia CS 9694, 1969):
This Guy's In Love With You
Do You Know The Way To San Jose?
The Look Of Love

Bobby Vinton

MR. LONELY
(Epic LN 2413, 1965):
Forever Yours I Remain

Dionne Warwick

PRESENTING DIONNE WARWICK
(Scepter SPS 508, 1963):
This Empty Place
Wishin' And Hopin'
I Cry Alone

Make The Music Play
Don't Make Me Over
It's Love That Really Counts
I Smiled Yesterday
Make It Easy On Yourself
The Love Of A Boy

ANYONE WHO HAD A HEART
(Scepter SPS 517, 1963):
Anyone Who Had A Heart
I Could Make You Mine
Please Make Him Love Me
Don't Make Me Over
I Cry Alone
Any Old Time Of The Day
This Empty Place

MAKE WAY FOR DIONNE WARWICK
(Scepter SPS-523, 1964):
A House Is Not A Home
(They Long To Be) Close To You
The Last One To Be Loved
Land Of Make Believe
Reach Out For Me
You'll Never Get To Heaven (If You Break My Heart).
Walk On By
Wishin' And Hopin'
I Smiled Yesterday

THE SENSITIVE SOUND OF DIONNE WARWICK
(Scepter SPS-528, 1965):
How Many Days Of Sadness
Is There Another Way To Love You?
Wives And Lovers
Don't Say I Didn't Tell You So
Only The Strong, Only The Brave
Forever My Love
That's Not The Answer

HERE I AM
(Scepter SPS-531, 1966):
Are You There (With Another Girl)
Don't Go Breaking My Heart
How Can I Hurt You
If I Ever Make You Cry
In Between The Heartaches
Long Day, Short Night
Window Wishing.

Burt Bacharach & Hal David

HERE WHERE THERE IS LOVE
(Scepter SPS-555, 1967):
Go With Love
Here Where There Is Love
Trains And Boats And Planes
What The World Needs Now Is Love;

THE WINDOWS OF THE WORLD
(Scepter SPS-563, 1967):
Another Night
The Beginning Of Loneliness
(There's) Always Something There To Remind Me
Walk Little Dolly
Windows Of The World

VALLEY OF THE DOLLS
(Scepter SPS-568, 1968):
As Long As There's An Apple Tree
Do You Know The Way To San Jose?
Let Me Be Lonely
Where Would I Go
Walking Backwards Down The Road

PROMISES, PROMISES
(Scepter SPS-571):
Promises, Promises
This Girl's In Love With You
Who Is Gonna Love Me
Whoever You Are, I Love You
Wanting Things

I'LL NEVER FALL IN LOVE AGAIN
(Scepter SPS-581, 1970)
The Wine Is Young
I'll Never Fall In Love Again
Raindrops Keep Fallin' On My Head
Loneliness Remembers What Happiness Forgets
Paper Maché
Knowing When To Leave
Let Me Go To Him

VERY DIONNE
(Scepter SPS-587, 1970):
Check Out Time
The Green Grass Starts To Grow
Make It Easy On Yourself
They Don't Give Medals To Yesterday's

Heroes
Walk the Way You Talk

DIONNE
(Warner Bros. 2585, 1972):
I Just Have To Breathe
The Balance Of Nature
If You Never Say Goodbye
Close To You
Be Aware
One Less Bell To Answer
Hasbrook Heights

FROM WITHIN
(Scepter SPS-598, 1972):
All Kinds Of People (medley)

**GO WITH LOVE:
DIONNE WARWICK SINGS THE SONGS OF BURT BACHARACH AND HAL DAVID**
(Columbia House P2S 5524)
What the World Needs Now Is Love
Walk On By
The Beginning Of Loneliness
Long Day, Short Night
Close To You
Another Night
Don't Go Breaking My Heart
How Can I Hurt You
Are You There With Another Girl
Window Wishing
Here Where There Is Love
Raindrops Keep Fallin' on My Head
Go With Love
Looking With My Eyes
If I Ever Make You Cry
Walkin' Backwards Down The Road
How Many Days Of Sadness
Windows Of The World
As Long As There's an Apple Tree
In Between The Heartaches
Walk Little Dolly
Is There Another Way To Love You

Timi Yuro:

THE BEST OF TIMI YURO
(Liberty 7286):
If I Never Get To Love You

Burt Bacharach - Selected U.S. Discography:

Singles:

Searching Wind / Roseanne (Cabot 108, 1958)
Move It On The Backbeat / A Felicidade (Big Top 3087)
(as Burt and the Backbeats)
Saturday Sunshine / And So Goodbye My Love (Kapp 532, 1963)
Don't Go Breaking My Heart / Trains And Boats And Planes (Kapp 657, 1965)
What's New Pussycat? / My Little Red Book (Kapp 685, 1965)
Nikki / Juanita's Place (Liberty 55934, 1966)
Alfie / Bond Street (A&M 845, 1967)
Fox Trot / Ukeatalia (United Artists 50123, 1967)
The Look Of Love / Reach Out For Me (A&M 888, 1967)
Message To Michael / Are You There (With Another Girl) (A&M 931, 1968)
The Bell That Couldn't Jingle / What The World Needs Now Is Love (A&M 1004, 1968)
I'll Never Fall In Love Again / Pacific Coast Highway (A&M 1064, 1969)
Wanting Things / She's Gone Away (A&M 1117, 1969)
Come Touch The Sun / Raindrops Keep Fallin' On My Head (A&M 1153, 1969)
Any Day Now / A House Is Not A Home (A&M 1222, 1970)
All Kinds of People / She's Gone Away (A&M 1241, 1971)
Freefall / One Less Bell To Answer (A&M 1290, 1971)
Something Big / Living Together, Growing Together (A&M 1489, 1973)
Living Together, Growing Together / Reflections (A&M 1512, 1974)
I Took My Strength From You / Time And Tenderness (A&M 1921, 1977)
Futures / No One Remembers My Name (A&M 1960, 1977)
New York Lady / Riverboat (A&M 2161, 1979)

LPs:

HIT MAKER! BURT BACHARACH PLAYS THE BURT BACHARACH HITS
(Kapp KSI 3447, 1966)
Don't Make Me Over
Walk On By
Don't Go Breaking My Heart
Blue On Blue
The Last One To Be Loved
There's Always Something There To Remind Me
What's New Pussycat?
24 Hours From Tulsa

My Little Red Book (All I Do Is Talk About You)
Trains And Boats And Planes
Wives And Lovers
Anyone Who Had A Heart

BURT BACHARACH PLAYS HIS HITS
(Kapp KS 3577, 1966)
Trains And Boats And Planes
My Little Red Book (All I Do Is Talk About You)
Anyone Who Had A Heart
There's Always Something There To Remind Me
24 Hours From Tulsa
Walk On By
Wives And Lovers
Don't Make Me Over
Blue On Blue
Don't Go Breaking My Heart
What's New Pussycat?

BURT BACHARACH PLAYS HIS HITS
(MCA MCL 1738, 1966)
Trains And Boats And Planes
My Little Red Book (All I Do Is Talk About You)
Anyone Who Had A Heart
There's Always Something There To Remind Me
24 Hours From Tulsa
Walk On By
Wives And Lovers
Don't Make Me Over
Blue On Blue
Don't Go Breaking My Heart
What's New Pussycat?

BURT BACHARACH PLAYS HIS HITS
(MCA MCL 1738, 1966)
Don't Make Me Over
Walk On By
Don't Go Breaking My Heart
Blue On Blue
The Last One To Be Loved
There's Always Something There To Remind Me

Burt Bacharach & Hal David

24 Hours From Tulsa
Trains And Boats And Planes
Wives And Lovers
Saturday Sunshine
A House Is Not A Home
Anyone Who Had A Heart

REACH OUT
(A&M SP 4131, 1967)
Reach Out For Me
Alfie
Bond Street
Are You There (With Another Girl)
What The World Needs Now Is Love
The Look Of Love
A House Is Not A Home
I Say A Little Prayer
The Windows Of The World
Lisa
Message To Michael

MAKE IT EASY ON YOURSELF
(A&M SP 4188, 1969)
Promises, Promises;
I'll Never Fall In Love Again
Knowing When To Leave
Any Day Now
Wanting Things
Whoever You Are, I Love You
Make It Easy On Yourself
Do You Know The Way To San Jose?
Pacific Coast Highway
She's Gone Away
This Guy's In Love With You

BURT BACHARACH
(A&M SP 3501, 1971)
Mexican Divorce
(They Long To Be) Close To You
Nikki
Wives And Lovers
All Kinds Of People
And The People Were With Her (Suite For Orchestra)
The April Fools

Hasbrook Heights
Freefall
One Less Bell To Answer

LIVING TOGETHER
(A&M SP 3527, 1973)
Something Big
Monterey Peninsula
I Come To You
Walk The Way You Talk
The Balance Of Nature
Living Together, Growing Together
Reflections
Lost Horizon
Long Ago Tomorrow
I Might Frighten Her Away

BURT BACHARACH'S GREATEST HITS
(A&M SP 3661, 1974)
I'll Never Fall In Love Again
Make It Easy On Yourself
This Guy's In Love With You
Reach Out For Me
The Look Of Love
What The World Needs Now Is Love
I Say A Little Prayer
Alfie
Raindrops Keep Fallin' On My Head
Wives And Lovers
(They Long To Be) Close To You
Living Together, Growing Together

BURT BACHARACH IN CONCERT
(A&M 68279, 1974)
Medley: Alfie / Do You Know The Way To San Jose?
Walk On By
Come Touch The Sun
Raindrops Keep Fallin' On My Head
The Look Of Love
Medley: Don't Make Me Over / Anyone Who Had A Heart / What's New Pussycat? / Wives And Lovers / 24 Hours From Tulsa
This Guy's In Love With You
I'll Never Fall In Love Again
(They Long To Be) Close To You

Burt Bacharach & Hal David

Bond Street
A House Is Not A Home
Alfie
What The World Needs Now Is Love
Promises, Promises
What The World Needs Now Is Love (reprise)

FUTURES
(A&M 64622, 1977)
I Took My Strength From You (I Had None)
Futures
Us
Where Are You?
We Should Have Met Sooner
No One Remembers My Name
The Young Grow Younger Every Day
Another Spring Will Rise
Seconds
When You Bring Your Sweet Love To Me
Time And Tenderness

WOMAN
(A&M AMLK63709, 1979)
Summer Of '77
Woman
Riverboat
Magdalena
New York Lady
There Is Time
The Dancing Fool
I Live In The Woods

Soundtracks:

(Soundtracks from films and shows featuring songs by Bacharach and David, and/or scores composed by Burt Bacharach. All are LPs unless otherwise specified.)

WHAT'S NEW, PUSSYCAT?
(United Artists UAS-5128, 1965)
What's New, Pussycat? - Tom Jones
School For Anatomy - Bookworm (medley)
High Temperature, Low Resistance
Downhill And Shady
Stripping Isn't Really Sexy, Is It?
Marriage, French Style - Here I Am (medley)
Here I Am - Dionne Warwick
Marriage, French Style
My Little Red Book - Manfred Mann
Pussycats On Parade
A Walk On The Wild Wharf
Chateau Chantel
Catch As Catch Can

AFTER THE FOX
(United Artists UAS-5148, 1966)
After The Fox - Peter Sellers and the Hollies
Making A Movie In Sevalio
Gold, Gold, Who's Got The Gold?
World Of Make Believe
Italian Fuzz
The Fox In Sevalio
Wheeler Dealer
Tourist Trap
After The Fox
Hot Gold
The Via Veneto
Making A Movie In Sevalio
Love x 2
Ukeatalia
Visiting Day
Bird Bath
Grotta rosa

ON THE FLIP SIDE
(Decca DL7-4836, 1966)
It Doesn't Matter Anymore - Rick Nelson
Fender Mender - Joanie Sommers & The Celestials
They Don't Give Medals (To Yesterday's Heroes) - Rick Nelson
Try to See It My Way - Joanie Sommers

Burt Bacharach & Hal David

Juanita's Place Montage
Take A Broken Heart - Rick Nelson
They're Gonna Love It - Donna Jean Young
Try To See It My Way - Rick Nelson & Joanie Sommers
Juanita's Place - The Celestials
They Don't Give Medals (To Yesterday's Heroes)

CASINO ROYALE
(Colgems 5005, 1967)
Casino Royale Theme - Herb Alpert & The Tijuana Brass
The Look Of Love - Dusty Springfield
Money Penny Goes For Broke
Le Chiffre's Torture Of The Mind
Home James, Don't Spare The Horses
Sir James' Trip To Find Mata
The Look Of Love
Hi There Miss Goodthighs
Little French Boy
Flying Saucers - First Stop Berlin
The Venerable Sir James Bond
Dream On James, You're Winning
The Big Cowboys and Indians Fight At Casino Royale
Casino Royale Theme

PROMISES, PROMISES (Original Cast)
(United Artists UAS-9902, 1968)
Overture
Half As Big As Life
Upstairs
You'll Think Of Someone
Our Little Secret
She Likes Basketball
Knowing When To Leave
Wanting Things
Turkey Lurkey Time
A Fact Can Be A Beautiful Thing
Grapes Of Roth
Whoever You Are I Love You
Where Can You Take A Girl?
Christmas Day
A Young Pretty Girl Like You
I'll Never Fall In Love Again
Promises, Promises

PROMISES, PROMISES (Studio Cast)
(Fontana SFL-13192, 1968)

PROMISES, PROMISES US promo LP
(United Artists SPOC-1)
(Same as regular LP, but with additional interview excerpts.)

PROMISES, PROMISES (British cast LP)
(United Artists UAS-29075)

PROMISES, PROMISES demo LP
(PP-77, unreleased)
Half As Big As Life
Upstairs,
You'll Think Of Someone
She Likes Basketball
Wanting Things
Whoever You Are
Christmas Day
A Young Pretty Girl Like You
Promises, Promises
What Am I Doing Here
Let's Pretend We're Grown Up
Tick Tock Goes The Clock
(Recorded in June 1968, the tracks on this album are demonstration recordings of the 12 songs originally written for Promises, Promises. They feature piano accompaniment by Burt Bacharach and vocals by Rose Marie Jun, Kenny Karen, Bernie Knee and Leslie Miller. 10 of the 12 tracks were later included on the CD BROADWAY FIRST TAKE VOLUME 2.)

BUTCH CASSIDY & THE SUNDANCE KID
(A&M SP-4227, 1969)
The Sundance Kid
Raindrops Keep Fallin' On My Head - B.J. Thomas
Not Goin' Home Anymore
South American Getaway
Raindrops Keep Fallin' On My Head (instrumental)
On a Bicycle Built For Joy - B.J. Thomas
Come Touch The Sun
The Old Fun City (N.Y. sequence)
Not Goin' Home Anymore

LOST HORIZON
(Bell B-1300, 1973)
Lost Horizon
Share The Joy
The World Is A Circle
Living Together, Growing Together

I Might Frighten Her Away
The Things I Will Not Miss
If I Could Go Back
Where Knowledge Ends (Faith Begins)
Question Me An Answer
I Come To You
Reflections

LOST HORIZON score
(unreleased)
The Hijacking
Refueling In The Desert
The Crash
Rescue Party
Himalayan Trek
Valley Of The Blue Moon
Arrival In Shangri-La
Dinner With Chang
Conway And Chang
Sally And To-Leen
The Truce Is Over
The High Lama
George And Maria
The Waterway
Return To High Lama
Funeral Procession
The Mystery Of Maria
The Avalanche

ISN'T SHE GREAT (CD)
(Polygram, 2000)
On My Way - Dionne Warwick
Love Theme
Lunch At Lindy's
Guy's Theme
Mass Love
Sexual Me, Sexual You
Yes, They Said Yes!
The Big Pitch
Are You My Friend?
Hello, Connecticut
For Mimsy
Heartache Revisited
The Book Tour (On My Way, reprise)
About Expectations
The Late Lunch
Victory At A Price
Open Your Heart - Vanessa Williams

Compact Discs – Selected Discography:

I have included four categories in the CD section of the discography: **CDs by Burt Bacharach, CDs by Dionne Warwick, various artists compilations** and **discs by other individual artists.** I have not included CDs that are straight reissues of albums listed in the LP section. I have also not limited this section to just Bacharach/David recordings.

Burt Bacharach CDs:

PAINTED FROM MEMORY
(Burt Bacharach & Elvis Costello)
(Mercury 538 002-2, 1998)
In The Darkest Place
Toledo
I Still Have That Other Girl
This House Is Empty Now
Tears At The Birthday Party
Such Unlikely Lovers
My Thief
The Long Division
Painted From Memory
The Sweetest Punch
What's Her Name Today?
God Give Me Strength

20TH CENTURY MASTERS
(Interscope, 1999)
The Look Of Love
Raindrops Keep Fallin' On My Head
This Guy's In Love With You
I'll Never Fall In Love Again
Do You Know The Way To San Jose?
What the World Needs Now Is Love
Alfie
(They Long To Be) Close To You
I Say A Little Prayer
One Less Bell To Answer
Reach Out For Me
Don't Make Me Over

BURT BACHARACH PLAYS HIS HITS
(MCA, 1997):
Don't Make Me Over
Walk On By

Burt Bacharach & Hal David

Don't Go Breaking My Heart
Wives And Lovers
Anyone Who Had A Heart
The Last One To Be Loved
(There's) Always Something There To Remind Me
24 Hours From Tulsa
Trains And Boats And Planes
Blue On Blue
A House Is Not A Home
What's New Pussycat?
My Little Red Book (All I Do Is Talk About You)
Saturday Sunshine
And So Goodbye, My Love

BURT BACHARACH PLAYS HIS HITS
(Japan, 1997, different cover and track line-up from above version):
Trains And Boats And Planes
My Little Red Book
Anyone Who Had A Heart
Always Something There To Remind Me
24 Hours From Tulsa
Walk On By
Wives And Lovers
Don't Make Me Over
Blue On Blue
Don't Go Breaking My Heart
What's New Pussycat?
A House Is Not A Home
The Last One To Be Loved
Saturday Sunshine
And So Goodbye My Love
Sail Along Silv'ry Moon

CLASSICS
(A&M 2521, 1987)
I Say A Little Prayer
The Look Of Love
Raindrops Keep Fallin' On My Head
(They Long To Be) Close To You
This Guy's In Love With You
Promises, Promises
Living Together, Growing Together
A House Is Not A Home
Message To Michael

The Sundance Kid
New York Lady
One Less Bell To Answer
Alfie
Reach Out For Me
What The World Needs Now Is Love
Make It Easy On Yourself
I'll Never Fall In Love Again
Wives And Lovers
No One Remembers My Name

**THE BEST OF BURT BACHARACH
(A&M, 1999):**
This Guy's In Love With You
The Look Of Love
I'll Never Fall In Love Again
Do You Know The Way To San Jose?
What The World Needs Now Is Love
Alfie
Promises, Promises
(They Long To Be) Close To You
Make It Easy On Yourself
I Say A Little Prayer
Any Day Now
Pacific Coast Highway
Raindrops Keep Fallin' On My Head
Trains And Boats And Planes
One Less Bell To Answer
Wives And Lovers
Don't Make Me Over
Living Together, Growing Together
Knowing When To Leave
Windows Of The World

Burt Bacharach & Hal David

Various artists CDs:

GREAT JEWISH MUSIC: BURT BACHARACH
(Tzadik, 1997):

Close to You
Don't Go Breaking My Heart - Marc Ribot Ensemble
Wives And Lovers - Dave Douglas
Who Gets The Guy/This Guy's In Love With You - Guy Klucevsek
Walk On By - Kramer
Promises, Promises - Erik Friedlander
Alfie - Joey Baron
Freefall - Zeena Parkins
Don't Go Breaking My Heart - Marc Ribot
Trains And Boats And Planes - Fred Frith
Do You Know The Way to San Jose? - Martin Medeski
The Man Who Shot Liberty Valance - Elliott Sharp
I Say A Little Prayer - Marie McAuliffe
She's Gone Away - Mike Patton
I Just Don't Know What To Do With Myself - Lloyd Cole
A House Is Not A Home - Anthony Coleman
The Look Of Love - Yuka Honda
What's New Pussycat? - Shelley Hirsch
What The World Needs Now Is Love - Bill Frisell
I Took My Strength From You - Eyvind Kang

TRIBUTE TO BURT BACHARACH
(Nippon Columbia COCA-12166, 1994)

I'll Never Fall In Love Again - 5th Garden
The Look Of Love - Soul Bossa Trio
With A Smile - Burt Bacharach (Vocal by Jane Miller)
Are You There With Another Girl - Carnation
Make It Easy On Yourself - Kyoto Jazz Massive
Mulino Bianco - Burt Bacharach
Me Japanese Boy - Pizzicato Five
Bond Street - Les 5-4-3-2-1 with K-taro Takanami
The April Fools - The Cozy Coners

EASY LISTENING BACHARACH
(Columbia 485125 2, 1996)

Promises, Promises - Percy Faith
Send Me No Flowers - Doris Day
Alfie - Tony Bennett
Wives And Lovers - Andy Williams

I'll Never Fall In Love Again - Patti Page
Walk On By - Mel Torme
Close To You - Johnny Mathis
Trains And Boats And Planes - Anita Harris
Do You Know The Way To San Jose? - Robert Goulet
A House Is Not A Home - Georgie Fame
This Girl's In Love With You - Salena Jones
Make It Easy On Yourself - Tony Bennett
Blue on Blue - Bobby Vinton
Raindrops Keep Fallin' on my Head - Peter Nero
My Little Red Book - Mel Torme
I Say A Little Prayer - Anita Harris
The Look Of Love - Johnny Mathis
The Story Of My Life - Marty Robbins
If I Could Go Back - Andy Williams
What The World Needs Now Is Love - Tony Bennett

THE LOOK OF LOVE - THE BURT BACHARACH COLLECTION
(Rhino four-CD box set R2 75339, 1998)

The Story Of My Life - Marty Robbins
Magic Moments - Perry Como
The Blob - The Five Blobs
Please Stay - The Drifters
I Wake Up Crying - Chuck Jackson
Tower Of Strength - Gene McDaniels
Baby It's You - The Shirelles
Mexican Divorce - The Drifters
(The Man Who Shot) Liberty Valance - Gene Pitney
Any Day Now (My Wild Beautiful Bird) - Chuck Jackson
Make It Easy On Yourself - Jerry Butler
I Just Don't Know What To Do With Myself - Tommy Hunt
It's Love That Really Counts - The Shirelles
Only Love Can Break A Heart - Gene Pitney
(There Goes) The Forgotten Man - Jimmy Radcliffe
Don't Make Me Over - Dionne Warwick
Let The Music Play - The Drifters
Blue On Blue - Bobby Vinton
True Love Never Runs Smooth - Gene Pitney
Blue Guitar - Richard Chamberlain
Reach Out For Me - Lou Johnson
24 Hours From Tulsa - Gene Pitney
Anyone Who Had A Heart - Dionne Warwick
A House Is Not A Home - Brook Benton
Wives And Lovers - Jack Jones
Wishin' And Hopin' - Dusty Springfield

Burt Bacharach & Hal David

Walk On By - Dionne Warwick
(There's) Always Something There To Remind Me - Lou Johnson
Me Japanese Boy I Love You - Bobby Goldsboro
To Wait For Love - Tony Orlando
Kentucky Bluebird - Lou Johnson
Land Of Make Believe - Dionne Warwick
The Last One To Be Loved - Lou Johnson
Fool Killer - Gene Pitney
Don't Go Breaking My Heart - Burt Bacharach
What The World Needs Now Is Love - Jackie DeShannon
Trains And Boats And Planes - Burt Bacharach
What's New Pussycat? - Tom Jones
My Little Red Book - Manfred Mann
Here I Am - Dionne Warwick
A Lifetime Of Loneliness - Jackie DeShannon
Made In Paris - Trini Lopez
Promise Her Anything - Tom Jones
Are You There (with Another girl) - Dionne Warwick
Come And Get Me - Jackie DeShannon
Alfie - Cilla Black
In Between The Heartaches - Dionne Warwick
Nikki - Burt Bacharach
So Long Johnny - Jackie DeShannon
The Windows Of The World - Dionne Warwick
Take A Broken Heart - Rick Nelson
I Say A Little Prayer - Dionne Warwick
Casino Royale - Herb Alpert and The Tijuana Brass
The Look Of Love - Dusty Springfield
Do You Know The way To San Jose? - Dionne Warwick
This Guy's In Love With You - Herb Alpert
Knowing When To Leave - Jill O'Hara
Promises, Promises - Dionne Warwick
Pacific Coast Highway - Burt Bacharach
Raindrops Keep Fallin' On My Head - B J Thomas
Odds And Ends - Dionne Warwick
Everybody's Out Of Town - B J Thomas
I'll Never Fall In Love Again - Dionne Warwick
(They Long To Be) Close To You - The Carpenters
Paper Machè - Dionne Warwick
One Less Bell To Answer - The 5th Dimension
Check Out Time - Dionne Warwick
Hasbrook Heights - Burt Bacharach
The Balance Of Nature - Dionne Warwick
Living Together, Growing Together - The 5th Dimension
You'll Never Get To Heaven - The Stylistics
Arthur's Theme - Christopher Cross
On My Own - Patti LaBelle and Michael McDonald

That's What Friends Are For - Dionne and Friends
God Give Me Strength - Burt Bacharach and Elvis Costello

BURT BACHARACH: ONE AMAZING NIGHT
(Attic N2K 1998)
One Less Bell To Answer - Sheryl Crow
Always Something There To Remind Me - All Saints
God Give Me Strength - Elvis Costello
Baby It's You/Message To Michael - Chrissie Hynde
What's New Pussycat? - Mike Myers
Anyone Who Had A Heart - Wynonna
Raindrops Keep Fallin' On My Head - Ben Folds Five
(They Long To Be) Close To You - Barenaked Ladies
The Windows Of The World/What The World Needs Now - Luther Vandross
Wives And Lovers - David Sanborn
Walk On By/I Say A Little Prayer/Do You Know The Way To San Jose - Dionne Warwick
Alfie - Burt Bacharach

THE BURT BACHARACH SONGBOOK
(Varese, 1998)
What The World Needs Now Is Love
(They Long to Be) Close to You
A House Is Not A Home
The Look Of Love
I'll Never Fall In Love Again
Wives And Lovers
One Less Bell To Answer
I Just Don't Know What to Do With Myself
Make It Easy On Yourself
(There's) Always Something There to Remind Me
Only Love Can Break a Heart
You'll Never Get to Heaven (If You Break My Heart)
Anyone Who Had A Heart
Do You Know The Way to San Jose?
Alfie
Don't Make Me Over
Message To Michael

WHAT THE WORLD NEEDS NOW -
BIG DEAL ARTISTS PERFORM THE SONGS OF BURT BACHARACH
(Big Deal, 1998)
Raindrops Keep Falling On My Head - Shonen Knife
(There's) Always Something There To Remind Me - Absolute Zeros
I'll Never Fall In Love Again - Splitsville

Don't Go Breaking My Heart - Wondermints
Make It Easy On Yourself - Idle
It Doesn't Matter Anymore - BMX Bandits
Promise Her Anything - Gladhands
Baby It's You - Michael Shelley
Trains And Boats And Planes - Dan Kibler
Walk On By - Cockeyed Ghost
Wishin' And Hopin' - Vandalias
It's Love That Really Counts - Barely Pink
(They Long To Be) Close To You - Hannah Cranna
I Say A Little Prayer - Mitchell Rasor

BROADWAY SINGS THE BEST OF BURT BACHARACH
(Varese, 1998):
What's New Pussycat? - Jason Graae
Are You There With Another Girl - Farah Alvin
I'll Never Fall In Love Again - Guy Haines
My Little Red Book - Melba Joyce
One Less Bell To Answer - Christiane Noll
The Blob/The Man Who Shot Liberty Valance/Hot Spell - Plaids
Alfie - Michelle Nicastro
The Look Of Love - Jane Krakowski
Anyone Who Had A Heart - La Chanze
Whoever You Are, I Love You - Susan Egan
Window Wishing - Alet Oury
A House Is Not A Home - Linda Purl
A Bacharach Love Story - Medley - Shauna Hicks
That's What Friends Are For - Helen Reddy

THE MAGIC OF BURT BACHARACH
(Charly, UK, 1999):
24 Hours From Tulsa - Gene Pitney
Baby It's You - The Shirelles
Any Day Now - Chuck Jackson
Make It Easy On Yourself - Jerry Butler
Raindrops Keep Fallin' on My Head - B.J. Thomas
I Just Don't Know What To Do With Myself - Tommy Hunt
I Cry Alone - Maxine Brown
I Wake Up Crying - Gene Chandler
You're Telling Our Secrets - Dee Clark
The Man Who Shot Liberty Valence - Gene Pitney
It's Love That Really Counts - The Shirelles
Wishin' and Hopin' - The Merseybeats
The Breaking Point - Chuck Jackson
Please Stay - The Drifters

Only Love Can Break A Heart - Timi Yuro
The Answer To Everything - Del Shannon
Message To Martha - Jerry Butler
I Just Don't Know What To Do With Myself - Big Maybelle
Trains And Boats And Planes - Billy J. Kramer and The Dakotas
The Look Of Love - Buddy Greco
This Guy's In Love With You - B.J. Thomas
Alfie - Bill Evans

THE REEL BURT BACHARACH
(Hip-O, 1999):
Raindrops Keep Fallin' On My Head - Burt Bacharach
The Look Of Love - Dusty Springfield
Lost Horizon - Shawn Phillips
Something Big - Mark Lindsay
The April Fools - Marvin Hamlisch
Finder Of Lost Loves - Dionne Warwick
What's New Pussycat? - Tom Jones
A House Is Not A Home - Burt Bacharach
Rome Will Never Leave You - Richard Chamberlain
(The Man Who Shot) Liberty Valance - Gene Pitney
Casino Royale - Herb Alpert & The Tijuana Brass
Made In Paris - Trini Lopez
Long Ago Tomorrow - B.J. Thomas
Seconds - Gladys Knight
Arthur's Theme - Christopher Cross
Love Is My Decision - Chris DeBurgh
The Best Of Times - Burt Bacharach

THE LOVE SONGS OF BURT BACHARACH
(Hip-O, 1999):
I Say A Little Prayer - Aretha Franklin
Do You Know The Way To San Jose? - Dionne Warwick
I Just Don't Know What To Do With Myself - Dusty Springfield
Raindrops Keep Fallin' On My Head - B.J. Thomas
What The World Need Now Is Love - Jackie DeShannon
The Look Of Love - Sergio Mendes
What's New Pussycat? - Tom Jones
Baby It's You - The Shirelles
Magic Moments - Perry Como
Make It Easy On Yourself - Jerry Butler
Wishin' And Hopin' - Dusty Springfield
You'll Never Get to Heaven - The Stylistics
Arthur's Theme - Christopher Cross
Always Something There To Remind Me - Naked Eyes

Walk On By - Isaac Hayes
Anyone Who Had A Heart - LuTher Vandross
On My Own - Patti Labelle
This House Is Empty Now - Elvis Costello

THE LOVE SONGS OF BURT BACHARACH
(Polygram UK, 1999):
Walk On By - Gabrielle
I Say A Little Prayer - Aretha Franklin
Do You Know The Way To San Jose? - Dionne Warwick
Make It Easy On Yourself - The Walker BroThers
The Look Of Love - Gladys Knight
I'll Never Fall In Love Again - Deacon Blue
Wishin' and Hopin' - Dusty Springfield
(There's) Always Something There To Remind Me - Sandie Shaw
You'll Never Get to Heaven (If You Break My Heart) - The Stylistics
What The World Needs Now Is Love - Jackie DeShannon
This Guy's In Love With You - Burt Bacharach
Trains And Boats And Planes - Billy J. Kramer and The Dakotas
Let The Music Play - The Drifters
24 Hours From Tulsa - Gene Pitney
One Less Bell To Answer - The 5th Dimension
Raindrops Keep Fallin' On My Head - B.J. Thomas
What's New Pussycat? - Tom Jones
Arthur's Theme (Best That You Can Do) - Christopher Cross)
Anyone Who Had A Heart - LuTher Vandross
(They Long To Be) Close To You - Burt Bacharach
Magic Moments - Perry Como
I Just Don't Know What To Do With Myself - Elvis Costello

BROADWAY FIRST TAKE, VOL. 2
(Slider, 2000):
Promises, Promises
What Am I Doing Here?
Upstairs
You'll Think Of Someone
She Likes Basketball
Let's Pretend We're Grown Up
Wanting Things
Tick Tock Goes The Clock
Whoever You Are, I Love You
Christmas Day

(This CD includes most of the June 1968 demo recordings for PROMISES, PROMISES. Also includes recordings from FLOWER DRUM SONG and LA CAGE AUX FOLLES.)

THE VERY BEST OF BURT BACHARACH
(Rhino, 2001):
Baby It's You - The Shirelles
Only Love Can Break A Heart - Gene Pitney
Anyone Who Had A Heart - Dionne Warwick
(There's) Always Something There To Remind Me - Sandie Shaw
Walk On By - Dionne Warwick
What The World Needs Now Is Love - Jackie DeShannon
Alfie - Dionne Warwick
What's New Pussycat? - Tom Jones
I Say A Little Prayer - Dionne Warwick
The Look Of Love - Dusty Springfield
Do You Know The Way To San Jose - Dionne Warwick
Raindrops Keep Fallin' On My Head - B.J. Thomas
One Less Bell To Answer - The Fifth Dimension
Arthur's Theme - Christopher Cross
That's What Friends Are For - Dionne Warwick, Elton John, Gladys Knight and Stevie Wonder

LOST IN BOSTON (THE ULTIMATE COLLECTION)
(Varese, 2001):
What Am I Doing Here? - Liz Callaway
Tick Tock Goes The Clock - Lisa Mayer, Judy Malloy, Debbie Pavelka
(New recordings of two numbers cut from Promises, Promises and other non-Bacharach and David songs cut from Broadway shows.).

A TRIBUTE TO BURT BACHARACH AND HAL DAVID
(2002):
This Guy's In Love With You
Raindrops Keep Fallin' On My Head
A House Is Not A Home
Wishin' And Hopin'
Close To You
Don't Make Me Over
Alfie
What's New Pussycat?

Burt Bacharach & Hal David

24 Hours From Tulsa
I Just Have To Breathe
Wives And Lovers
Do You Know The Way To San Jose?
Make It Easy On Yourself
One Less Bell To Answer
The Look Of Love
Reach Out For Me
I Just Don't Know What To Do With Myself
Walk On By
I Say A Little Prayer
Do You Know The Way To San Jose
Anyone Who Had A Heart
What The World Needs Now Is Love

BURT BACHARACH'S 60 GREATEST HIT SONGS
(EMI, 2002):
The Story Of My Life - Michael Holliday
A House Is Not A Home - Shirley Bassey
Only Love Can Break A Heart - Gene Pitney
Raindrops Keep Fallin' On My Head - B.J. Thomas
Any Day Now (My Wild Beautiful Bird) - Chuck Jackson
24 Hours From Tulsa - Gene Pitney
(Theres) Always Something There To Remind Me - Sandie Shaw
What The World Needs Now Is Love - Jackie Deshannon)
Trains And Boats And Planes - Billy J Kramer and The Dakotas
Alfie - Cilla Black
The Look Of Love - Shirley Bassey
Be True To Yourself - Bobby Vee
Baby It's You - The Shirelles
Everybody's Out Of Town - B.J. Thomas
I Wake Up Crying - Chuck Jackson
Anyone Who Had A Heart - Cilla Black
I'll Never Fall In Love Again - Bobbie Gentry
Close To You - Englebert Humperdinck
This Guy's In Love With You - Al Martino
What's New Pussycat? - Tom Jones
Keep Me In Mind - Alma Cogan
Long Ago Tomorrow - B.J. Thomas
Make It Easy On Yourself - Cilla Black
True Love Never Runs Smooth - Gene Pitney
Keep Away From Other Girls - Helen Shapiro)
Long After Tonight Is All Over - Jimmy Radcliffe
My Little Red Book (All I Do Is Talk About You) - Manfred Mann
Blame It On Me - Peabo Bryson
Please Stay - The Drifters

After The Fox - The Hollies with Peter Sellers
Sandy - The Swinging Blue Jeans
If I Never Get To Love You - Timi Yuro
Tower Of Strength - Gene McDaniels
Wives And Lovers - Julie London
I Just Don't Know What To Do With Myself - Tommy Hunt
Magic Potion - The Searchers
Come And Get Me - Jackie Deshannon
They Don't Give Medals (To Yesterday's Heroes) - Chuck Jackson
You Belong In Someone Else's Arms - David Whitfield
Long Day, Short Night - The Shirelles
(The Man Who Shot) Liberty Valance - Gene Pitney
Don't Make Me Over - Tommy Hunt
Crazy Times - Gene Vincent
Maybe - Peabo Bryson and Roberta Flack
The Love Of A Boy - Timi Yuro
Walk On By - Helen Shapiro
It's Love That Really Counts - The Shirelles
Reach Out For Me - Nancy Wilson
This Empty Place - The Searchers
(There Goes) The Forgotten Man - Jimmy Radcliffe
Anonymous Phone Call - Frank Ifield
Another Tear Falls - Gene McDaniels
A Lifetime Of Loneliness - Jackie Deshannon
Live Again - Irma Thomas
Me Japanese Boy I Love You - Bobby Goldsboro
The Answer To Everything - Del Shannon
The Breaking Point - Chuck Jackson
Windows And Doors - Jackie Deshannon
Wishin' And Hopin' - The Merseybeats
Magic Moments - Jula De Palma

BLUE BACHARACH
(Blue Note, 1999)
This Guy's In Love With You – Stanley Turrentine
Wives And Lovers – Nancy Wilson
I Say A Little Prayer – Reuben Wilson
The Look Of Love – The Three Sounds
What The World Needs Now Is Love – Stanley Turrentine
They Don't Give Medals to Yesterday's Heroes – Lou Rawls
I'll Never Fall In Love Again – Grant Green
Do You Know The Way To San Jose? – Richard 'Groove' Holmes
Walk On By – Stanley Turrentine
Promises, Promises – Jazz Crusaders
Knowing When To Leave – Ernie Watts Quintet
Always Something There To Remind Me – Stanley Turrentine
Wives And Lovers – Grant Green
Alfie – Nancy Wilson

CDs by individual artists:

Stan Getz:
WHAT THE WORLD NEEDS NOW - STAN GETZ PLAYS BACHARACH & DAVID
(Polygram, 1998):
Wives And Lovers
Windows Of The World
The Look Of Love
Any Old Time Of The Day
Alfie
In Times Like These
A House Is Not A Home [Master Take]
Trains And Boats And Planes
What The World Needs Now Is Love
In Between The Heartaches [Edited Master Take]
Walk On By
A House Is Not A Home [Alternate Take]
In Between Heartaches [Partial Alternative Take]
My Own True Love
Tara's Theme

The Anita Kerr Singers:
REFLECT ON THE HITS OF BURT BACHARACH AND HAL DAVID / VELVET VOICES AND
BOLD BRASS
(Collector's Choice, 1999):
What's New Pussycat?
Alfie
Are You There (With Another Girl)
In Between The Heartaches
The Windows of The World
Do You Know The Way to San Jose?
Don't Make Me Over
Walk On By
Whoever You Are, I Love You
I Say A Little Prayer
The Look Of Love
A House Is Not A Home
What The World Needs Now Is Love
(Also features other, non-Bacharach and David, tracks.)

Marie McAuliffe:
REFRACTIONS
(Avant, 1998):
I Say A Little Prayer
Promises, Promises
Do You Know The Way To San Jose?
In Between The Heartaches
Are You There (With Another Girl)
Wives And Lovers
Alfie
A House Is Not A Home
In The Land Of Make Believe
Trains And Boats And Planes
Where Are You
The Look Of Love
One Less Bell To Answer

Cal Tjader:
SOUNDS OUT BURT BACHARACH
(DCC, 1998)
Moneypenny Goes for Broke
What The World Needs Now Is Love
Anyone Who Had A Heart
Don't Make Me Over
A Message To Michael
My Little Red Book
I Say A Little Prayer
Walk On By
You'll Never Get To Heaven

McCoy Tyner:
WHAT THE WORLD NEEDS NOW - THE MUSIC OF BURT BACHARACH
(GRP, 1997):
(They Long To Be) Close To You
What The World Needs Now Is Love
You'll Never Get To Heaven (If You Break My Heart)
The Windows Of The World
One Less Bell To Answer
A House Is Not A Home
(There's) Always Something There to Remind Me
Alfie
The Look Of Love

Dionne Warwick CDs:

THE DIONNE WARWICK COLLECTION - HER ALL-TIME GREATEST HITS
(Rhino, 1989):
Don't Make Me Over
This Empty Place
Anyone Who Had A Heart
Walk On By
You'll Never Get To Heaven (If You Break My Heart)
A House Is Not A Home
Reach Out For Me
Who Can I Turn To (When Nobody Needs Me)
Looking With My Eyes
Are You There (With Another Girl)
Message To Michael
Trains And Boats And Planes
I Just Don't Know What To Do With Myself
Another Night
Alfie
The Windows Of The World
I Say A Little Prayer
Valley Of The Dolls
Do You Know The Way To San Jose?
(There's) Always Something There To Remind Me
Promises, Promises
The April Fools
I'll Never Fall In Love Again
The Green Grass Starts To Grow

DEFINITIVE COLLECTION
(Arista, 1999):
Anyone Who Had A Heart
Don't Make Me Over
Walk On By
Message To Michael
Alfie
I Say A Little Prayer
The Windows Of The World
Do You Know The Way To San Jose?
I'll Never Fall In Love Again
Then Came You
I'll Never Love This Way Again
Déjà Vu
After You
No Night So Long
Heartbreaker

How Many Times Can We Say Goodbye
Will You Love Me Tomorrow
Love Power
Reservations For Two
That's What Friends Are For

HIDDEN GEMS - THE BEST OF DIONNE WARWICK VOL. 2
(Rhino R2 70329, 1992)
I Smiled Yesterday
Wishin' And Hopin'
Unlucky
Make It Easy On Yourself
I Cry Alone
Make The Music Play
Any Old Time Of Day
(They Long To Be) Close To You
In The Land Of Make Believe
How Many Days Of Sadness
You Can Have Him
Here I Am
This Little Light
What The World Needs Now Is Love
Let Me Be Lonely
Who Is Gonna Love Me?
This Girl's in Love With You
Slaves
The Look Of Love
Let Me Go To Him

FRIENDS CAN BE LOVERS
(Arista, 1993):
Sunny Weather Lover
Age Of Miracles
Where My Lips Have Been
Friends Can Be Lovers
Love Will Find A Way
Much Too Much
'Til The End Of Time
The Woman That I Am
Fragile
I Sing At Dawn

Burt Bacharach & Hal David

DIONNE WARWICK SINGS THE BACHARACH & DAVID SONGBOOK
(Empire, 1995):
Do You Know The Way To San Jose?
What The World Needs Now Is Love
Alfie
Message To Michael
I Just Don't Know What To Do With Myself
I Say A Little Prayer
You'll Never Get To Heaven
Anyone Who Had A Heart
I'll Never Fall In Love Again
Walk On By
Trains And Boats And Planes
Make It Easy On Yourself
A House Is Not A Home
(There's) Always Something There To Remind Me
The Look Of Love
Raindrops Keep Fallin' On My Head
Wishin' And Hopin'
Only Love Can Break A Heart
Promises, Promises
Wives And Lovers
Reach Out For Me
Windows Of The World

PRESENTING DIONNE WARWICK/ANYONE WHO HAD A HEART
(Castle, 1995):
This Empty Place
Wishin' And Hopin'
I Cry Alone
Zip-A-Dee-Doo-Dah
Make The Music Play
If You See Bill
Don't Make Me Over
It's Love That Really Counts (In The Long Run)
Unlucky
I Smiled Yesterday
Make It Easy On Yourself
The Love Of A Boy
Anyone Who Had A Heart
Shall I Tell Her
Gettin' Ready For The Heartbreak
Oh Lord, What Are You Doing To Me
Any Old Time Of Day
Mr. Heartbreak
Put Yourself In My Place

I Could Make You Mine
Please Make Him Love Me

HERE I AM/HERE WHERE THERE IS LOVE
(Castle, 1995):
Here I Am
In Between The Heartaches
If I Ever Make You Cry
(Here I Go Again) Lookin' With My Eyes
Once In A Lifetime
This Little Light
Don't Go Breaking My Heart
Window Wishing
Long Day, Short Night
Are You There (With Another Girl)
How Can I Hurt You?
I Loves You, Porgy
Go With Love
What The World Needs Now Is Love
I Just Don't Know What To Do With Myself
Here Where There Is Love
Trains And Boats And Planes
Alfie
As Long As He Needs Me
I Wish You Love
I Never Knew What I Was up To
Blowin' In The Wind

MAKE WAY FOR DIONNE WARWICK/THE SENSITIVE SOUND OF DIONNE WARWICK
(Castle, 1995):
A House Is Not A Home
People
(They Long To Be) Close To You
The Last One To Be Loved
Land Of Make Believe
Reach Out For Me
You'll Never Get To Heaven
Walk On By
Wishin' And Hopin'
I Smiled Yesterday
Get Rid Of Him
Make The Night A Little Longer
Unchained Melody
Who Can I Turn To

How Many Days Of Sadness
Is There Another Way To Love You
Where Can I Go Without You
You Can Have Him
Wives And Lovers
Don't Say I Didn't Tell You
Only The Strong, Only The Brave
Forever My Love
That's Not The Answer

HER CLASSIC SONGS
(Curb, 1997):
Walk On By
Anyone Who Had A Heart
Message To Michael
Theme From Valley Of The Dolls
Alfie
Trains And Boats And Planes
I'll Never Fall In Love Again
Promises, Promises
A House Is Not A Home
(There's) Always Something There To Remind Me

HER CLASSIC SONGS, VOLUME 2
(Curb, 1998):
I Say A Little Prayer
Do You Know The Way To San Jose?
This Girl's In Love With You
Reach Out For Me
Close To You
If We Only Have Love
Do You Believe In Love At First Sight
Once You Hit The Road
Don't Ever Take Your Love Away
Do I Have To Cry

DIONNE SINGS DIONNE
(Platinum, 1998):
Walk On By
Love Begins With You
Reach Out for Me
High Upon This Love (from The Bold And The Beautiful)
I Say A Little Prayer For You
Always Something There To Remind Me

If I Want To
Aquarela Do Brazil
I Promise You
Be My Neighbor
All Kinds Of People
What The World Needs Now Is Love
Do You Know The Way To San Jose?
Humbly I Pray

DIONNE SINGS DIONNE II
(JVC Japan, 2001):
I'll Never Fall In Love Again
Anyone Who Had A Heart
What A Fool Believes
In Between The Heartaches
The Look Of Love
I Say A Little Prayer
Close To You
Don't Make Me Over
Then Came You
Message To Michael
You'll Never Get To Heaven (If You Break My Heart)

LOVE SONGS
(Rhino, 2001):
You'll Never Get To Heaven (If You Break My Heart)
I Say A Little Prayer
Forever My Love
Here Where There Is Love
For The Rest Of My Life
Whoever You Are, I Love You
Dream Sweet Dreamer
The Wine Is Young
One Less Bell To Answer
Love Song
Close To You
You Are The Heart Of Me
Sure Thing
Jealousy
World Of My Dreams
I Didn't Mean To Love You

THE VERY BEST OF DIONNE WARWICK
(Rhino, 2000):
Don't Make Me Over
Anyone Who Had A Heart
Walk On By
Reach Out For Me
Are You There (With Another Girl)
Message To Michael
Trains And Boats And Planes
Alfie
The Windows Of The World
Valley Of The Dolls
I Say A Little Prayer
Do You Know The Way To San Jose?
Promises, Promises
This Girl's In Love With You
I'll Never Fall In Love Again
Then Came You

DEFINITIVE COLLECTION
(Arista, 1999):
Anyone Who Had A Heart
Don't Make Me Over
Walk On By
Message To Michael
Alfie
I Say A Little Prayer
The Windows Of The World
Do You Know The Way To San Jose?
I'll Never Fall In Love Again
Then Came You
I'll Never Love This Way Again
Déjà Vu
After You
No Night So Long
Heartbreaker
How Many Times Can We Say Goodbye
Will You Love Me Tomorrow
Love Power
Reservations For Two
That's What Friends Are For

The Hits:

Hit recordings of songs by Bacharach and David. All chart positions from BILLBOARD's Hot 100 And Bubbling Under charts.

Herb Alpert and the Tijuana Brass:
Casino Royale (No. 24, 1967)
This Guy's In Love With You (No. 1, 1968)
To Wait For Love (No. 51, 1968)

Burt Bacharach:
Saturday Sunshine (No. 93, 1963)
I'll Never Fall In Love Again (No. 93, 1969)
All Kinds Of People (No. 116, 1971)

Tony Bennett:
Living Together, Growing Together (No. 111, 1972)

Brook Benton:
A House Is Not A Home (No. 75, 1964)

Cilla Black:
Alfie (No. 95, 1966)

Jerry Butler:
Make It Easy On Yourself (No. 20, 1962)

Jerry Butler And Brenda Lee Yeager:
(They Long To Be) Close To You (No. 91, 1972)

Glen Campbell And Anne Murray:
I Say A Little Prayer/By The Time I Get To Phoenix (No. 81, 1971)

The Carpenters:
(They Long To Be) Close To You (No. 1, 1970)

Richard Chamberlain:
Blue Guitar (No. 42, 1963)
Rome Will Never Leave You (No. 99, 1964)

Perry Como:
Magic Moments (No. 4, 1958)

Doris Day:
Send Me No Flowers (No. 135, 1964)

Jackie DeShannon:
What The World Needs Now Is Love (No. 7, 1965)
A Lifetime Of Loneliness (No. 66, 1965)

Come And Get Me (No. 83, 1966)
Windows And Doors (No. 108, 1966)

The 5th Dimension:
One Less Bell To Answer (No. 2, 1970)
Living Together, Growing Together (No. 32, 1973)

The Four Coins:
Wendy Wendy (No. 72, 1958)

Aretha Franklin:
I Say A Little Prayer (No. 10, 1968)

Gloria Gaynor:
Walk On By (No. 98, 1975)

Bobby Goldsboro:
Me Japanese Boy I Love You (No. 74, 1964)

R.B. Greaves:
Always Something There To Remind Me (No. 27, 1970)

George Hamilton:
Don't Envy Me (No. 134, 1963)

Isaac Hayes:
Walk On By (No. 30, 1969)
The Look Of Love (No. 79, 1971)

Englebert Humperdinck:
I'm a Better Man (No. 38, 1969)

Tommy Hunt:
I Just Don't Know What To Do With Myself (No. 119, 1964)

Lou Johnson:
Kentucky Bluebird (No. 104, 1964)

Trini Lopez:
Made In Paris (No. 113, 1966)

Manfred Mann:
My Little Red Book (No. 124, 1965)

Johnny Mathis:
Make It Easy On Yourself (No. 103, 1972)

Sergio Mendes and Brasil '66:
I Say A Little Prayer (No. 106, 1968)

The Shirelles:
It's Love That Really Counts (No. 102, 1962)

Dusty Springfield:
In The Land Of Make Believe (No. 113, 1969)

The Swinging Blue Jeans:
Don't Make Me Over (No. 116, 1966)

Bobby Vee:
Anonymous Phone Call (No. 110, 1963)

Dionne Warwick:
Don't Make Me Over (No. 21, 1962)
This Empty Place (No. 84, 1963)
Make The Music Play (No. 81, 1963)
Anyone Who Had A Heart (No. 8, 1963)
Walk On By (No. 6, 1964)
You'll Never Get To Heaven (No. 34, 1964)
A House Is Not A Home (No. 71, 1964)
Reach Out For Me (No. 20, 1964)
Here I Am (No. 65, 1965)
Looking With My Eyes (No. 64, 1965)
Are You There (With Another Girl) (No. 39, 1965)
Message To Michael (No. 8, 1966)
Trains And Boats And Planes (No. 22, 1966)
I Just Don't Know What To Do With Myself (No. 26, 1966)
Another Night (No. 49, 1966)
Alfie (No. 15, 1967)
The Beginning Of Loneliness (No. 79, 1967)
The Windows Of The World (No. 32, 1967)
I Say A Little Prayer (No. 4, 1967)
Do You Know The Way To San Jose? (No. 10, 1968)
Let Me Be Lonely (No. 71, 1968)
Who Is Gonna Love Me (No. 33, 1968)
(There's) Always Something There To Remind Me (No. 65, 1968)
Promises, Promises (No. 19, 1968)
This Girl's In Love With You (No. 7, 1969)
The April Fools (No. 37, 1969)
Odds And Ends (No. 43, 1969)
I'll Never Fall In Love Again (No. 6, 1969)
Let Me Go To Him (No. 32, 1970)
Paper Maché (No. 43, 1970)
Make It Easy On Yourself (live recording) (No. 37, 1970)
The Green Grass Starts To Grow (No. 43, 1970)
Who Gets The Guy? (No. 57, 1971)
Only Love Can Break A Heart (No. 109, 1977)

Bacharach and David With Others:

What follows is a selected list of songs Bacharach and David wrote with other songwriters.

Hal David With Others:

A Girl Can't Say
(Hal David/Leon Carr)
Eydie Gormé

Above The Tears, Beyond The Pain
(Hal David/Archie Jordan)
Orsa Lia
(1979)

America Is
(Hal David/Joe Raposos)
B.J. Thomas
(1985)

American Beauty Rose
(Hal David-Redd Evans-Arthur Altman)
Frank Sinatra
(1961)

As I Was Walking
(Hal David/Sherman Edwards)
Johnny Janis
(1961)

Baby Elephant Walk
(Hal David/Henry Mancini)
Pat Boone, Lawrence Welk

Bell Bottom Blues
(Hal David-Leon Carr)
Teresa Brewer
(1953)

Bing Bang Boom
(Hal David-Leon Carr)
Lu Ann Simms:
(1954)

Blue Roses
(Hal David-Paul Lekytie)
Ray Charles Singers
(1966)

Broken Hearted Melody
(Hal David-Sherman Edwards)
Sarah Vaughan
(1959)

Call Me Careless
(Hal David/Leon Carr)
Joan Weber

The Charanga
(Hal David/Marco Rizo)
Merv Griffin
(1961)

Do You Know How Christmas Trees Are Grown?
(Hal David/John Barry)
Jackie DeShannon
(1969)

Donna Means Heartbreak
(Hal David-Paul Hampton)
Gene Pitney
(1962)

Don't Let It Happen To Us
(Hal David-Sherman Edwards)
The Shirelles
(1963)

Early Morning Strangers
(Hal David/Barry Manilow)
Cher
(1976)

Everything That Happens To You
(Hal David/Michel Legrand)
Lena Horne
(1974)

The Face, Not The Image
(Hal David-Albert Hammond)
Albert Hammond
(1975)

False Friends
(Hal David-Sherman Edwards)
Gene McDaniels
(1963)

The Four Winds And The Seven Seas
(Hal David-Don Rodney)
Vic Damone
(1949)

Girls In The Summertime
(Hal David-Sherman Edwards)
Paul Petersen
(1963)

The Good Times Are Comin'
(Hal David-John Barry)
Mama Cass Elliot
(1970)

Got A Locket In My Pocket
(Hal David/Lee Pockriss)
The Four Lads
(1959)

Have A Hope, Have A Wish, Have A Prayer
(Hal David-Leon Carr)
Delta Rhythm Boys
(1954)

Home Is Where The Heart Is
(Hal David/Sherman Edwards)
Elvis Presley
(1962)

I Can't Hold On
(Hal David/Archie Jordan)
Orsa Lia
(1979)

If I Could Hold You In My Arms
(Hal David-Robert Colby)
Kathy Linden
(1958)

It Was Almost Like A Song
(Hal David-Archie Jordan)
Ronnie Milsap
(1977)

A Job Is A Home To A Homeless Man
(Hal David-Albert Hammond)
Albert Hammond
(1975)

Johnny Get Angry
(Hal David-Sherman Edwards)
Joanie Sommers
(1962)

Judy Says
(Hal David-Lee Pockriss)
Arena Twins
(1961)

Lay The Music Down
(Hal David-Albert Hammond)
Albert Hammond
(1975)

Listen My Love
(Hal David-Sid Lipman)
Rod Lauren
(1960)

Love Isn't Love Till You Give It Away
(Hal David-Albert Hammond)
Albert Hammond
(1975)

Love Me Good
(Hal David/Archie Jordan)
Orsa Lia
(1979)

A Man And A Train
(Hal David/Frank De Vol)
Marty Robbins
(1973)

The Melancholy Trumpet
(Hal David/Leon Carr)
Harry James

Moonraker
(Hal David-John Barry)
Shirley Bassey
(1979)

My Baby's Got Such Lovin' Ways
(Hal David-Leon Carr)
The McGuire Sisters
(1955)

My Heart Is An Open Book
(Hal David-Lee Pockriss)
Carl Dobkins, Jr.
(1959)

New In The Ways Of Love
(Hal David-Lee Pockriss)
Tommy Edwards
(1959)

99 Miles From L.A.
(Hal David-Albert Hammond)
Art Garfunkel
(1975)

One Life
(Hal David-Albert Hammond)
Albert Hammond
(1975)

One Little Girl At a Time
(Hal David-Neal Hefti)
Ed Ames
(1967)

(Otto Drives Me Crazy) Otto's Gotta Go
(Hal David/Leon Carr/S. Wayne)
Guy Mitchell

Outside My Window
(Hal David-Sherman Edwards)
The Fleetwoods
(1960)

River River
(Hal David-Leon Carr)
Jimmy Mosby
(1960)

Rivers Are For Boats
(Hal David/Albert Hammond)
Albert Hammond
(1974)

Santa Barbara
(Hal David/Archie Jordan)
Ronnie Milsap

Saturday's Kisses
(Hal David-Leon Carr)
Charlie Applewhite
(1958)

Sea Of Heartbreak
(Hal David-Paul Hampton)
Don Gibson
(1961)

Send A Little Love My Way
(Hal David/Henry Mancini)
Frank Sinatra

Thank You Lord
(Hal David/Archie Jordan)
B.J. Thomas

To All The Girls I've Loved Before
(Hal David-Albert Hammond)
Willie Nelson And Julio Iglesias
(1984)

To Love A Child
(Hal David/Joe Raposo)
Frank Sinatra

The Two Of Us
(Hal David-Sherman Edwards)
George Hamilton IV
(1959)

Until
(Hal David/Harry James/Alvin Homes)
The Clark Sisters

Using Things And Loving People
(Hal David/Archie Jordan)
B.J. Thomas

Valerie
(Hal David-Sherman Edwards)
James Darren
(1961)

What Do You See In Her
(Hal David-Frank Weldon)
Jeri Southern
(1955)

When The Boys Get Together
(Hal David-Sherman Edwards)
Joannie Sommers
(1962)

A Whistlin' Tune
(Hal David/Sherman Edwards)
Elvis Presley
(1961)

Who Could Love Me
(Hal David-Bruno Canfora-Antonio Amurri)
Shirley Bassey
(1966)

Wonderful Wasn't It
(Hal David-Don Rodney)
The Mills Brothers
(1951)

You Only See What You Wanna See
(Hal David-Paul Hampton)
Jack Scott
(1962)

Burt Bacharach With Others:

The Answer To Everything
(Burt Bacharach/Bob Hilliard)
Del Shannon
(1961)

Any Day Now (My Wild Beautiful Bird)
(Burt Bacharach/Bob Hilliard)
The Drifters, Chuck Jackson, Elvis Presley

Arthur's Theme
(Burt Bacharach/Christopher Cross/Carole Bayer Sager/Peter Allen)
Christopher Cross
(1981)

Baby It's You
(Burt Bacharach/Mack David/Barney Williams)
The Shirelles (1961)
The Beatles (1963)

Beauty Isn't Everything
(Burt Bacharach/Edward Heyman)
June Valli
(1956)

The Bell That Couldn't Jingle
(Burt Bacharach/Larry Kusik)
Bobby Helms
(1957)

Blame It On Me
(Burt Bacharach/Carole Bayer Sager)
Peabo Bryson and Roberta Flack
(1983)

The Blob
(Burt Bacharach/Mack David)
The Five Blobs
(1958)

Captives Of The Heart
(Burt Bacharach/John Bettis)
Dionne Warwick
(1994)

A Chance For Heaven
(Burt Bacharach/Carole Bayer Sager/Christopher Cross)
Christopher Cross
(1984)

Charlie
(Burt Bacharach/Bobby Russell)
Bobby Vinton
(1975)

Close
(Burt Bacharach/Sydney Shaw)
Gals And Pals
(1967)

Come Completely To Me
(Burt Bacharach/Paul Hampton)
Steve Rossi
(1961)

Crazy Times
(Burt Bacharach/Paul Hampton)
Gene Vincent
(1959)

Desperate Hours
(Burt Bacharach/Wilson Stone)
Mel Torme
(1955)

Don't Say Goodbye Girl
(Burt Bacharach/Narada Michael Walden/Sally Jo Dakota)
Tevin Campbell
(1993)

Don't You Believe It
(Burt Bacharach/Bob Hilliard)
Andy Williams
(1962)

Dream Big
(Burt Bacharach/Paul Hampton)
Sonny James
(1959)

Dreamin' All The Time
(Burt Bacharach/Bob Hilliard)

Jack Jones
(1962)

Easy To Love
(Burt Bacharach/Carole Bayer Sager)
Carole Bayer Sager
(1981)

Everchanging Times
(Burt Bacharach/Carole Bayer Sager/William Conti Jr)
Siedah Garrett
(1987)

Extravagant Gestures
(Burt Bacharach/Carole Bayer Sager)
Dionne Warwick
(1985)

Faithfully
(Burt Bacharach/Sydney Shaw)
Johnny Mathis
(1960)

Find Love
(Burt Bacharach/Paul Anka)
Jackie DeShannon
(1979)

Finder Of Lost Loves
(Burt Bacharach/Carole Bayer Sager)
Dionne Warwick with Glenn Jones
(1985)

Fool Me Again
(Burt Bacharach/Carole Bayer Sager)
Nicolette Larson
(1981)

Front Page Story
(Burt Bacharach/Carole Bayer Sager/Neil Diamond)
Neil Diamond
(1982)

Girls Know How
(Burt Bacharach/Carole Bayer Sager/David Foster)
Al Jarreau
(1982)

God Give Me Strength
(Burt Bacharach/Elvis Costello)
Elvis Costello and Burt Bacharach
(1996)

Heartlight
(Burt Bacharach/Carole Bayer Sager/Neil Diamond)
Neil Diamond
(1982)

Heavenly
(Burt Bacharach/Sydney Shaw)
Johnny Mathis
(1958)

Hot Spell
(Burt Bacharach/Mack David)
Margaret Whiting
(1958)

How About
(Burt Bacharach/Jack Wolf)
Della Reese
(1957)

How Long?
(Burt Bacharach/Carole Bayer Sager)
Dionne Warwick
(1985)

Hurricane
(Burt Bacharach/Carole Bayer Sager/Neil Diamond)
Neil Diamond
(1982)

I Don't Need You Anymore
(Burt Bacharach/Paul Anka)
Jackie Deshannon
(1979)

I Still Have That Other Girl
(Burt Bacharach/Elvis Costello)
Burt Bacharach and Elvis Costello
(1998)

I'll Bring Along My Banjo
(Burt Bacharach/Norman Gimbel)
Johnnie Ray
(1961)

I'll See You On The Radio (Laura)
(Burt Bacharach/Carole Bayer Sager/Neil Diamond)
Neil Diamond
(1986)

I'm Guilty
(Burt Bacharach/Carole Bayer Sager/Neil Diamond)
Neil Diamond
(1982)

I've Got My Mind Made Up
(Burt Bacharach/Paul Anka)
Michael McDonald
(1979)

In A World Such As This
(Burt Bacharach/Carole Bayer Sager/Bruce Roberts)
Dionne Warwick
(1987)

In Ensenada
(Burt Bacharach/Carole Bayer Sager/Neil Diamond)
Neil Diamond
(1982)

In My Reality
(Burt Bacharach/Carole Bayer Sager)
Natalie Cole
(1987)

In The Darkest Place
(Burt Bacharach/Elvis Costello)
Elvis Costello and Burt Bacharach
(1998)

In Tune
(Burt Bacharach/Libby Titus)

Libby Titus And Burt Bacharach
(1979)

Indoor Sport
(Burt Bacharach/Frederick Tobias)
Petula Clark
(1960)

It's Only Love
(Burt Bacharach/Carole Bayer Sager/Stephen Bishop)
Stephen Bishop
(1981)

Keep Me In Mind
(Burt Bacharach/Jack Wolf)
Patti Page
(1954)

Let Me Be The One
(Burt Bacharach/Carole Bayer Sager/Taja Sevelle)
Gladys Knight And The Pips
(1987)

Like No One In The World
(Burt Bacharach/John Bettis)
Johnny Mathis
(1996)

Little Betty Falling Star
(Burt Bacharach/Bob Hilliard)
Gene Pitney
(1963)

Lost Among The Stars
(Burt Bacharach/Carole Bayer Sager/Neil Diamond)
Neil Diamond
(1982)

Love Always
(Burt Bacharach/Carole Bayer Sager/Bruce Roberts)
El Debarge
(1986)

Love Is Fire (Love Is Ice)
(Burt Bacharach/Carole Bayer Sager)
Gladys Knight and the Pips
(1987)

Love Is My Decision
(Burt Bacharach/Carole Bayer Sager/Chris De Burgh)
Chris De Burgh
(1988)

Love Light
(Burt Bacharach/Carole Bayer Sager)
Barbra Streisand
(1988)

Love Power
(Burt Bacharach/Carole Bayer Sager)
Dionne Warwick And Jeffrey Osborne
(1987)

Love Too Good To Last
(Burt Bacharach/Carole Bayer Sager/Peter Allen)
The Pointer Sisters
(1980)

Making Love
(Burt Bacharach/Carole Bayer Sager/Bruce Roberts)
Roberta Flack
(1982)

Maybe
(Burt Bacharach/Carole Bayer Sager/Marvin Hamlisch)
Peabo Bryson And Roberta Flack
(1983)

Me Beside You
(Burt Bacharach/Carole Bayer Sager/Neil Diamond)
Neil Diamond
(1986)

Mexican Divorce
(Burt Bacharach/Bob Hilliard)
The Drifters
(1961)

The Miracle Of St. Marie
(Burt Bacharach/Bob Hilliard)
The Four Coins
(1961)

Burt Bacharach & Hal David

Need A Little Faith
(Burt Bacharach/Carole Bayer Sager)
Patti Labelle
(1989)

Night Shift
(Burt Bacharach/Carole Bayer Sager/Marvin Ross)
Quarterflash
(1982)

Obsession
(Burt Bacharach/Desmond Child)
Desmond Child
(1991)

On My Own
(Burt Bacharach/Carole Bayer Sager)
Patti Labelle and Michael McDonald
(1985)

One Part Dog, Nine Parts Cat
(Burt Bacharach/Bob Hilliard)
Dick Van Dyke
(1961)

Out Of My Continental Mind
(Burt Bacharach/Sydney Shaw)
Lena Horne
(1961)

Over You
(Burt Bacharach/Carole Bayer Sager/Ray Parker Jr.)
Ray Parker Jr.
(1987)

Overnight Success
(Burt Bacharach/Carole Bayer Sager)
Gladys Knight And The Pips
(1987)

Painted From Memory
(Burt Bacharach/Elvis Costello)
Elvis Costello and Burt Bacharach
(1998)

Perfect Lovers
(Burt Bacharach/Carole Bayer Sager/Nathan East)

Ray Parker Jr.
(1987)

Pick Up The Pieces
(Burt Bacharach/Bob Hilliard)
Jack Jones
(1962)

Please Stay
(Burt Bacharach/Bob Hilliard)
The Drifters
(1961)

Poor Rich Boy
(Burt Bacharach/David Pack/Joseph Puerta)
Ambrosia
(1981)

Power Of Your Love
(Burt Bacharach/Carole Bayer Sager/Taja Sevelle)
Taja Sevelle
(1991)

Seconds
(Burt Bacharach/Neil Simon)
Gladys Knight
(1974)

Sleep With Me Tonight
(Burt Bacharach/Carole Bayer Sager/Neil Diamond)
Neil Diamond
(1984)

Somebody's Been Lying
(Burt Bacharach/Carole Bayer Sager)
The Carpenters
(1981)

Someone Else's Eyes
(Burt Bacharach/Carole Bayer Sager/Bruce Roberts)
Aretha Franklin and Michael McDonald
(1991)

Sometimes Late At Night
(Burt Bacharach/Carole Bayer Sager)
Carole Bayer Sager
(1981)

Split Decision
(Burt Bacharach/Carole Bayer Sager)
Natalie Cole
(1987)

Stay Devoted
(Burt Bacharach/Carole Bayer Sager)
Dionne Warwick
(1985)

Stronger Than Before
(Burt Bacharach/Carole Bayer Sager/Bruce Roberts)
Carole Bayer Sager
(1981)

Such Unlikely Lovers
(Burt Bacharach/Elvis Costello)
Elvis Costello and Burt Bacharach
(1998)

The Sweetest Punch
(Burt Bacharach/Elvis Costello)
Elvis Costello and Burt Bacharach
(1998)

Take Good Care Of You And Me
(Burt Bacharach/Carole Bayer Sager/Gerry Goffin)
Dionne Warwick and Jeffrey Osborne
(1989)

Take Me To Your Ladder
(Burt Bacharach/Bob Hilliard)
Buddy Clinton
(1960)

Tears At The Birthday Party
(Burt Bacharach/Elvis Costello)
Elvis Costello and Burt Bacharach
(1998)

Tell Her
(Burt Bacharach/Carole Bayer Sager/Peter Allen)
Carole Bayer Sager
(1981)

Tell It To Your Heart
(Burt Bacharach/Tonio K)
Randy Crawford
(2000)

That's What Friends Are For
(Burt Bacharach/Carole Bayer Sager)
Dionne and Friends
(1985)

They Don't Make Them Like They Used To
(Burt Bacharach/Carole Bayer Sager)
Kenny Rogers
(1986)

This Doesn't Feel Like Love Anymore
(Burt Bacharach/Carole Bayer Sager/Joyce Irby)
Klymaxx
(1993)

This House Is Empty Now
(Burt Bacharach/Elvis Costello)
Elvis Costello and Burt Bacharach
(1998)

Three Wheels On My Wagon
(Burt Bacharach/Bob Hilliard)
Dick Van Dyke
(1961)

Toledo
(Burt Bacharach/Elvis Costello)
Elvis Costello and Burt Bacharach
(1998)

Tower Of Strength
(Burt Bacharach/Bob Hilliard)
Gene McDaniels
(1961)

Two Hearts
(Philip Bailey/Maurice White)
Earth, Wind And Fire
(1993)

Uninvited Dream
(Burt Bacharach/Sammy Gallop)

Peggy Lee
(1957)

Us
(Burt Bacharach/Robert Russell)
Tom Jones
(1975)

Waiting For Charlie To Come
(Burt Bacharach/Bob Hilliard)
Etta James
(1962)

Walking Tall
(Burt Bacharach/Tim Rice)
Lyle Lovett
(1999)

What's Her Name Today?
(Burt Bacharach/Elvis Costello)
Elvis Costello and Burt Bacharach
(1998)

Where Did The Time Go?
(Burt Bacharach/Carole Bayer Sager)
The Pointer Sisters
(1980)

Who's Got The Action?
(Burt Bacharach/Bob Hilliard)
Phil Colbert
(1965)

Wild Again
(Burt Bacharach/Carole Bayer Sager)
Carole Bayer Sager
(1981)

You And Me For Always
(Burt Bacharach/Carole Bayer Sager)
Barbra Streisand
(1988)

Robin Platts

You Belong In Someone Else's Arms
(Burt Bacharach/Paul Hampton)
David Whitfield
(1963)

You Don't Know Me
(Burt Bacharach/Carole Bayer Sager)
Carole Bayer Sager
(1981)

You're Following Me
(Burt Bacharach/Bob Hilliard)
Peter Gordeno
(1961)

Look for these other books from Collector's Guide Publishing Inc.

**GENESIS
INSIDE & OUT
By Robin Platts**

Genesis: Inside & Out" tells the whole story, from their humble beginnings at Charterhouse School, through Phil Collins' departure, right up to the present day, when the group seems to have split up. Author Robin Platts covers the band's history in great detail, drawing from his own interviews with past Genesis members and associates, and from extensive archival research.

The book explores Genesis' career in great depth, including details about: the making of each album; how the group developed their songwriting approach and how it changed over three decades; why various members left and how the group survived those departures; details of bootlegs, demo tapes and unreleased recordings; information about each tour, including set lists; critical reaction to their records and concerts; a comprehensive discography; and many photos of rare record sleeves and memorabilia.

**PINK FLOYD
THE PRESS REPORTS
By Vernon Fitch**

"Pink Floyd – The Press Reports 1966-1983" is an historical look at Pink Floyd, as seen through press reports of the major music papers during the years 1966 through 1983. Reported in this book are record reviews, band member interviews, reviews of live performances, reports of band projects, and more, in a chronological history culled from news articles of the time.

Perhaps most interesting are the interviews with the band members that are featured throughout the book. Read interviews with Syd Barrett, David Gilmour, Nick Mason, Roger Waters, Richard Wright, and others, as they give rare insights into events as they were taking place. These interviews are a history of Pink Floyd by the band members themselves, as the events were happening. For anyone interested in Pink Floyd, this is a revealing book about one of the most significant bands in the history of rock music.

20TH CENTURY ROCK AND ROLL PROGRESSIVE ROCK
By Jerry Lucky

For progressive rock aficionados and all lovers of classical rock music, this book highlights the 50 most influential and important progressive rock bands, past and present, from around the world.

Exploring the artists and their music, from its origins to current prog music, the history and discography are presented in knowledgeable detail.

Veteran author Jerry Lucky shares with us his vast experience in the Progressive Rock world detailing the development of Prog by looking closely at the players as well as their music.

Progressive rock music combines and transends the various music genrés to a greater extent than possibly any other type of music. This book will take you straight to the very best that Prog has to offer and make you comfortable with its roots and where it's going next.

THE PROGRESSIVE ROCK FILES
By Jerry Lucky

After years of research, musicologist and broadcaster Jerry Lucky has created a definitive guide to Progressive Rock music.

Everything from the history and the critical thrashing, to the complex development this musical genre has gone through from it's beginnings in 1967 to the present day.

Also included is a comprehensive A-Z listing of over 1400 Progressive Rock bands each with a brief musical description and recored discography to aid in your discovery of this challenging and adventurous musical art-form.

Jerry Lucky is a broadcaster and musicologist with a love of Progressive Rock music. He has authored articles on such diverse interests as music, marketing and drag racing. His work on The Progressive Rock Files began in 1983 while hosting a Prog radio show called Exposure. He currently resides in Victoria, BC with his family and an ever growing collection of Progressive Rock albums and CDs.

FROM GRAND FUNK TO GRACE
THE AUTHORIZED BIOGRAPHY OF MARK FARNER
By Kristofer Engelhardt

Mark Farner is a founding member, lead guitarist-vocalist and primary creative force of the international famous rock group Grand Funk Railroad. By the mid-1970s they had become "the American band." In total, they've sold over 25-million records.

In this authorized biography, the fiercely private Mark Farner, talks about conflicts within his family and Grand Funk Railroad, his drug use, "sex-capades," touring with "the American band," marital infidelities, a child out of wedlock, divorce, his teenage bride, bitter lawsuit, losing a fortune, the breakup and reunions of Grand Funk, and much more!

INCLUDES: Bonus music CD of songs written and recorded by Mark Farner.

URBAN LEGENDS OF ROCK & ROLL
YOU NEVER CAN TELL
By Dale Sherman

"You Never Can Tell" covers the gauntlet of great rock and roll myths. From the tales that are just peculiar to legends so outlandish they can hardly be believed; from the stories made up for publicity, to stories invented to destroy a performer's career; from the beginning of rock and roll, up to the present and beyond.

* The rock artist who had a couple of ribs removed to make himself more "flexible." * And many, many more!

"You Never Can Tell" is packed with incredible stories about fame, music, money, sex, conspiracies, death, and everything in between! Which are true? Which are false?

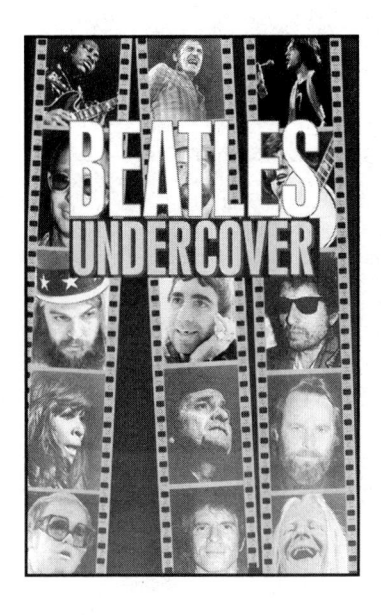

BEATLES UNDERCOVER
By Kristofer Engelhardt

"Beatles Undercover" is a reference book, which explores the origins and evolution of The Beatles' contributions to other artists' music, along with a brief biographical sketch of each of these artists. In short, this book is about The Beatles' admiration for and generous support of their friends and fellow musicians. It's neither a price guide nor a discography per se. It does not seek to expose the artists' personal lives or critique their work.

INCLUDES: CD of unreleased recordings produced and/or written by John Lennon.

"This book stands alone as the last word on The Beatles' work for other artists. The research and attention to detail are astounding." — Roy Cicala – Lennon's recording engineer.

THE PINK FLOYD ENCYCLOPEDIA
By Vernon Fitch

The Pink Floyd Encyclopedia is an in-depth reference work covering all the people, places and history of the musical group Pink Floyd.

From the earliest days of the band to the present, this book explains band relationships, from The Abdabs to Zee. The Pink Floyd Encyclopedia is a must for every Pink Floyd enthusiast, from the casual fan to the obsessive collector.

INCLUDES: A Hawkwind exclusive tribute CD.

"Fitch has taken it upon himself to assemble just about every known item of information about Pink Floyd and, as such, his book is a triumph."
— Record Collector Magazine U.K.

**LED ZEPPELIN
THE PRESS REPORTS
By Robert Godwin**

In "Led Zeppelin – The Press Reports..." noted Led Zeppelin expert Robert Godwin has collected and reviewed nearly a thousand articles from around the globe. Reports of the band's activities from Tokyo to New York and from Sydney to London are all synopsised and presented in chronological order.

Never before has the band's day by day history been organized and scrutinized in this way, with the band themselves speaking in interviews from around the world.

INCLUDES: Jimmy Page interview from 1977 on CD.

"... outrageously exhaustive ..."
— Brad Tolinski – Guitar World.

**THE ILLUSTRATED COLLECTOR'S GUIDE TO LED ZEPPELIN
By Robert Godwin**

For the collector it is not uncommon to stumble across Led Zeppelin CD's that they have never heard of or seen before, this is the shady world of bootlegs.

Since 1984 Robert Godwin has attempted to shine a light into the dark places to help the collector identify these historical snapshots.

This book includes hundreds of new listings from around the world including solo albums, Yardbirds, Coverdale-Page and, of course, Led Zeppelin.

**For more information visit us at
www.cgpublishing.com**